Islamic Historiography

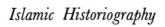

ISLAMIC HISTORIOGRAPHY

THE HISTORIES OF MAS'ŪDĪ

by

Tarif Khalidi

STATE UNIVERSITY OF NEW YORK PRESS

ALBANY 1975

Islamic Historiography
First published in 1975
State University of New York Press
99 Washington Avenue, Albany, New York 12210

Library of Congress Cataloging in Publication Data

Khalidi, Tarif, 1938-
Islamic historiography.
Includes index.
1. al-Mas'ūdī, d. 956? I. Title.
DS37. 5. M35K45 907'. 2'024 [B] 75-5933
ISBN 0-87395-282-0
ISBN 0-87395-283-9 (microfiche)

To

A. S. K., A. S. K.

and the memory of

A. S. K.

ACKNOWLEDGMENTS

This study grew out of a doctoral dissertation submitted to the University of Chicago in 1970. When I first began my studies there, I was granted a generous fellowship from the Center for Middle Eastern Studies which enabled me to work in pleasant and stimulating surroundings. To the then director, Professor William R. Polk, I extend my heartfelt thanks. This study owes most to Professor Muhsin Mahdi, formerly of Chicago and now the James Richard Jewett Professor of Arabic at Harvard. His incisive critical comments guided my research and his interest and encouragement sustained my labours. It is a pleasant privilege to have been his student. Professors Wilferd Madelung and Jaroslav Stetkevych of the Department of Near Eastern Languages and Civilizations of the University of Chicago, also read the entire work and encouraged me at every stage of writing. Professor Madelung was particularly helpful on problems of Islamic theology while Professor Stetkevych took great interest in the chapter on *adab* and both amended and deleted much that would have made this study more imperfect than it is. Professor Nabia Abbott of the Oriental Institute, though not directly involved in this study, was a constant source of inspiration throughout my years at Chicago. The staff of the library of the Oriental Institute was invariably helpful and I would like in particular to thank the librarian, Miss Shirley Lyon, for many hours of patience and courtesy.

In Beirut, my colleague, Professor Constantine K. Zurayk, read the entire work and made numerous and pertinent suggestions for improving it. My brother, Professor Walid Khalidi of the Institute for Palestine Studies, while not directly involved in the present work, has over the years been a stimulating intellectual mentor over a wide spectrum of topics.

In preparing this study for publication, I again received generous help from many quarters. Mr. Norman Mangouni, Director of the State University of New York Press, extended his interest and gracious assistance at every stage and Mr. W. Bruce Johnson, copy-editor, applied expert revision to the text. I am also deeply grateful for the encouragement and advice of Professor George F. Hourani of the Department of Philosophy of the State University of New York at Buffalo. Mr. Zahi Khuri, Director of Publications at the American University of Beirut, gently shepherded the often bewildered author through the intricacies of publication. My aunt, Mrs. Salwa Jeha Khalidi, typed the manuscript with her usual loving care. Mrs. Suha Tamim, godmother to many books already, compiled the index as a task of friendship. No blame, however, can possibly attach to any of these ladies and gentlemen for my errors of omission or commission. Their labor merits, alas, a more plenteous harvest.

Finally, to my wife, Amal Saidi Khalidi, I owe a debt of gratitude which public acknowledgment does little to repay. She and I alone can settle that account if indeed that account can ever be settled.

Tarif Khalidi

Department of History
American University of Beirut

CONTENTS

INTRODUCTION

This work is a study of al-Mas'ūdī, a major figure in Muslim historical writing of the Middle Ages. It was motivated in part by the high regard in which the Muslim scholarly community has held him and by the relatively small number of studies on Muslim historiography in general. Mas'ūdī was an Iraqi historian of the tenth century who lived in Egypt for the greater part of his working life and traversed the length and breadth of the Muslim empire and beyond. He belonged to a new school of historiography which numbered among its ranks men like al-Muṭahhar ibn Ṭāhir al-Maqdisī and Ibn Miskawayhi. This school of historians was concerned with the broader theoretical implications of their field of study and may be said to have in part prepared the way for Ibn Khaldūn, some four centuries later.

From its earliest origins, Muslim historiography had maintained a close relationship with the other religious sciences in Islam, particularly Tradition or Ḥadīth. The two disciplines fed from the same source, that is, the early history of the Muslim community, so that the work of some of the early historians of Islam is at times almost indistinguishable from Tradition. But Tradition soon became technical in the sense that it came to concentrate increasingly upon the sayings and doings of the Prophet, whereas historiography expanded its domain in both space and time. This parting of the ways may be dated roughly to the early ninth century, when the newly founded cities of Iraq began to prosper in the heart of a vast Abbasid Empire and a commercial network linked this empire eastward to China and westward to the British Isles.

This multinational Empire bred problems on a new scale to both the scholar and the administrator. The Muslim scholar was faced with cultures, nations and creeds which challenged him, sometimes tacitly and sometimes explicitly, to justify the truth of his faith. In fact, the ninth century may be called the Age of the Great Debate in

Muslim intellectual history. The sources of the period preserve some of these debates between the Muslims and the non-Muslims. At every turn, the Muslim scholar had to refine his polemical skills, to delve into the history and dogma of his enemies and, of course, to answer the critics of his own community. The administrator, on the other hand, wanted guidance in the increasingly complex affairs of state, and history itself was often the only guide to precedent. For both scholar and administrator, secular history was essential.

Tradition, however, became the preserve of the more conservative Muslim scholars. Working within the logic of their own discipline, with time they concerned themselves less with polemics and cultural challenges and more with the transmission of an accurate record of the *res gestae* of the Prophet, whose status was enhanced by the passage of years. Polemical theology became suspect to this type of scholar, and philosophy and science were, at best, irrelevant. The resulting tension between the Traditionists and their opponents, the "Modernists," is reflected in Mas'ūdī as well as other scholars of the Middle Ages. Many of the Modernist historians, theologians and scientists felt that Tradition was a field which lacked logical rigor. It was, so to speak, the soft underbelly of the Muslim faith, through which atheists, charlatans, and other enemies of Islam could infiltrate the minds of the simple folk and corrupt their hearts. It was precisely from this standpoint that a historian like al-Muṭahhar ibn Ṭāhir al-Maqdisī wrote his *Kitāb al-Bad' wa'l Ta'rīkh.* He wanted to establish as accurate a record as possible of the history of the community and of near-by nations and to provide his reader with a rational theological guide which would enable him to protect himself against dangerous allegorization of, or insidious attacks upon, the cosmology and eschatology of the faith.

The Modernists strove to come to terms with "wisdom," that is the Greek, Indian, and Persian corpus of philosophy and science, and to adapt therefrom whatever was suitable for the strengthening of the rational foundations of Islam. The historians among them dropped not only the methodology and style of Tradition but also its horizons. New themes were broached, such as Byzantine and Indian history. New ways were sought to present an accurate and readable account of the external physical world as well as its history. For this reason, some combined geography with history and felt that the history of man could not be completed without at least some account of the environment in which this history unfolds. It is not unlikely that some, Ya'qūbī for example, fell under the influence of the Greek classification of the sciences and therefore gave a portrait, roughly historical in character, of each of these sciences to round out the history of man himself. It is to this category of Modernist historians that Mas'ūdī belongs, and his work grew out of the intellectual turmoil of the Age of the Great Debate.

Historians may be studied meaningfully in either of two ways. One can either determine their general reliability as sources or one can, as in the present study, attempt to determine their view of history and its theoretical foundations, to rethink their thoughts, as R.G. Collingwood[1] might phrase it. The present study is not concerned so much with the life and works of Mas'ūdī as with rethinking his thoughts. He is in many respects the most readable and fascinating of Muslim historians. His easy style and frequent digressions have led many of his readers, both ancient and modern, to regard him as little more than a delightful raconteur. This study, on the contrary, was undertaken in the belief that Mas'ūdī was one of the earliest Muslim historians to reflect thoughtfully on the method and purpose of history. The most frustrating obstacle which faces the student of Mas'ūdī is the loss of his more theoretical works on history and the sciences, where his observations are set forth in greater detail, and to which he so frequently refers his reader. But this obstacle has been set aside in this study in the belief that, in his extant works, Mas'ūdī provides his reader with enough clues to his thinking to warrant the attempt to understand and analyze it.

Intellectually, Mas'ūdī was encyclopaedic. A reconstruction of the contents of his lost works from the references he makes to them (see Appendix B) reveals him to have been interested in almost all the sciences of his day, both philosophic and natural. He was also a tireless traveller who seems to have taken a keen interest in all that he saw and heard of the marvels of the world, so much so in fact, that some later books of marvels were fathered upon him. To many of these marvels and physical phenomena he attempted to apply some of the scientific principles and explanations which he had learnt from

[1] R. G. Collingwood, *The Idea of History* (Oxford: Clarendon Press, 1961), pp. 218-19.

the Graeco-Muslim philosophical and scientific tradition. But Mas'ūdī was also a sectarian Muslim, a Twelver Shī'ite who seems to have accepted at face value the theosophical theology and cosmology of Shī'ism which taught, among other things, the continuity of divine inspiration among the Prophet's progeny, the twelve imāms. Theology co-existed peacefully with Greek and Indian philosophy and science. To explain this co-existence, one would need to review the history of the relationship between Reason and Revelation in Islam, a task beyond the scope of this study. How a Muslim historian like Mas'ūdī tackled this problem needs a brief explanation.

Historians like Ya'qūbī, Dīnawarī, Maqdisī and Mas'ūdī faced a corpus of history, both pre-and non-Islamic, to which they had to evolve a certain attitude, particularly since some of this pre-Islamic history was found in the Koran. To one side stood the Traditionists who, while practising an inner criticism of *matn* and *isnād*, often allowed into the corpus of Ḥadīth, and thus into the religion itself, stories and commentaries which were of a legendary or supernatural character. This laxity was not mental laziness but was born of the desire to stress the omnipotence of God or the miraculous nature of prophecy. To another side stood the small circle of Muslim philosophers and scientists, best represented in this context by Muḥammad ibn Zakariyyā al-Rāzī, who continued the Greek philosophical and scientific tradition and often came close to denying prophecy itself, certainly its miraculous aspect. In the middle stood the polemical theologians, primarily the Mu'tazilites, who attempted, in general, to steer a middle course between faith and philosophy, to find rational grounds for belief in God and prophecy but to limit the sphere of the miraculous within the narrower confines of the laws of nature. Maqdisī, a Mu'tazilite historian, condemns Rāzī in one place for his rejection of miracles but refers his readers to the works of Rāzī for a better understanding of the natural characteristics of the physical universe. Mas'ūdī too, while not, strictly speaking, a Mu'tazilite, would have found no necessary contradiction between a belief in the theosophy of Shī'ism and the "miraculous" intervention of God on behalf of the family of 'Alī on the one hand and a belief in the systematic and rational ordering of the universe understood within the Graeco-Indian philosophical tradition on the other. The charge of credulity levelled so often against Mas'ūdī must also be seen in this light, viz. that belief in natural law did not necessarily exclude belief in the Divine breaking of that law, often for reasons known only to the Divinity.

These are some of the major themes of this study. The study itself is divided into five chapters. In chapter 1, an attempt is made to describe Mas'ūdī's literary affinities, sources and style. Mas'ūdī used his sources carefully and criticized or commended previous historians for reasons which had to do with his own conception of a historian's responsibilities: accuracy, originality, and concision. This reflects itself in his views on belles lettres (*adab*) where he championed the "moderns" in their fight against the supremacy of the "ancients" because he recognized that the moderns represented an originality of thought which was not confined to the realm of belles lettres.

In chapter 2, an attempt is made to describe his reflections on historical method and the bases of these reflections and views. Mas'ūdī was influenced by the method of the natural scientists and consequently emphasized the importance of continued research and critical inquiry into the causes of events. But some attention will also be devoted to the limitations of this method and to the question of fables and natural oddities, which have often disturbed his critical readers. In chapter 3, I try to discover how Mas'ūdī dealt with such issues as man's place in the universe, the activity of God in history and the growth and development of societies. Certain themes and patterns recur which seem to indicate that Mas'ūdī chose an encyclopaedic form for his histories because he believed that man could not be studied meaningfully except within the context of his place in his environment. Chapters 4 and 5, devoted respectively to the pre-Islamic nations and Islam, seek to apply the conclusions reached earlier to his treatment of these two subjects. Appendix A provides the fragments of a biography, while Appendix B seeks to reconstruct the contents of his lost works from references and citations found in Mas'ūdī's extant works.

Muslim historiography of the Middle Ages is a field of immense richness which has received little attention from Arabists and Islamicists. It is hoped that this study of a major Muslim historian would, with all its short-comings, prove to be of some interest in a *terra* which is, in many respects, almost *incognita*.

LIST OF ABBREVIATIONS

This list is divided into three sections:

1. Mas'ūdī's works.
2. Other primary Arabic sources.
3. Journals, encyclopaedias and other reference works.

1. The edition of the *Murūj* by Charles Pellat is now (1974) completed in five volumes. This is a revised edition of the earlier edition by C. Barbier de Meynard and Pavet de Courteille (Paris: Société Asiatique, 1861-77). The Pellat edition reproduces the pagination of the earlier edition in the text.

2. The editions in this section are arranged alphabetically according to the name or surname by which their authors have been most widely known. Under each author, his works are arranged alphabetically according to the abbreviated forms used in the footnotes. Further biographical and bibliographical information about the works or authors cited can be located in Brockelmann, *Geschichte* and Sezgin, *Geschichte*, through the use of title or author indexes.

3. Entries in this section include items abbreviated in the footnotes. Bibliographical data on secondary sources which are partially abbreviated may be found in the places where they are first cited in the footnotes.

1. Mas'ūdī's Works

Murūj — *Kitāb Murūj al-Dhahab wa Ma'ādin al-Jawhar* (*Les Prairies d'Or*) [The meadows of Gold and Mines of Gems]. Edited by C. Barbier de Meynard and Pavet de

Courteille, revised and corrected by Charles Pellat. 5 vols. Beirut: Publications de l'Université Libanaise, Section des Études Historiques. Vol. 11. 1966-74.

Tanbīh — *Kitāb al-Tanbīh wa al-Ishrāf*. Edited by M. J. de Goeje. Bibliotheca Geographorum Arabicorum, Vol. 8. Leiden: E. J. Brill, 1894.

2. Other Primary Arabic Sources

'Abd al-Jabbār ibn Aḥmad, al-Qāḍī (d. 415/1025):

Sharḥ — *Sharḥ al-Uṣūl al-Khamsa*. Edited by 'Abd al-Karīm 'Uthmān. Cairo: Maktabat Wahba, 1965.

Aristotle (d. 322 B.C.):

Arabic Meteorology — *The Arabic Version of Aristotle's Meteorology*. Edited by Casimir Petraitis. Beirut: Dār al-Mashriq, 1967.

Ash'arī, Abū al-Ḥasan 'Alī ibn Ismā'īl al- (d. 324/935):

Maqālāt — *Maqālāt al-Islāmiyyīn*. Edited by Helmut Ritter. 2 vols. Istanbul: Maṭba'at al-Dawla, 1929-30.

Baghdādī, 'Abd al-Qāhir ibn Ṭāhir al-(d. 429/1037):

Farq — *Kitāb al-Farq bayn al-Firaq*. Edited by Muḥammad Badr. Cairo: Maṭba'at al-Ma'ārif, 1328/1910.

Uṣūl — *Kitāb Uṣūl al-Dīn*. Istanbul: Maṭba'at al-Dawla, 1346/1928.

Balādhurī, Aḥmad ibn Yaḥyā al- (d. 279/892):

Futūḥ — *Kitāb Futūḥ al-Buldān*. Edited by Raḍwān Muḥammad Raḍwān. Cairo: Dār al-Ma'ārif, 1932.

Bukhārī, Muḥammad ibn Ismā'īl al- (d. 256/870):

Ṣaḥīḥ — *Ṣaḥīḥ al-Bukhārī*. Edited by Ludolf Krehl. 4 vols. Leiden: E.J. Brill, 1862-1908.

Dhahabī, Shams al-Dīn Muḥammad ibn Aḥmad al- (d. 749/1348):

Duwal — *Kitāb Duwal al-Islām*. Haidarabad: Dā'irat al-Ma'ārif, 1918.

'Ibar — *Kitāb al-'Ibar fī khabari man ghabar*. Edited by Fu'ād al-Sayyid. 3 vols. Kuwayt: Dā'irat al-Maṭbū'āt, 1960-61.

Mushtabih — *Kitāb al-Mushtabih fī al-Rijāl*. Edited by 'Alī Muḥammad al-Bajawī. 2 vols. Cairo: 'Īsā al-Bābī al-Ḥalabī, 1962.

Dīnawarī, Abū Ḥanīfa Aḥmad ibn Dāwūd al- (d. 282/895):

Akhbār — *Kitāb al-Akhbār al-Ṭiwāl*. Edited by Vladimir Guirgass. Leiden: E.J. Brill, 1888.

Eutychius (Sa'īd ibn al-Biṭrīq) (d. 328/939):

Annales — *Annales*. Edited by Louis Cheikho. Corpus Scriptorum Christianorum Orientalium, Scriptores Arabici, ser. 3, vols. 6-7. 2 vols. Beirut: Imprimerie Catholique, 1905-06.

Fārābī, Abū Naṣr Muḥammad ibn Muḥammad ibn Ṭarkhān al- (d. 339/950):

Fuṣūl — *Fuṣūl al-Madanī*; *'Aphorisms of the Statesman'*. Edited and translated by D. M. Dunlop. Cambridge: Cambridge University Press, 1961. (References are to the Arabic text).

Iḥṣā' — *Iḥṣā' al-'Ulūm*. Edited by 'Uthmān Amīn. Cairo: Dār al-Fikr al-'Arabī, 1948.

Milla — *Kitāb al-Milla*. Edited by Muḥsin Mahdī. Beirut: Dār al-Mashriq, 1968.

Fīrūzābādī, Muḥammad ibn Ya'qūb al- (d. 818/1415):

Qāmūs — *al-Qāmūs al-Muḥīṭ*. 4 vols. Būlāq: al-Maṭba'a al-Mīriyya, 1884-85.

Ḥajjī Khalīfa, Muṣṭafā ibn 'Abdallāh (d. 1069/1657):

Kashf — *Kashf al-Ẓunūn*; *'Lexicon Bibliographicum et encyclopaedicum'*. Edited by Gustav Flügel. Oriental Translation Fund of Great Britain and Ireland No. 42. 7 vols. London, 1835-58.

Ibn 'Abd Rabbihi, Aḥmad ibn Muḥammad (d. 328/940):

'Iqd — *Kitāb al-'Iqd al-Farīd*. Edited by Aḥmad Amīn. 7 vols. Cairo: Lujnat al-Ta'līf, 1940-53.

Ibn Abī al-Ḥadīd, 'Abd al-Ḥamīd ibn Hibat Allāh (d. 656/1258):

Sharḥ — *Sharḥ Nahj al-Balāgha*. Edited by Muḥam-. mad Abū al-Faḍl Ibrāhīm. 20 vols. Cairo: 'Īsā al-Bābī al-Ḥalabī, 1959-64.

Ibn Abī Uṣaybi'a, Aḥmad ibn al-Qāsim (d. 669/1270):

'Uyūn — *Kitāb 'Uyūn al-Anbā' fī Ṭabaqāt al-Aṭibbā'*. Edited by August Müller. 2 vols. Cairo/Königsberg: al-Maṭba'a al-Wahbiyya, 1882-84.

Ibn Bābawayh, Muḥammad ibn 'Alī (d. 381/991 or 992):

Ma'ānī — *Ma'ānī al-Akhbār*. Edited by 'Alī Akbar al-Ghaffārī. Teheran: Maktabat al-Ṣadūq, 1959.

Tawḥīd — *Kitāb al-Tawḥīd*. Najaf: al-Maṭba'a al-Ḥaydariyya, 1386/1966.

Ibn Ḥajar al-'Asqalānī, Aḥmad ibn 'Alī (d. 853/1449):

Lisān — *Kitāb Lisān al-Mīzān*. 6 vols. Haidarabad: Dā'irat al-Ma'ārif, 1911-13.

Ibn Ḥazm, Abū Muḥammad 'Alī (d. 456/1064):

Jamhara — *Jamharat Ansāb al-'Arab*. Edited by 'Abd al-Salām Muḥammad Hārūn. Cairo: Dār al-Ma'ārif, 1962.

Ibn Hishām, 'Abd al-Malik (d. 218/834):

Tījān — *Kitāb al-Tījān fī Mulūk Ḥimyar*. Haidarabad: Dā'irat al-Ma'ārif, 1347/1928.

Ibn al-'Imād, 'Abd al-Ḥayy ibn Aḥmad (d. 1090/1679):

Shadharāt — *Shadharāt al-Dhahab fī Akhbāri man Dhahab*. 8 vols. Cairo: Maktabat al-Qudsī, 1931-33.

Ibn Ja'far, Qudāma (d. ca. 322/933):

Naqd — *Kitāb Naqd al-Shi'r*. Edited by Seger Adrianus Bonebakker. Leiden: E. J. Brill, 1956.

Ibn Khaldūn, 'Abd al-Raḥmān (d. 808/1406):

Muqaddima — *Tārīkh Ibn Khaldūn*: *al-Muqaddima*. Vol. 1. Beirut: Dār al-Kitāb al-Lubnānī, 1961.

Ibn Khallikān, Aḥmad ibn Muḥammad (d. 681/1282):

Wafayāt — *Kitāb Wafayāt al-A'yān*. Edited by Muḥammad Muḥyiddīn 'Abd al-Ḥamīd. 6 vols. Cairo: Maktabat al-Nahḍa, 1948.

Ibn Manẓūr, Muḥammad ibn Mukarram (d. 711/1311 or 1312):

Lisān — *Lisān al-'Arab*. 15 vols. Beirut: Dār Ṣādir, 1955-56.

Ibn al-Murtaḍā, Aḥmad ibn Yaḥyā (d. 840/1437):

Ṭabaqāt — *Ṭabaqāt al-Mu'tazila*. Edited by Susanna Diwald-Walzer. Beirut: Imprimerie Catholique, 1961.

Ibn al-Mu'tazz, 'Abdallāh (d. 295/908):

Badī' — *Kitāb al-Badī'*. Edited by Ignatius Kratchkovsky. E.J.W. Gibb Memorial Series, New Series. Vol. 10. London: Luzac and Co., 1935.

Rasā'il — *Rasā'il ibn al-Mu'tazz*. Edited by Muḥammad Khaffājī. Cairo: Muṣṭafā al-Bābī al-Ḥalabī, 1365/1946.

Ṭabaqāt — *Kitāb Ṭabaqāt al-Shu'arā' al-muḥdathīn*. Reproduced in facsimile with notes by Abbas Eghbal. E.J.W. Gibb Memorial Series, New Series, Vol. 13. London: Luzac and Co., 1939.

Ibn al-Nadīm, Muḥammad ibn Abī Ya'qūb (d. after 377/987):

Fihrist — *Kitāb al-Fihrist*. Edited by Gustav Flügel. Leipzig: F.C.W. Vogel, 1871-72.

Ibn Qurra, Ibrāhīm ibn Sinān ibn Thābit (d. 335/946):

Rasā'il — *Rasā'il ibn Sinān.* Haidarabad: Dā'irat al-Ma'ārif, 1367/1948.

Ibn Qutayba, Abū Muḥammad 'Abdallāh ibn Muslim (d. 276/889):

Ma'ārif — *Kitāb al-Ma'ārif.* Edited by Tharwat 'Ukāsha. Cairo: Maṭba'at Dār al-Kutub, 1960.

al-Shi'r — *Kitāb al-Shi'r wa al-Shu'arā'*. 2 vols. Beirut: Dār al-Thaqāfa, 1964.

'Uyūn — *'Uyūn al-Akhbār.* 4 vols. Cairo: photocopy of the Dār al-Kutub edition of 1924-30, 1963.

Ibn Taghrībirdī, Abū al-Maḥāsin Yūsuf (d. 874/1469):

Nujūm — *al-Nujūm al-Zāhira.* 12 vols. Cairo: Wizārat al-Thaqāfa, 1963.

Ikhwān al-Ṣafā' (fl. ca. 10th cent.):

Rasā'il — *Rasā'il Ikhwān al-Ṣafā'*. Edited by Khayr al-Dīn al-Ziriklī. 4 vols. Cairo: al-Maktaba al-Tijāriyya, 1928.

Jāḥiẓ, Abū 'Uthmān 'Amr ibn Baḥr al- (d. 255/868):

Bayān — *Kitāb al-Bayān wa al-Tabyīn.* Edited by Ḥasan al-Sandūbī. 3 vols. Cairo: al-al-Maktaba al-Tijāriyya, 1947.

Majmū' — *Majmū' Rasā'il al-Jāḥiẓ.* Edited by Paul Kraus and Muḥammad Ṭāha al-Ḥājirī. Cairo: Lujnat al-Ta'līf, 1943.

Rasā'il — *Rasā'il al-Jāḥiẓ.* Edited by Ḥasan al-Sandūbī. Cairo: al-Maktaba al-Tijāriyya, 1933.

Rasā'il, ed. Hārūn — *Rasā'il al-Jāḥiẓ.* Edited by 'Abd al-Salām Muḥammad Hārūn. 2 vols. Cairo: Maktabat al-Khānjī, 1964-65.

Thalāth Rasā'il — *Thalāth Rasā'il.* Edited by J. Finkel. Cairo: al-Maṭba'a al-Salafiyya, 1926.

Jawharī, Ismā'īl ibn Ḥammād al- (d. 394/1003?):

Ṣiḥāḥ — *Tāj al-Lugha wa Ṣiḥāḥ al-'Arabiyya*. 2 vols. Būlāq: al-Maṭba'a al-'Āmira, 1865.

Khayyāṭ, Abū al-Ḥasan 'Abd al-Raḥmān ibn Muḥammad al- (d. ca. 300/912):

Intiṣār — *Kitāb al-Intiṣār*. Edited by Albert Nader. Beirut: Imprimerie Catholique, 1957.

Kindī, Ya'qūb ibn Isḥāq al- (d. ca. 260/873):

Rasā'il — *Rasā'il al-Kindī al-Falsafiyya*. Edited by Muḥammad 'Abd al-Hādī Abū Rīda. Cairo: Dār al-Fikr al-'Arabī, 1950.

Kulaynī, Muḥammad ibn Ya'qūb al- (d. 328/939):

Kāfī — *al-Uṣūl min al-Kāfī*. Edited by 'Alī Akbar al-Ghaffārī. Vol. 1. Teheran: n. p., 1381/1961.

Kutubī, Muḥammad ibn Shākir al- (d. 764/1363):

Fawāt — *Fawāt al-Wafayāt*. Edited by Muḥammad Muḥyiddīn 'Abd al-Ḥamīd. 2 vols. Cairo: Maktabat al-Nahḍa, 1951.

Manbijī, Maḥbūb (Agapius) ibn Qusṭanṭīn al- (fl. 10th cent.):

'Unwān — *Kitāb al-'Unwān*. Edited by Louis Cheikho. Corpus Scriptorum Christianorum Orientalium, Scriptores Arabici, ser. 3, vol. 5. Beirut: Imprimerie Catholique, 1912.

Maqdisī, al-Muṭahhar ibn Ṭāhir al- (fl. ca. 355/966):

Bad' — *Kitāb al-Bad' wa al-Ta'rīkh*. Edited and translated by Clement Huart. 6 vols. Paris: E. Leroux, 1899-1919. (References are to pages of Arabic text.)

Najāshī, Aḥmad ibn 'Alī al- (d. 450/1058):

Rijāl — *Kitāb al-Rijāl*. Edited by Jalāl al-Dīn al-Gharawī al-Āmulī. Teheran: Markaz Nashr Kitāb, n.d.

Nawbakhtī, al-Ḥasan ibn Mūsā al- (d. 310/922):

Firaq	*Kitāb Firaq al-Shī'a*. Edited by Helmut Ritter. Istanbul: Staats Druckerei, 1931.

Ṣā'id (Ibn Ṣā'id) al-Andalusī (d. 462/1069):

Ṭabaqāt	*Kitāb Ṭabaqāt al-Umam*. Edited by Louis Cheikho. Beirut: Imprimerie Catholique, 1912.

Shahrastānī, Muḥammad ibn 'Abd al-Karīm al- (d. 548/1153):

Milal	*Kitāb al-Milal wa al-Niḥal*. Edited by Aḥmad Fahmī Maḥmūd. 3 vols. Cairo: Maktabat al-Ḥusayn, 1948-49.

Sijistānī, Abū Ya'qūb Isḥāq ibn Aḥmad al- (d. after 361/971):

Ithbāt	*Kitāb Ithbāt al-Nubū'āt*. Edited by 'Ārif Tāmir. Beirut: Imprimerie Catholique, 1966.

Subkī, Tāj al-Dīn 'Abd al-Wahhāb ibn 'Alī al- (d. 722/1370):

Ṭabaqāt	*Ṭabaqāt al-Shāfi'iyya al-Kubrā*. 6 vols. Cairo: al-Maṭba'a al-Ḥusayniyya, 1905-06.

Ṣūlī, Muḥammad ibn Yaḥyā al- (d. 335/946):

Adab	*Adab al-Kuttāb*. Edited by Muḥammad Bahjat al-Atharī. Cairo: al-Maṭba'a al-Salafiyya, 1341/1922.
Akhbār Abī Tammām	*Akhbār Abī Tammām*. Edited by Khalīl Maḥmūd 'Asākir et al. Cairo: n.p., 1356/1937.
Akhbār al-Buḥturī	*Akhbār al-Buḥturī*. Edited by Ṣalāḥ al-Ashtar. Damascus: Publications de L'Academie arabe de Damas, 1378/1958.
Awrāq	*Kitāb al-Awrāq*; *Qism Akhbār al-Shu'arā'*; *'Section on Contemporary Poets'*. Edited by J. Heyworth Dunne. London: Luzac and Co., 1934.

Ṭabarī, Abū Ja'far Muḥammad ibn Jarīr al- (d. 310/923):

Annales	*Annales*. Edited by M. J. de Goeje et

al. Editio photomechanice iterata. 13 vols. Lugduni Batavorum: E. J. Brill, 1964-65.

Tafsīr — *Jāmiʿ al-Bayān fī Tafsīr al-Qurʾān.* 30 vols. Cairo: n. p., 1321/1903.

Tawḥīdī, Abū Ḥayyān ʿAlī ibn Muḥammad al- (fl. late 10th cent.):

Imtāʿ — *Kitāb al-Imtāʿ wa al-Muʾānasa.* Edited by Aḥmad Amīn and Aḥmad al-Zayn. 3 vols. Cairo: Lujnat al-Ta'līf, 1939.

Yaʿqūbī, Aḥmad ibn Abī Yaʿqūb ibn Wāḍiḥ al- (d. ca. 284/897):

Historiae — *Historiae.* Edited by M. Th. Houtsma. 2 vols. Leiden: E.J. Brill, 1883.

Yāqūt ibn ʿAbdallāh al-Ḥamawī (d. 626/1229):

Muʿjam — *Muʿjam al-Udabāʾ al-Musammā bi Irshād al-Arīb ilā maʿrifat al-Adīb.* 20 vols. Cairo: Maṭbaʿat Dār al-Ma'mūn, 1936-38.

Zabīdī, al-Murtaḍā al- (d. 1206/1791):

Sharḥ — *Sharḥ al-Qāmūs al-Musammā Tāj al-ʿArūs min Jawāhir al-Qāmūs.* 10 vols. Cairo: al-Maṭbaʿa al-Khayriyya, 1889-90.

Zamakhsharī, Maḥmūd ibn ʿUmar al- (d. 538/1144):

Asās — *Asās al-Balāgha.* Cairo: n.p., 1327/1909.

3. Journals, Encyclopaedias and Other Reference Works

Der Islam — *Der Islam.* Berlin, 1910----.

Encyclopaedia, ed. Houtsma et al. — *The Encyclopaedia of Islam.* Edited by M. Th. Houtsma et al. 4 vols. Leiden: E. J. Brill, 1913-34.

Encyclopaedia, Supplement — *The Encyclopaedia of Islam. Supplement.* Edited by M. Th. Houtsma et al. Leiden: E. J. Brill, 1938.

Encyclopaedia, ed. Gibb et al. — *The Encyclopaedia of Islam.* Edited by H.A.R. Gibb et al. New Edition. Leiden: E. J. Brill, 1960----.

Brockelmann, *Geschichte*	Brockelmann, Carl. *Geschichte der arabischen Literatur; Zweite den Supplementbände angepasste Auflage*. 2 vols. Leiden: E. J. Brill, 1943-49.
Brockelmann, *Supplement*	Ibid. *Supplementbände*. 3 vols. Leiden: E. J. Brill, 1937-42.
Sezgin, *Geschichte*	Sezgin, Fuat. *Geschichte des arabischen Schrifttums*. Vol. 1. Leiden: E.J. Brill, 1967.
Historians of the Middle East	Lewis, Bernard and Holt, P. M., eds. *Historians of the Middle East*. London: Oxford University Press, 1962.
Islamic Culture	*Islamic Culture*. Hayderabad, Deccan, 1927----.
Islamic Quarterly	*Islamic Quarterly*. London, 1954----.
Journal Asiatique	*Journal Asiatique*. Paris, 1822----.
Journal of the American Oriental Society	*Journal of the American Oriental Society*. New Haven, 1843---.
Journal of The Pakistan Historical Society	*Journal of the Pakistan Historical Society*. Karachi, 1953---.
Al-Mas'ūdī, ed. Ahmad and Rahman	Ahmad, S. Maqbul and Rahman, A., eds. *Al-Mas'ūdī Millenary Commemoration Volume*. Aligarh: Indian Society for the History of Sciences and Institute of Islamic Studies, Aligarh Muslim University, 1960.
Majallat	*Majallat al-Majma' al-'Ilmī al-'Irāqī*. Baghdad, 1950---.
Muslim World	*The Muslim World*. Hartford, 1911---.
S E I	*Shorter Encyclopaedia of Islam*. Edited by H.A.R. Gibb and J. H. Kramers. Leiden: E. J. Brill, 1953.
Studia Islamica	*Studia Islamica*. Paris, 1953---.
Wiener Zeitschrift	*Wiener Zeitschrift für die Kunde des Morgenlandes*. Wien, 1887----.
Zeitschrift für die Kunde	*Zeitschrift für die Kunde des Morgenlandes*. Göttingen, 1837-50.
Zeitschrift für Semitistik	*Zeitschrift für Semitistik*. Leipzig, 1922-35.

1. SOURCES AND STYLE

Range of Sources

As an introduction to the present study of Mas'ūdī's history, this chapter proposes to examine the range of Mas'ūdī's sources and his handling of them, together with some salient features of his style and his literary affinities. Such a survey will help to elucidate his working method as a historian and to point to certain of his important theoretical reflections on history which are to be elaborated in later chapters. Mas'ūdī was concerned to obtain his information from the best available sources and passed frequent judgments on the reliability (or otherwise) of these sources. These judgments provide a valuable clue to his methods of gathering and sifting the information he obtained. On the other hand, his literary style will be examined through an analysis of his literary affinities. Mas'ūdī was keenly aware of the literary movements and controversies of his day. His style was therefore the product of his own views on contemporary literature. The analysis of his style, which will serve to complement the analysis of the handling of his sources, throws light on Mas'ūdī's historical craft, his practice of history. With these preliminary observations, we now turn to examine his sources.

The fabric of Mas'ūdī's histories is sustained by three main categories of sources: written, oral and experiential. It was primarily in the latter two categories that Mas'ūdī believed his unique contribution to historiography to lie:

> [For there can be no comparison between] one who lingers among his own kinsmen and is satisfied with whatever information reaches him about his part of the world, and another who spends a lifetime in travelling the world, carried to and fro by his

journeys, extracting every fine nugget from its mine and every valuable object from its place of seclusion.[1]

To symbolize this quest for the "gems" of knowledge, Mas'ūdī chose an appropriate title for his major surviving work of history: *Murūj al-Dhahab wa Ma'ādin al-Jawhar* [The Meadows of Gold and Mines of Gems]. He likens himself to one who found gems of various kinds scattered about from which he fashioned a necklace (*'iqd*) and a precious adornment (*'ilq*) to be treasured by the one who seeks it.[2] His work, therefore, is not the compilation of an armchair historian

[1] Mas'ūdī, *Murūj*, sec. 7.

[2] Mas'ūdī, *Murūj*, sec. 3609. A minor controversy has arisen over the exact translation of the word *Murūj*. The usual translation of meadows was first challenged by J. Gildemeister, "Über den Titel des Masudischen Werkes *Murūj al-Dhahab*", *Zeitschrift fur die kunde*, 9: 202-204. Gildemeister's arguments are of considerable interest and may be summarized as follows: (1) There is a logical contradiction between meadow (*marj*) and gold (*dhahab*). (2) Mas'ūdī gives one no reason to ascribe such a strange and false image to him. (3) Even if one grants that the term is a poetic metaphor, what is to be done with the prosaic parallel "... and mines of gems" (*wa ma'ādin al-jawhar*)? Gildemeister then proposes that the clue to the riddle is in a variant reading (cf. Mas'ūdī, *Murūj*, sec. 217) found in a MS, "*wa bi nahr al-Multān marj al-dhahab*", which he, relying on some accounts of the geography of India, translates as "and in the river of Multān there is sifting of gold." Therefore, he concludes, 'goldwashings' (*Goldwäschen*) is not only more accurate from a geographical and historical point of view, but is in keeping with the author's intention in his work — to derive value from an unruly mass of facts. Thus by "washing the gold" one is led to the gems themselves.

Carl Brockelmann in the first edition of his *Geschichte der Arabischen Literatur* ([Leipzig: C. F. Amelangs, 1901], p. 110), adopts this interpretation and translates the title as "Die Goldwäschen und Edelsteingruben." (See also *idem*, "al-Mas'ūdī," *Encyclopaedia*, ed. Gibb et al., 3: 403.) George Sarton in his *Introduction to the History of Science* ([Baltimore: Carnegie Institute of Washington, 1927–48], 1: 638) writes: "The translation of Murūj by 'meadows' does not seem to fit the sense or the parallelism. It has been suggested that it means washings in the mining sense."

Despite the obvious attraction of this interpretation of the title, it has serious linguistic and stylistic shortcomings, some of which are indicated by Charles Pellat in his revised translation of the Barbier de Maynard and Pavet de Courteille edition *Les Prairies d'Or* (Paris: Société Asiatique, 1962), Avant-Propos, pp. I-II. Pellat retains meadows (*prairies*) in the title because he could not find any lexicographical justification for translating *murūj* by "washings." He further quotes *Murūj*, sec. 796 where Mas'ūdī speaks of a land sprouting gold (*tunbit al-dhahab*) as an example of the imagery which may have suggested itself to the author.

In accepting the validity of Pellat's remarks one may add that *murūj* and *ma'ādin* appear, grammatically speaking, to be two contrasting *nomina loci*. Whether

but the careful record of a man who actively pursued knowledge back to its sources.

The oral information was gleaned from debates as well as interrogations. Debates were, no doubt, an invaluable source of information, especially on the beliefs of the various non-Muslim religions. Masʿūdī records that he held public debates with Christians, Jews and Khurramiyya, in Iraq, Palestine and Persia.[1] He was conversant enough with the theologies of these creeds to be able to appraise the worth of his various disputants to many of whom he was generous in his praise.[2] Masʿūdī also interrogated a great number of people from all walks of life whom he met on his travels. Merchants, seamen, scholars and travellers provided him with geographical and historical information untapped by earlier historians. In several cases,

or not gold was sifted in the river Multān, Gildemeister's objections may be countered as follows: (1) The MSS, consulted by both Barbier de Maynard and Pellat read "and the meaning of Multān is the house of gold" (*wa al-Multān farj al-dhahab*). (See also Masʿūdī, *Tanbīh*, p. 55 and Maqdisī, *Bad'*, 4: 77). The root *mrj* does not mean to sift or wash but to mix. Thus, even if one were able to derive *murūj* as a *nomen actionis* from *mrj*, this would mean "the mixing of gold" rather than "gold-washings."

One further point may be made in this regard. An examination of the titles of books cited by Ibn al-Nadīm in the *Fihrist* reveals that images of gardens and of gold or gems recur frequently, e.g., "The Well-groomed Gardens" (*al-Riyāḍ al-Mu'niqa*), p. 59; "The Chain of Gold" (*Silsilat al-Dhahab*), p. 83; "The Gems of Reports" (*Jawāhir al-Akhbār*), p. 113; "The Sifting of Gems" (*Muntakhal al-Jawāhir*), p. 100; "The Basket of Gems" (*Safaṭ al-Jawhar*), p. 151. Other titles which refer to gardens or gems may be found in *Fihrist*, pp. 116, 117, 146, 148, 149, 317. Thus, the imagery in Masʿūdī's title appears to belong to the conventions of his day and age. The words *murūj al-dhahab* suggest an image of gold neatly spread out like a well-groomed lawn. In comparing his book to a necklace (*ʿiqd*), Masʿūdī is evoking a similar aesthetic tableau.

[1] Masʿūdī, *Tanbīh*, pp. 155, 113–14, 353–54. On the Khurramiyya, see Baghdādī, *Farq*, pp. 251–52.

[2] Ibn al-Murtaḍā in his *Ṭabaqāt*, p. 88, mentions a debate with a Jew in Baghdad on the abrogation of religious laws, which probably took place in the early years of the 4th/10th century. This may well have been one of the debates to which Masʿūdī refers in *Tanbīh*, pp. 113–14. For the record of a famous debate held in 326, which may be regarded as typical of its kind and period, see Abū Ḥayyān al-Tawḥīdī, *Imtāʿ*, 1: 107 ff. Cf. also Gustave E. von Grunebaum, *Medieval Islam* (Chicago: Phœnix Books, 1966), p. 248, n. 63; Shawqī Ḍayf, *al-ʿAṣr al-ʿAbbāsī al-Awwal* (Cairo: Dār al-Maʿārif, 1966), pp. 457–64 (hereafter referred to as *al-ʿAṣr al-ʿAbbāsī*). In at least one instance, Masʿūdī seems to have actively sought out his disputants, for he mentions that the debate with the Christian was held in a church in Takrīt (Masʿūdī, *Tanbīh*, p. 155).

these informants supplied him with or corrected data about countries which he was unable to visit.[1] The information which he accepted came from men whom he often refers to as knowledgeable, discriminating, or cultured.[2]

The range of Mas'ūdī's written sources is very extensive. It encompasses not only the well-known Muslim works on history, geography, astronomy, philosophy and theology but also a wealth of other, non-Muslim material. Translations of Greek scientific and philosophical works are extensively quoted, as well as Indian, Persian, Christian, Jewish and other sectarian works. In some instances, Mas'ūdī makes mention of government archives as sources of information.[3]

Mas'ūdī's own observations form a valuable part of his work. In contrast to Ṭabarī, who provides little or no information on the lands and peoples of his own day, Mas'ūdī often corroborated or

[1] E.g., Mas'ūdī, *Murūj*, secs. 228, 295–96, 349, 367, 822, 895, 1395; Mas'ūdī, *Tanbīh*, pp. 89, 110, 174. Cf. Jawād 'Alī, "Mawārid Ta'rīkh al-Ṭabarī," *Majallat* 2 (1951): 174; Lewicki, "al-Mas'ūdī on the Slavs," *Al-Mas'ūdī*, ed. Ahmad and Rahman, pp. 11–13, who conjectures that the numerous Slavonic slaves in Muslim lands supplied Mas'ūdī with his information on matters Slavic; S. Maqbūl Aḥmad, "Travels of Abu'l Ḥasan 'Alī b. al-Ḥusayn al-Mas'ūdī," *Islamic Culture* 28 (1954): 509–24; *idem*, "al-Mas'ūdī on the Kings of India," *Al-Mas'ūdī*, ed. Ahmad and Rahman, pp. 97 ff.

[2] Mas'ūdī, *Tanbīh*, pp. 110, 384; Mas'ūdī, *Murūj*, secs. 296, 739.

[3] E.g., Mas'ūdī, *Murūj*, secs. 8–14: a general historical and geographical bibliography; *Murūj*, secs. 719, 1293, 1405 and Mas'ūdī, *Tanbīh*, pp. 154–55: Christian sources; *Murūj*, secs. 541, 586, 644 and *Tanbīh*, pp. 106, 110: Persian sources; *Tanbīh*, p. 135: Manichaean sources; *Tanbīh*, p. 384: Qarmatian sources; *Tanbīh*, pp. 40, 190: government archives; *Murūj*, sec. 167: Indian sources; *Murūj*, secs. 547–49: Zoroastrian sources; *Murūj*, secs. 733, 1422: Roman sources; *Murūj*, sec. 914: Frankish sources; *Tanbīh*, pp. 94, 112: Jewish sources. There is a valuable assessment of some of these sources in D. M. Dunlop, *Arab Civilization to A.D. 1500* (London: Longman, 1971), pp. 99-114 (hereafter referred to as *Arab Civilization*). References to Greek philosophical and scientific works are found *passim*. These works were either written in, or translated into, Arabic. Mas'ūdī evidently knew no Greek (*Murūj*, sec. 193). Cf. S. M. Stern, "Al-Mas'ūdī and the Philosopher al-Fārābī," *Al-Mas'ūdī*, ed. Ahmad and Rahman, pp. 32, n. 1 and 39, n. 1, who points out mistranslations of Greek names. Fehmi Jadaane, *L'Influence du Stoïcisme sur la Pensée Musulmane* (Beirut: Imprimerie Catholique, 1968), pp. 58–59, argues on the basis of Mas'ūdī's statement in *Tanbīh*, p. 115, that he probably knew Greek. But this is dubious. Whether he knew Persian or not is an open question. See *Murūj*, secs. 539, 571, 618, 637, 650, 1116, 1299, 1416; *Tanbīh*, pp. 86, 95, 103–4. We incline to think that he did.

rejected geographical and other data acquired second-hand.[1] At least one of his lost books, his *K. al-Qaḍāyā wa al-Tajārib*, is a record of the experiences encountered on his voyages, for in describing that book, he writes:

> We described therein all that we saw and experienced in our travels over lands and kingdoms and all reports we heard of the world of nature, animal, vegetable and mineral and their effect upon marvels of buildings, monuments and countries.[2]

The Historian's Craft

To describe the historian's craft, especially his activity as a compiler, Mas'ūdī chose a curious phrase: a "woodcutter by night" (*ḥāṭib layl*).[3] In Arabic dictionaries, this phrase is said to apply to those who mix the weighty with the trivial in their discourse just as the woodcutter at night gathers in the good timber along with the bad.[4] At first sight, the choice of this particular image appears to be an unhappy one since it undermines the lofty conception which Mas'ūdī had of his own achievements as a historian. If the historian-compiler is no better than a woodcutter by night, then history itself becomes the idle pastime of the dilettante.

Nothing could be further from Mas'ūdī's purpose or method. The use of the phrase, despite its apparent incongruity, illuminates an important facet of his method as a historian. A historian for Mas'ūdī is one who brings together what is variegated or disparate (*muṣannif*). In order to be faithful to his profession, the historian must record all

1 E.g., *Murūj*, secs. 705, 502–3, 245-46, 295-96; *Tanbīh*, p. 66. For the contrast between the two historians, see Jawād 'Alī, "Mawārid Ta'rīkh al-Ṭabarī," *Majallat* 1 (1950): 170.

2 *Murūj*, sec. 815. The various kinds of knowledge together with Mas'ūdī's views will be discussed in chapter 2.

3 Mas'ūdī, *Murūj*, secs. 1205, 1354.

4 Ibn Manẓūr, *Lisān*, 1:322; Zamakhsharī, *Asās*, 1:96; Jawharī, *Ṣiḥāḥ*, 1:44; Fīrūzābādī, *Qāmūs*, 1:56; al-Murtaḍā al-Zabīdī, *Tāj*, 1:216. According to this latter, the phrase was first coined by Aktham ibn Ṣayfī, the pre-Islamic sage, who compared the talkative man to the woodcutter by night (*al-mikthār ḥāṭib layl*). Mas'ūdī quotes the adage as *al-mukthir ḥāṭib layl* which conveys the same sense (see Mas'ūdī, *Murūj*, sec. 892).

the diverse facts and opinions bearing upon a single theme which are known to him.[1] Furthermore, Mas'ūdī has in several places indicated that his two surviving books deal with reports (*khabar*, *akhbār*), not research and critical inquiry (*baḥth wa naẓar*). If the historian's work is to be comprehensive and all-inclusive, it would reflect the texture of life around him in all its diversity. Mas'ūdī, therefore, uses the phrase "woodcutter by night" not as an apology for being slovenly but rather as a reflection on the diversity of life itself.[2] The attempt to record the diversity of life is a characteristic of *adab* and its influence on Mas'ūdī, as will be seen below.

Information must be taken from all quarters. Mas'ūdī quotes with approval the saying of 'Alī ibn Abī Ṭālib: "Wisdom is the elusive desire of the believer. Seek your desire even among the polytheists".[3] This advice he follows to the letter. Wherever possible, Mas'ūdī collates divergent facts or opinions by introducing such words as "and a dispute arose concerning" or "and people disagree concerning" followed by the different versions. But two important factors limit and define such collation of reports.[4] To begin with, Mas'ūdī held that the mere recording of a fact or an opinion did not signify approval of its content or veracity.[5] This attitude to reports is basic to the science

[1] Mas'ūdī, *Murūj*, secs. 556, 1205.

[2] E.g., Mas'ūdī, *Murūj*, sec. 2958.

[3] *Murūj*, sec. 2848; cf. Ya'qūbī, *Historiae*, 2: 2–3; Ibn Qutayba, *'Uyūn*, I, *mīm*. Mas'ūdī is here paraphrasing the words of Ibn al-Mu'tazz as quoted in Ṣūlī, *Akhbār Abī Tammām*, p. 176.

[4] In overlooking these two factors, many medieval and modern commentators on Mas'ūdī have branded him as credulous and superstitious. We take it that the charge of credulity was first brought against Mas'ūdī by Ibn Khaldūn (for full references, see Walter J. Fischel, "Ibn Khaldūn and al-Mas'ūdī," *Al-Mas'ūdī*, ed. Ahmad and Rahman, p. 55, n. 1–6). It has since been taken up and repeated by several scholars both Eastern and Western: see, e.g., Jawād 'Alī, "Mawārid Ta'rīkh al-Ṭabarī," *Majallat* 2 (1951): 176; Grunebaum, *Medieval Islam*, p. 119; Mohibbul Ḥasan, "Al-Mas'ūdī on Kashmir," *Al-Mas'ūdī*, ed. Ahmad and Rahman, p. 26; Carl Brockelmann, "Mas'ūdī," *Encyclopaedia*, ed. Houtsma et al, 3: 403–4.

[5] This problem is dealt with in general terms in Franz Rosenthal, *A History of Muslim Historiography*, 2nd ed., rev., (Leiden: E. J. Brill, 1968), pp. 63–65, and, esp., p. 108 (hereafter referred to as *Muslim Historiography*), where Rosenthal writes: "In the opening chapter of the Murūj . . . al-Mas'ūdī also made it quite clear by implication that he was approaching a scientific subject which might even be in contradiction to the religious precepts of Islam." The passage in question, *Murūj*, sec. 42, does not bear out Rosenthal's interpretation. Mas'ūdī

of Tradition where "although the invention and wanton dissemination of false traditions was condemned by Muslims, alleviating elements were recognized in certain circumstances, particularly when it was a question of edifying sayings and moral teachings in the name of the Prophet".[1]

Muslim historiography displayed a similar attitude. The didactic value of legends of prophets was recognized by the earliest Muslim historians.[2] The mere inclusion of such legends cannot therefore be sufficient cause for convicting Mas'ūdī of credulity, especially since accounts of the creation and of pre-Islamic history, containing much legendary material, had come to occupy a firm place in the histories of Mas'ūdī's forerunners: Dīnawarī, Ya'qūbī and Ṭabarī.[3] Maqdisī, in recording such legends, often appended allegorical interpretations to them and thus explicitly consummated what was implicit in many of his predecessors.[4]

In the second place, Mas'ūdī repeatedly admonishes the reader to pay careful attention to his treatment of the subject matter, which he acknowledges to be brief but suggestive and thought-provoking. The manner in which various accounts or opinions are presented often suggests interesting clues to Mas'ūdī's intellectual affinities. Such stylistic clues are not, of course, sufficient of themselves to establish beyond doubt his views on certain issues raised in his histories. But they do reinforce the numerous passages in which Mas'ūdī explicitly states his views on such topics as the value of history, the scope of

merely states that his book contains a resume (*jumal*) of speculative, demonstrative and dialectical sciences (*'ulūm al-naẓar wa al-barāhīn wa al-jadal*) relating to many opinions and religions (*ārā' wa niḥal*) by way of historical report (*'alā ṭarīq al-khabar*). The only legitimate implication here is that Mas'ūdī does not necessarily subscribe to every opinion he records. Cf. Mas'ūdī, *Murūj*, secs. 212, 1327, 1345; Ṭabarī, *Annales*, 1: 6; Maqdisī, *Bad'*, 1: 154; 2: 25; Franz Rosenthal, *The Technique and Approach of Muslim Scholarship* (Rome: Pontificium Institutum Biblicum, 1947), pp. 42–43 (hereafter referred to as *Technique*).

1 T. W. Juynboll, "Ḥadīth", *SEI*, p. 117.

2 Cf. Nabia Abbott, *Studies in Arabic Literary Papyri*, vol. 1, *Historical Texts* (Chicago: The University of Chicago Press, 1957). (Hereafter referred to as *Studies*, 1).

3 Cf. Rosenthal, *Muslim Historiography*, pp. 133–36; *idem*, in *Historians of the Middle East*, ed. Bernard Lewis and P. M. Holt (London: Oxford University Press, 1962), pp. 40–44. Mas'ūdī's views on the value of history will be dealt with in chap. 2.

4 Cf. Maqdisī, *Bad'*, 2: 33–34.

knowledge, and the supernatural. Perhaps the most conspicuous of these clues in Mas'ūdī's presentation of conflicting reports or opinions is his tendency to preface these accounts with the one he subscribes to or deems the most reasonable. Numerous examples of this practice can be cited in earlier and contemporary Muslim historians.[1] In Mas'ūdī, this stylistic device assumes greater significance because of his more pronounced interest in the theoretical aspects of his subject. A mere literary device in earlier historians becomes a valuable intellectual pointer in the case of Mas'ūdī.[2]

However, it must be borne in mind that such stylistic idiosyncracies serve neither to establish nor to invalidate the views of Mas'ūdī but merely to corroborate them. A case in point is the use of the verb "to allege" (*za'ama*). It has been suggested that phrases like "some allege" (*za'ama ba'ḍuhum*) or "it is said" (*yuqāl*) indicate a certain scepticism in Ṭabarī and Ibn Isḥāq.[3] But due caution must be exercised in the case of Mas'ūdī. Broadly speaking, the verb *za'ama* is used in conjunction either with a false opinion or with an opinion concerning which Mas'ūdī is noncommittal.[4] For Mas'ūdī believed

[1] E.g., Balādhurī, *Futūḥ*, pp. 92, 94, 129, 148, 177, 181, 201, 286; Ṭabarī, *Annales*, 1: 52; Dīnawarī, *Akhbār*, pp. 30, 73, 129, 190; Maqdisī, *Bad'*, 4: 105–6.

[2] See Mas'ūdī's interesting presentation of the disputed question of the faith of the Prophet's grandfather, 'Abd al-Muṭṭalib (cf. Mas'ūdī, *Murūj*, secs. 1126 and 1138); the story of David and Uriah and the larger question of the sins of prophets or their immunity (*'iṣma*) thereform (Mas'ūdī, *Murūj*, sec. 104); the faith of the Pharaoh of Egypt who made Joseph the governor of his domains (*Murūj*, sec. 783); also *Murūj*, secs. 1113–18 on the genealogy of the Kurds; *Tanbīh*, p. 231 and *Murūj*, sec. 1463 on 'Alī as the first believer; *Murūj*, secs. 509 and 521 on the Siryān and Nabaṭ; *Murūj*, sec. 1207 on the explanation of phantom voices in the wilderness (*hawātif*); *Murūj*, sec. 76 on Abraham's knowledge of God; *Tanbīh*, p. 271 on the Prophet's declaration to 'Alī that he ('Alī) was to him as Hārūn was to Mūsā; *Murūj*, sec. 755 on the Byzantine Emperor who was reigning at the time of the Prophet's birth; in general, see *Tanbīh*, pp. 51, 239, 300.

[3] Cf. Jawād 'Alī, "Mawārid Ta'rīkh al-Ṭabarī," *Majallat* 1 (1950): 168; Alfred Guillaume, *Life of Muḥammad* (London: Oxford University Press, 1955), Introduction, pp. XIX, XX.

[4] For *za'ama* with false opinions, cf. Mas'ūdī, *Murūj*, secs. 295–96, 563–65, 1339, 1196–97, 1161,1117; *Tanbīh*, pp. 67, 144. For *za'ama* with non-committal opinions, see *Tanbīh*, pp. 62, 87; *Murūj*, secs. 826, 1321, 1345, 1358. Cf. Nabia Abbott, *Studies in Arabic Literary Papyri*, vol. 2, *Qur'ānic Commentary and Tradition* (Chicago: The University of Chicago Press, 1967), p. 63 (hereafter referred to as *Studies*, 2); 'Abdul Laṭīf Ṭībāwī, "Ibn Isḥāq's *Sīra*, a critique of Professor Guillaume's English Translation," *Islamic Quarterly* 3 (October, 1956): 208–9.

that he had taken the greatest care to ensure accuracy of presentation and had discerned the import of all that he had learnt. He further claimed that he did not champion any particular doctrine and had narrated only what reflected credit on people.[1]

Now accuracy of presentation for Masʻūdī entailed either a return to the sources of information or a reliance on the "specialists" in each branch of knowledge. The return to the sources meant, in the first place, a rejection of "imitation of authority" (*taqlīd*) especially insofar as it implied that only an ancient few possessed the necessary learning to derive knowledge from its sources.[2] It meant, in the second place, that particular nations or sects were preeminently qualified to provide accurate information on their own history or dogma.[3] Finally, and to a less pronounced degree, it meant a return to the Koran as an arbiter in certain questions of fact or theory.[4]

Masʻūdī's reliance on "specialists" in each field raises certain problems of historical method. Who are the best authorities in each subject, and why are they so? Leaving aside for the moment the larger implications of the second question, it appears that Masʻūdī drew his information from those sources which in his opinion had made a thorough and specialized study of their chosen subject or had been in the most ideal position to observe or record the facts they narrate. In the natural sciences, his authorities were the Muslim and Greek scientists and astronomers. As if to underline the authenticity of his information, Masʻūdī occasionally reminds his readers that such scientific data cannot be found in the works of jurists who reason by analogy (*al-fuqahāʼ al-qāʼisūn*). The same holds true for chronology, where Masʻūdī draws upon the tables of astronomers, especially for the post-Hijra era, because these astronomers, as opposed to historical reporters, have closely studied these dates and have mastered them with precision.[5]

1 Masʻūdī, *Murūj*, secs. 291, 3609; *Tanbīh*, pp. 50, 279.

2 Cf. Joseph Schacht, "Taḳlīd," *SEI*, p. 563. Masʻūdī's views on *taqlīd* will be discussed in chap. 2.

3 E.g., Masʻūdī, *Murūj*, secs. 562, 571, 1382, 1393, 1395, 1397, 2151, 2152; *Tanbīh*, pp. 80, 105–6, 110, 300.

4 E.g., Masʻūdī, *Murūj*, secs. 66, 1324, 1438 where Masʻūdī quotes the Koranic verses which militate against the exact computation of past ages. Ṭabarī's reliance on Koran and Ḥadīth to settle historical problems is far more pronounced.

5 *Murūj*, secs. 1221, 1510, 3621. Cf. Rosenthal, *Technique*, pp. 60 ff.

More light is thrown on Mas'ūdī's method when one examines the occasional critical references that he makes to his predecessors and attempts to determine his reasons for praising or blaming them. From the bibliography which he sets down at the beginning of the *Murūj* and in scattered references throughout his two surviving works, it is possible to reconstruct the qualities which Mas'ūdī particularly admired in earlier historians.[1] To begin with, Mas'ūdī praised the historians who were eyewitnesses to the events they record and consistently preferred their testimony over all others. Muḥammad ibn Yaḥyā al-Ṣūlī (d. 335/946) comes in for special praise, "since he records unusual events which befell no other man, and others which he alone records because he himself witnessed them".[2] In consequence, the few words of introduction by which Mas'ūdī occasionally presents his authorities to the reader often reflect his confidence in the competence of that authority to have witnessed and judged events at first hand. In the period of the Umayyad and Abbasid Caliphates, many of his authorities are learned men who kept the company of princes and Caliphs and were intimate and judicious observers of the court life around them.[3] Conversely, Mas'ūdī in one instance preferred an earlier to a later account of an incident largely by virtue of its antiquity.[4]

Of even greater significance to Mas'ūdī's own work is the praise he bestows on historians displaying breadth of vision, wide intellectual interests or encyclopaedic curiosity. Ibn Khurradādhbih's lost history is singled out as "the most painstaking of its genre, the most skillfully composed, the most instructive and with the most comprehensive account of the history of nations and kings, Persians as well as others." Balādhurī's *Futūḥ* is similarly extolled among other things for its description of lands in the four quarters of the earth. Ṭabarī's history outshines other works since it comprehends diverse kinds of historical

[1] Cf. Rosenthal, *Technique*, pp. 65–66, who comments as follows: "Historians occasionally maintain that the opportunity to use contemporary material and to be an eyewitness of the reported events constitutes a considerable advantage for historical writers. As-Sakhāwī thus declares that as-Ṣūlī's *History of the Wazirs* benefitted from the fact that its author was an eyewitness of many of the events he described." Al-Sakhāwī is quoting Mas'ūdī, *Murūj*, sec. 11; cf. Rosenthal, *Muslim Historiography*, p. 412, n. 5.

[2] Mas'ūdī, *Murūj*, sec. 11.

[3] E.g., *Murūj*, secs. 2471, 2613, 2621, 2685, 3042, 3140, 3291, 3543.

[4] *Tanbīh*, p. 344.

reports, traditions and sciences. Aḥmad ibn al-Ṭayyib al-Sarakhsī (d. 286/899), Muḥammad ibn Aḥmad al-Jayhānī (d. ca. 313/925), and Ibn Abī ʻAwn (d. 322/934) are likewise commended for works which embrace geographical as well as historical information on the world around them.[1] It may also be presumed that his esteem for Ibn Isḥāq and Wāqidī was derived from their novel and integrative approach to Islamic history.[2] It is interesting to add that such breadth of vision is detected and admired by Masʻūdī in Christian historians as well.[3]

In the third place Masʻūdī, being supremely conscious of his own contributions to historiography, displays a partiality to what is original in both the content and the literary style of earlier historians. Leaving aside for the moment the literary aspects of his work and his own literary preferences, Masʻūdī was not above criticizing Madā'inī for example, because he merely transmitted what he heard, whereas Jāḥiẓ's works were stimulating and well argued.[4] When criticizing his predecessors, Masʻūdī was, in the main, perturbed by their excursions into realms of knowledge of which they knew little or nothing. The lengthy broadside against Sinān ibn Thābit ibn Qurra (d. 331/943) is motivated by the latter's attempt at historical writing. By so doing he transgressed the bounds of his own specialty (*kharaja ʻan ṣināʻatih*) which was, in fact, geometry and astronomy. In addition he reported events which he alleged to be true although he did not witness them.[5]

But devastating criticism is alien to Masʻūdī, who more often coupled his critical remarks upon earlier writers with a few phrases of esteem. Ibn Khurradādhbih, for instance, is taken to task because

1 Masʻūdī, *Murūj*, secs. 9, 11; *Tanbīh*, pp. 75–76.

2 *Tanbīh*, p. 278. On the achievement of Ibn Isḥāq and Wāqidī, cf. ʻAbd al-ʻAzīz al-Dūrī, *Baḥth fī Nash'at ʻIlm al-Tārīkh ʻind al-ʻArab* (Beirut: Imprimerie Catholique, 1960), pp. 27–32 (hereafter referred to as *Baḥth*); David Samuel Margoliouth, *Lectures on Arabic Historians* (Calcutta: The University of Calcutta Press, 1930), chap. 5; Sir Hamilton Alexander Roskeen Gibb, "Ta'rīkh," *Encyclopaedia, Supplement*, pp. 233–45; Nabia Abbott, *Studies*, 1:9; Josef Horovitz, "The Earliest Biographies of the Prophet and Their Authors," *Islamic Culture* 2 (1928): 181–82, 514–21.

3 *Tanbīh*, pp. 154–55.

4 *Murūj*, sec. 3146.

5 *Murūj*, sec. 14. For reliance on "specialists" in every branch of knowledge, see Ikhwān al-Ṣafā', *Rasā'il*, 3: 290.

his *al-Masālik wa al-Mamālik* contains information which one would normally expect from court messengers (*fuyūj*) and mail carriers (*ḥummāl al-kharā'iṭ*) and because he failed to note that the revenue from Iraq fluctuated from one period to another. And yet, says Mas'ūdī, it is the best book in this field. Abū 'Ubayda Ma'mar ibn al-Muthannā, despite his backbiting and his vicious attack on Arab genealogy, wrote good books on the battle-days of the Arabs (*Ayyām al-'Arab*).[1] Mas'ūdī's critique of Jāḥiẓ deserves special treatment. His obvious admiration for Jāḥiẓ's style and originality of mind is mingled with grave reservations. As may be expected, Jāḥiẓ is censured for incorporating in his works much geographical and zoological information which he neither witnessed nor was able to confirm.[2] Affectation, dilettantism and frivolity were inexcusable in a serious writer. But perhaps the cardinal sin of Jāḥiẓ in the eyes of Mas'ūdī was his anti-'Alid sentiments.[3] Jāḥiẓ the polemicist irked Mas'ūdī's own sympathies. Jāḥiẓ the writer elicited Mas'ūdī's unqualified admiration for his splendid style and argumentation.

Mas'ūdī further expected from historians a scrupulous regard to bibliography and the citing of authorities. His own fulminations against plagiarists, which he inserted at the end of the *Murūj*, attest to the strength of his views on this issue. In this regard, it must be remembered that, by the time that Mas'ūdī came to write, the citing of bibliography was becoming increasingly important and "its existence or non-existence in a work indicated the degree of scholarship the author laid claim to".[4] Aside from his extensive bibliography introduced shortly after the opening of the *Murūj*, Mas'ūdī inserts occasional bibliographical references to establish the provenance of his ideas.[5] The charge of plagiarism which he levels against Ibn Qutayba stems from his own concern for the integrity of scholarship.[6]

[1] Mas'ūdī, *Murūj*, secs. 503, 2765. For further criticism of Ma'mar, cf. *Tanbīh*, p. 243. On Ma'mar's achievements, see Dūrī, *Baḥth*, pp. 44–46.

[2] E.g., *Murūj*, secs. 217, 432, 865. See Grunebaum, *Medieval Islam*, p. 333.

[3] *Murūj*, secs. 2280–82, 3146. For the views of Jāḥiẓ, see Charles Pellat, *Le Milieu basrien et la formation de Ǧāḥiẓ* (Paris: Adrien-Maisonneuve, 1953), pp. 188–94 (hereafter referred to as *Le Milieu basrien*).

[4] Rosenthal, *Muslim Historiography*, p. 134, n. 2. Cf. *idem*, *Technique*, pp. 41 ff.; Ya'qūbī, *Historiae*, 2: 344.

[5] *Murūj*, secs. 1328, 1365.

[6] *Murūj*, sec. 1327.

This integrity was to be preserved in part by the maintenance of the critical standards outlined above but also by addressing his works to the learned few, the élite, the scholars of his own and of succeeding generations. The *Murūj* is dedicated as an ornament (*tuḥfa*) to the illustrious among kings and wise men.[1] But this dedication is not a mere cliché or literary convention. Knowledge itself is transmitted from one generation of scholars to the next and it is for their sake, for the sake of men of critical inquiry and contemplation that books are written and knowledge is recorded.[2] This élitist conception of the historian's audience did not necessarily preclude the use of the work by men whose scholarly interests were limited:

> Men differ in their objective and in what they seek to acquire of knowledge. Some pursue a historical report, others are men of research and inquiry, still others are men of Tradition who scrutinize circumstances and pay heed to the death of such as we have mentioned. Therefore we have accommodated in our book all men of opinion.[3]

But this attitude did preclude the general public in whose competence Mas'ūdī had no faith. Scholarly contempt for the "common man" was widespread among many of Mas'ūdī's predecessors and contemporaries, and his credulousness, lack of discrimination and fickleness were commented upon and condemned.[4] Mas'ūdī's careful scrutiny of what he believed to be the best sources available to him led him to treat with scepticism the historical and doctrinal ideas prevalent among the masses.[5] There were two other characteristics

1 *Murūj*, sec. 16; in two instances in the *Tanbīh*, written thirteen years later, the dedication has crept into the full title of the *Murūj* which is cited as follows: *Kitāb Murūj al-dhahab wa ma'ādin al-jawhar fī tuḥaf al-ashrāf min al-mulūk wa ahl al-dirāyāt* (*Tanbīh*, pp. 1, 329).

2 *Tanbīh*, p. 77.

3 *Murūj*, sec. 2217; cf. sec. 3385.

4 E.g., Ya'qūbī, *Historiae*, 2: 242–43; Ibn Qutayba, *'Uyūn*, 1, *nūn*; Maqdisī, *Bad'*, 2: 50.

5 *Murūj*, secs. 1338–39, 1343; *Tanbīh*, pp. 93–94, 135, 302. The superstitions of of the anthropomorphists (*Ḥashwiyya*) among the Traditionists are also the object of Mas'ūdī's scorn (*Murūj*, sec. 288). The famous passage dealing with the common man (*Murūj*, secs. 1847–49) is a powerful piece of invective, a tour de force of great literary interest. Cf. I. Goldziher, *Muhammedanische Studien* (Halle: Max Niemeyer, 1888–93), 2: 163 ff. (*Muslim Studies*, ed. S. M. Stern,

displayed by the "common man" which were a bane to the historian. The first was the jealousy and rivalry betrayed by some ignorant writers, which made them vie with their contemporaries even in fields where these latter excelled. The second was the uncritical tendency of men to praise the old authors and condemn the new, even when these latter had written works of greater value and merit. Mas'ūdī writes:

> But this is a group to whom eminent men pay no heed. Rather one should be concerned with men of inquiry and contemplation who have accorded every issue its proper share of justice and given it its rightful due, neither exalting the old if it is defective nor downgrading the new if it is innovating. It is for such men that books are written and knowledge is recorded. [1]

History and adab

The Muslim historian of the 4th/10th century cannot be understood or judged apart from his literary style, and this for two reasons: first, because historians believed that history was, at least in part, written to entertain the reader, in the best sense of the term; secondly, because the historian was, in some sense, a belletrist (*adīb*) and thus was attentive to his own as well as other historians' styles. [2] Mas'ūdī's encyclopaedic interests, the breadth of his conception of history,

translated from the German by C. R. Barber and S. M. Stern [Chicago: Aldine, 1968–72 (Albany: State University of New York Press, 1968–72)], 2: 153 ff.).

1 *Tanbīh*, pp. 76–77; cf. Ibn Qutayba, *'Uyūn*, 1, *nūn*; Jāḥiẓ, *Majmū'*, pp. 100–101; Ṣūlī, *Akhbār Abī Tammām*, p. 6.

2 This question is dealt with by Rosenthal, *Muslim Historiography*, pp. 30–53; Grunebaum, *Medieval Islam*, pp. 250–57; André Miquel, *La Géographie humaine du monde musulman* (Paris–La Haye: Mouton, 1967), especially pp. 191 ff., 210 ff. (hereafter referred to as *La Géographie humaine*); I. Goldziher, "Arabic Literature During the Abbasid Period," *Islamic Culture* 31 (1957): 308; H.A.R. Gibb, *Arabic Literature*, 2nd ed., rev. (Oxford: Clarendon Press, 1962), pp. 78–79; see also *Alfarabi's Philosophy of Plato and Aristotle*, trans. Muhsin Mahdi (Ithaca: Cornell University Press, 1969), p. 73 (hereafter referred to as *Alfarabi's Philosophy*); Ibn 'Abd Rabbihi, *'Iqd*, 1: 3; Ibn Qutayba, *'Uyūn*, 1, *hā'*, *yā'*; Jāḥiẓ, *Majmū'*, pp. 40–41. The whole issue is more obfuscated than resolved by Charles Pellat, "Was Mas'ūdī a Historian or an Adīb?", *Journal of the Pakistan Historical Society* 9 (October 1961): 231-34; cf. below, p. 23, n. 2. Ibn Isḥāq's use of poetry to embellish his *Sīra* is discussed in Josef Horovitz, "Alter und Ursprung des Isnād," *Der Islam* 8 (1918): 41.

entailed a concern for belles lettres, especially of the Abbasid era, as well as for his own literary style. Both these concerns were, in his view, germane to his activity as a historian, the first because it fell within his scheme of recording the knowledge of past ages, and the second because it tallied with his express intention to achieve eloquence in his writing.[1]

The momentous poetical controversy of Mas'ūdī's age, a controversy which was of interest to him, was the conflict of the "moderns" (*muḥdathūn*) against the "ancients" (*mutaqaddimūn*). This conflict rested on two divergent conceptions of the creative domain of the human intellect. The party of the "ancients" viewed this domain as being circumscribed by the conventions established for all time by the classical poets. The party of the "moderns" encouraged, in varying degrees, a wider pursuit of novelty in both content and form.[2] The burden of self-justification usually falls upon those who break the bounds of the old in search of the new. In the context of the literary controversies of the ninth and tenth centuries, this process of self-justification led to the growth of a vigorous school of literary criticism whose major representatives sought to defend and popularize "modern" poetry.[3] But more was involved than the mere defence of poetry. Mistrust of "modernism" by the philologists, who were the principal

1 Mas'ūdī, *Murūj*, sec. 892.

2 A detailed discussion of this controversy, which lies beyond the scope of this study, may be found in Ibn al-Mu'tazz, *Ṭabaqāt*, pp. 3, 33, 109; *idem*, *Badī'* pp. 1, 3, 58; *idem*, *Rasā'il*, p. 23; Ibn Qutayba, *al-Shi'r*, pp. 10–11; Ṣūlī, *Akhbār Abī Tammām*, pp. 14–15, 17 ff.; Qudāma ibn Ja'far, *Naqd*, pp. 80–81, 100. See also Reynold Alleyne Nicholson, *A Literary History of the Arabs* (1907; reprint London: Cambridge University Press, 1969), pp. 285–336 (hereafter referred to as *Literary History*); Gibb, *Arabic Literature*, pp. 60–63, 77–78, 85–88; G. E. von Grunebaum, "Growth and Structure of Arabic Poetry A.D. 500–1000," in *The Arab Heritage*, ed. Nabih Amin Faris (Princeton: Princeton University Press, 1944), pp. 121–141; I. Goldziher, *Abhandlungen zur arabischen Philologie* (Leiden: E. J. Brill, 1896), 1: 122–174 (hereafter referred to as *Abhandlungen*); *idem*, "Arabic Literature During the Abbasid Period," *Islamic Culture* 31 (1957): 301–4; Ḍayf, *al-'Aṣr al-'Abbāsī*, pp. 146–86; Amjad Trabulsi, *La Critique poétique des Arabes* (Damascus: Institut Français de Damas, 1956), pp. 67–73 (hereafter referred to as *La Critique*).

3 The literary critics of the tenth century are discussed in G. E. von Grunebaum "Arabic Literary Criticism in the 10th Century A.D.," *Journal of the American Oriental Society* 61 (1941): 51–57. Grunebaum pays insufficient attention to the conceptual foundations of the new school of literary criticism. See also Nazirul-Islam, *Die Aḫbār über Abū Tammām von as-Ṣūlī* (Breslau, 1940), pp. 7–16 (hereafter referred to as *Die Aḫbār*).

opponents of the "modern" poets, extended to "modernism" in literature as a whole.[1] What is at stake here is the conflict between "imitation" (*taqlīd*), and "innovation" (*tajdīd*), whose effects were neither confined to the realm of literature nor limited to the ninth and tenth centuries.

Mas'ūdī's interest in poetry embraced a concern for the theory of literary criticism. In his use and selection of poetry he was not content with the mere citation of verse but delivered himself of critical judgements which have an important bearing on his historical thought as well as his literary style.[2] The corpus of poetry in the *Murūj* falls into two distinct categories. The bulk of verse in the pre-Abbasid section is essentially an extension of the historical incident, cited in order to throw light on a historical situation or character.[3] In the Abbasid section, much of the poetry is cited for its own sake and critical comments are appended to it.

This fact is in itself somewhat baffling. The celebrated poets of the Jāhiliyya and Umayyad periods are quoted, along with other, lesser known versifiers, only in order to place men and events in a historical perspective. Thus, a reader of Mas'ūdī who knew nothing of Arabic poetry would be unable to judge the poetical merits of the poets of this early period. To account for this neglect of earlier poets, two explanations may be put forward. The first can be discussed only in brief since it anticipates certain aspects of Mas'ūdī's ethical views, while the second is connected with the rise of the schools of literary criticism and Mas'ūdī's relationship thereto.

Mas'ūdī's antagonism towards the Umayyads will be discussed at greater length elsewhere. In the present context, it may be asserted that the studied neglect of a critical assessment of Umayyad poetry was, in part, due to Mas'ūdī's hostile treatment of that period

[1] Goldziher, *Abhandlungen*, 1: 141, who quotes *Tanbīh*, p. 76, where Mas'ūdī relates how Jāḥiẓ was forced by popular taste to ascribe some of his books to ancient writers in order to gain currency for them. Cf. Ibn Qutayba, *al-Shi'r*, p. 674.

[2] The only discussion of this question occurs in H. Ghulam Mustafa, "Use of Poetry by al-Mas'ūdī in his works," *Al-Mas'ūdī*, ed. Ahmad and Rahman, pp. 77–83. This essay is descriptive and there is little attempt at systematic analysis.

[3] E.g., Mas'ūdī, *Murūj*, secs. 52, 91, 145, 397, 567, 758, 948, 1032, 1089, 1142–49, 1258–60, 1378, 1411, 1464, 1585, 1661–64, 1787–88, 1829, 1882–83, 1966–67, 2195, 2244.

as a whole. The famous Umayyad poets, Jarīr, Akhṭal and Farazdaq, were close to the imperial government and "shared in the general psychological instability and conflict of principles and parties."[1] Insofar as they reflected much of the spirit of Umayyad rule, a rule which Mas'ūdī scorned as a kingdom (*mulk*)[2] to distinguish it from the Abbasid Caliphate (*khilāfa*), their art was unworthy of his attention.

In the realm of literary criticism, important advances had been made by the middle of the tenth century, with many of which Mas'ūdī was in contact. It therefore becomes necessary to retrace in outline some of the developments which have a particular relevance to Mas'ūdī's thought and style. Ibn Qutayba (d. 276/889) is generally credited with being the "first critic of importance to declare that ancients and moderns should be judged on their merits without regard to their age."[3] In the introduction to his *Kitāb al-Shi'r wa al-Shu'arā'*, Ibn Qutayba states that he has rejected imitation in his choice of poetry and has not been bound by the literary taste of other men. No ancient poet was to be revered merely for being ancient and no modern poet to be despised merely for being modern. The only criterion for inclusion was the excellence of the poetry.[4] This critical attitude, even though embryonic, was elaborated and refined by critics like Ibn al-Mu'tazz (d. 296/908), Qudāma ibn Ja'far (d. ca. 322/933) and Muḥammad ibn Yaḥyā al-Ṣūlī (d. 335/946), all of whom applied themselves, in varying degrees, to the controversy of "ancients" and "moderns." Ibn al-Mu'tazz claimed to have been the first to collect and define the figures of speech (*al-badī'*) in his book *Kitāb al-Badī'*. In that book he attempted to show that figures of speech were not unknown to the "ancients." In his *Kitāb Ṭabaqāt al-Shu'arā' al-Muḥdathīn*, Ibn al-Mu'tazz chose to concentrate on the "new" poets because of their popularity but did not thereby reject the "ancients".[5] His

1 Gibb, *Arabic Literature*, p. 43. Cf. Nicholson, *Literary History*, pp. 238–46.

2 E.g., *Tanbīh*, p. 328; *Murūj*, secs. 1683, 1858, 2275. Cf. Goldziher, *Muhammedanische Studien* 2: 31 ff. (*Muslim Studies*, trans. Barber and Stern, 2: 40 ff.).

3 Nicholson, *Literary History*, p. 286. Cf. Gibb, *Arabic Literature*, pp. 77–78; Goldziher, *Abhandlungen*, 1:156–59.

4 Ibn Qutayba, *al-Shi'r*, pp. 10–11.

5 Ibn al-Mu'tazz, *Badī'*, pp. 1, 3, 58. Cf. *idem*, *Ṭabaqāt*, pp. 33–51. See also the statistical list of "ancient" and "modern" poets quoted in the *Ṭabaqāt*, drawn up in Goldziher, *Abhandlungen*, 1: 167.

critical views on the controversy of "ancient" vs. "modern" were more consistent than those of Ibn Qutayba. Qudāma ibn Ja'far endeavoured in his *Naqd al-Shi'r* to demonstrate, for the first time, how good poetry could be distinguished from bad and was not directly concerned with the controversy except to claim in one place that the "new" poets had excelled in certain figures of speech.[1] But the critic who went furthest in his espousal of the "new" poetry was undoubtedly Muḥammad ibn Yaḥyā al-Ṣūlī. This distinguished critic and historian, who was esteemed very highly by Mas'ūdī, upheld the unequivocal superiority of the "new" poets, claiming that "scarcely any poetical idea (*ma'nā*) had been taken over by a new poet from an ancient one without his improving it." Ṣūlī does not deny that in certain areas of poetic experience, the "ancients" were superior to the "moderns."[2] But the main thrust of his argument points to the progressive enrichment of poetic diction.

These critics, and especially the last, exercised a considerable influence on Mas'ūdī's literary ideas and tastes. Their advocacy of the "new" poetry, whether tentative and apologetic as in Ibn Qutayba, or vigorous and sophisticated as in al-Ṣūlī, helps to explain Mas'ūdī's predilection for "modern" poetry, and the prominence he accorded to it in the *Murūj*. Of even greater importance to Mas'ūdī's general historical outlook is the fact that these critics, by championing the "modern" school of poetry, had implicitly or explicitly rejected imitation and had thereby broadened the confines of the human imagination.[3]

1 Qudāma ibn Ja'far, *Naqd*, pp. 80–81.

2 Ṣūlī, *Akhbār Abī Tammām*, pp. 16–17. Cf. Nazirul-Islam, *Die Aḫbār*, p. 29.

3 The following are the most significant references to these critics: Ibn Qutayba (Mas'ūdī, *Murūj*, sec. 11); Qudāma ibn Ja'far (*Murūj*, sec. 12); Ibn al-Mu'tazz (*Murūj*, sec. 3399); Ṣūlī (*Murūj*, secs. 11, 2850, 3469-71). Mas'ūdī's remarks in *Tanbīh*, p. 76, on "ancients" and "moderns" reflect the ideas in Ṣūlī, *Akhbār Abī Tammām*, pp. 16–17. In another passage, *Murūj*, secs. 2849–50, Mas'ūdī paraphrases the critical comments of Ibn al-Mu'tazz as quoted in Ṣūlī, *Akhbār Abī Tammām*, pp. 176–77. Mas'ūdī's use of Muḥammad ibn Yazīd al-Mubarrad as one of his main sources for Abbasid literary anecdotes is also worthy of note. Al-Mubarrad was a philologist, not a critic, but he did not share the hostility towards the "moderns" displayed by many of his fellow philologists (cf. Goldziher, *Abhandlungen*, 1: 167 and n. 1; Ṣūlī, *Akhbār Abī Tammām*, p. 97). Mas'ūdī's reliance on al-Mubarrad was, therefore, in keeping with his literary preferences. Mas'ūdī's appreciation of these critics is reflected in *Tanbīh*, pp. 75–76.

Mas'udī's Style

Mas'ūdī's literary style may either be analyzed in isolation or it may be viewed in the light of his own literary judgements and preferences, and those of his age. Comments on his style have tended to be of the first variety and are, therefore, generalized and of little value.[1] It may therefore be useful, as an introduction to Mas'ūdī's style, to review some of the features of style most admired by those critics whom Mas'ūdī esteemed, and to determine how far these features are reflected in Mas'ūdī's own literary judgements and style.[2]

Pride of place in literary prose belongs, in Mas'ūdī's view, to Jāḥiẓ. Their relationship has been mentioned above and this must now be examined further. While Jāḥiẓ was not a systematic literary critic in the same sense as Ibn al-Mu'tazz, Qudāma or al-Ṣūlī, it is possible to reconstruct those qualities which Jāḥiẓ held in esteem. Foremost among those qualities which make for good literature are the brevity (*ījāz*), clarity (*īḍāḥ*) and lack of affectation (*takalluf*) in literary style, whether in poetry or prose. Such, according to Jāḥiẓ, are the primary constituents of eloquence (*balāgha*, *bayān*).[3] As far as contemporary poetry was concerned, Jāḥiẓ preferred that poetry which expressed religious ideas or philosophical opinions: hence the importance of the verses he cites for a study of the complex political and religious milieu of his times.[4]

Some or all of these preferences were reflected in the literary taste of Jāḥiẓ's successors, and some or all of them went into the making of the poetry of the "moderns." Thus, Ibn Qutayba expressed a distinct partiality for poetry which was free of affectation, clear in

1 E.g., Etienne Marc Quatremère, "Notice sur la vie et les ouvrages de Masoudi," *Journal Asiatique*, ser. 3, 7: 21.

2 A useful discussion of the criteria on which criticism was based may be found in Grunebaum, "Arabic Literary Criticism in the 10th Century A.D.," *Journal of the American Oriental Society* 61 (1941): 51–57. Surprisingly, however, Grunebaum takes little notice of al-Ṣūlī.

3 Cf., e.g., Jāḥiẓ, *Bayān*, 1: 30, 90–92, 97–98, 110–11, 126–27; 3: 328–30. Mas'ūdī considered the *Bayān* to be Jāḥiẓ's finest work (Mas'ūdī, *Murūj*, sec. 3147). The two words *balāgha* and *bayān* are both used by Jāḥiẓ to mean eloquence (see Pellat, *Le Milieu basrien*, p. 116).

4 Pellat, *Le Milieu basrien*, p. 163.

meaning and smooth in diction.[1] In his writings one finds the oft-expressed affinity for the poets by nature (*maṭbūʿūn*) as opposed to poets by affectation. In like manner, Ibn al-Muʿtazz condemns "modern" poets who use odd (*gharīb*) phraseology, for such oddity in "modern" verse is all the more conspicuous. He criticizes Abū Tammām for affectation and believes that simplicity, clarity and concision are essential to eloquence.[2] Qudāma's literary theory, although visibly different in its procedure from that of contemporaneous critics by reason of its Aristotelean foundation, still makes use of conventional terms of literary criticism when denoting praise or blame. Thus the verbal expression, according to Qudāma, should be smooth (*sahl, samḥ*). "Modern" poets who use uncouth and incongruous expressions (*lafẓ waḥshī*) are guilty of affectation. Eloquence consists in the perfect matching of verbal expression to idea.[3] Ṣūlī shares the widespread appreciation for simplicity of poetic diction but, at the same time, does not condemn as affectation that poetry which is the result of great effort and concentration.[4] This helps to explain his admiration for Abū Tammām, as well as poets whose diction was considered simpler, like al-Buḥturī and Abū al-ʿAtāhiya. His taste was distinctly "modern," as seen in his selections and in the poets whose *akhbār* he chose to record.[5]

Upon examining Masʿūdī's own literary judgements and taste, it becomes evident that these were shaped largely by the views of the critics whose literary theories were outlined above. In Masʿūdī, there is the same predilection for simplicity and concision of diction,[6] to be seen at its most obvious in his esteem for the poetry of Abū al-ʿAtāhiya and the prose of Jāḥiẓ. His own definition of eloquence as constituted by clarity and brevity reflects the judgement of Jāḥiẓ and of later critics. On the controversy of "ancient" vs. "modern",

[1] Ibn Qutayba, *al-Shiʿr*, pp. 14–17, 22 ff., 32 ff., 46, 679, 712.

[2] Ibn al-Muʿtazz, *Rasāʾil*, pp. 23, 26, 62, 64. (*Gharīb* as used here by Ibn al-Muʿtazz presumably means archaic). See also *idem*, *Ṭabaqāt*, pp. 3, 5, 6, 92, 105, 109, 135.

[3] Qudāma ibn Jaʿfar, *Naqd*, pp. 10, 12, 17, 19, 80–81, 84, 100.

[4] For Ṣūlī's views on simplicity of diction, see *Akhbār al-Buḥturī*, p. 62; *idem*, *Akhbār Abī Tammām*, pp. 16–17. For his views on *takalluf*, see *Akhbār al-Buḥturī*, pp. 137–38.

[5] See Ṣūlī, *Akhbār al-Buḥturī*, pp. 22–26; Trabulsi, *La Critique poétique*, p. 19.

[6] E.g., *Murūj*, secs. 12, 1862, 2452, 2716, 3399.

Mas'ūdī's views must, to a certain extent, be determined by negative evidence. It has been noted above that "ancient" poets are under-represented in his work. His own critical comments bear a close resemblance to Ṣūlī's, in that he argues for the progressive refinement of knowledge without the outright rejection of the old.[1] Mas'ūdī also displays the familiar critical esteem for the poets by nature, among whom he numbers Abū 'Alī al-Baṣīr, 'Alī ibn al-Jahm, Ibn al-Mu'tazz and, above all Abū al-'Atāhiya.[2]

But together with simplicity of diction which was characteristic of the "poetry by nature," Mas'ūdī admired poetic inventiveness (*ikhtirā'*) and originality.[3] It is this which explains his devotion to poets as diverse in their style and spirit as Abū al-'Atāhiya and Abū Tammām.[4] This latter, according to Ṣūlī, was condemned out of hand by many who did not take the trouble to fathom the conceptual difficulties of his verse.[5] But Mas'ūdī was alive to the subtlety and novelty of thought in poets like Abū Tammām and Ibn al-Rūmī and detected in this latter, for example, the influence of Greek philosophy and Islamic theology.[6]

Simplicity and originality, then, were the hallmarks of the style cherished by Mas'ūdī. His own lucid prose, perhaps consciously modelled on that of Jāḥiẓ, is free from the ornate rhymed prose (*saj'*) which was becoming increasingly popular in the tenth century.[7]

1 Mas'ūdī, *Tanbīh*, p. 76.

2 References to these poets may be found in *Murūj*, secs. 3020, 2934, 3399, and 2452, respectively.

3 E.g., *Murūj*, secs. 3020, 3376, 3399, 3404–5, 3459; on the concept of originality, see Grunebaum, "Arabic Literary Criticism," *Journal of the American Oriental Society* 61 (1941): 54–55.

4 Here too, one may detect the influence of Ṣūlī who, as may be expected, was keenly alive to poetic originality (cf. Ṣūlī, *Akhbār al-Buḥturī*, p. 175; *idem*, *Akhbār Abī Tammām*, pp. 17, 118). Ṣūlī, it should be remembered, admired both Abū Tammām and Abū al-'Atāhiya.

5 Ṣūlī, *Akhbār Abī Tammām*, pp. 14–16.

6 On Abū Tammām, see *Murūj*, secs. 2839-41, 2849-50. On Ibn al-Rūmī, see *Murūj*, sec. 3376 ff.

7 On the popularity of *saj'* in the tenth century, see Gibb, *Arabic Literature*, pp. 89–90; Zakī Mubārak, *al-Nathr al-Fannī fī al-Qarn al-Rābi'*, 2d printing (Cairo al-Maktaba al-Tijāriyya, 1957), vol. 1; Goldziher, "Arabic Literature During the Abbasid Period," *Islamic Culture* 31 (1957): 309 ff.; Ḍayf, *al-'Aṣr al-'Abbāsī*, pp. 441 ff. (who suggests that the influence of Mu'tazilism made for a more precise language).

His fidelity to his sources impels him to reproduce the jargon of his informants and also to explain the odd or technical terms he is occasionally driven to use.[1]

The most recurrent charge brought against his style is its frequent digressions. It has been repeated so often by modern writers that account must be taken of it.[2] To this end, the problem will be considered first in its general literary context, and then viewed more closely in the case of Mas'ūdī.

Considering the pivotal position of Jāḥiẓ in the development of Arabic belles lettres and the praise which Mas'ūdī lavishes on his literary accomplishments, it would be fitting to scrutinize the divagations of Jāḥiẓ in order to determine their true import. Now *adab* in general strives to adopt from all branches of learning what is necessary for culture and an understanding of the past. *Adab*, therefore, tends to be encyclopaedic in nature and avoids "unilateral professionalism".[3] Thus the digressions which characterize the works of Jāḥiẓ and later men of letters are germane to their literary purpose of furnishing, in the words of Ibn al-Mu'tazz, "from every report its kernel and from every necklace its gem".[4] Moving from one subject to another, the *adīb* is anxious not to bore his reader but to lead him gently through the various branches of knowledge necessary for his edification as well as entertainment. Jāḥiẓ, having in mind both the reader and the listener, deliberately varies the mood of his discourse in order to maintain the interest of his audience.[5] The discursive style is, therefore, integral to *adab* as practiced by Jāḥiẓ and subsequent literati like Ibn Qutayba and Ibn al-Mu'tazz.

1 E.g., Mas'ūdī, *Murūj*, secs. 362, 364, 374, 379, 594, 784, 1396; *Tanbīh*, pp. 103–4, 116–22, 138–39, 159, 168.

2 E.g., Carl Brockelmann, "Mas'ūdī," *Encyclopaedia*, ed. Houtsma et al., 3: 403; Gibb, *Arabic Literature*, p. 82; Nicholson, *Literary History*, p. 353; Mohammad Shafi, "al-Mas'ūdī as a Geographer," *Al-Mas'ūdī*, ed. Ahmad and Rahman, p. 72; Ghulam Mustafa, "Use of Poetry by al-Mas'ūdī in his works," *ibid.*, p. 77; E. M. Quatremère, "Notice sur la vie et les ouvrages de Masoudi," *Journal Asiatique*, ser. 3, 7: 22. On literary digressions, see G. E. von Grunebaum, *Islam*: *Essays in the Nature and Growth of a Cultural Tradition* (London: Kegan Paul, 1955), pp. 87–98, 109, n. 2.

3 Goldziher, "Arabic Literature," *Islamic Culture* 31 (1957): 308.

4 Ibn al-Mu'tazz, *Ṭabaqāt*, p. 33.

5 See, e.g., Jāḥiẓ, *Bayān*, 2: 225–26; 3: 297–308.

Mas'ūdī was well aware of the digressive character of the style of Jāḥiẓ and its import.[1] Inasmuch as he planned his own historical works to be encyclopaedic in scope, his tendency to digress can be said to reflect the spirit of *adab*, although one must note that this spirit subserves rather than dominates his main historical theme.[2] Accordingly, Mas'ūdī informs his reader that the title of each chapter (*bāb*) might not tally with its contents in every respect. Mas'ūdī refers to these divagations as "passing thoughts" (*sāniḥ, sawāniḥ*).[3] In the main, they consist of anecdotes or brief excursions into topics which crop up in the course of the narrative. From the viewpoint of the author himself, these digressions are controlled and, in a sense, are reminiscent of the style of Eutychius, a near-contemporary historian.[4] In deliberately varying his tone, he, like Jāḥiẓ and later literati, strove to instruct but also to entertain his readers and thus to forestall the flagging of their interest.[5]

The isnād

To round out this examination of Mas'ūdī's style, some attention must be devoted to Mas'ūdī's use of the *isnād*. Islamic historians had, by Mas'ūdī's time, evolved a continuous narrative style based upon a chronological framework which normally revolved around pre-Islamic kings and Islamic caliphs.[6] Where a continuous historical narrative is concerned, it is generally presumed that Balādhurī was the first to dispense with the cumbersome, Tradition-like historiography to be seen in the works of Ibn 'Abd al-Ḥakam, for example,

1 *Murūj*, sec. 3146.

2 Pellat misses the point in arguing in the *Journal of the Pakistan Historical Society* 9 (October, 1961): 231–34, that Mas'ūdī was an *adīb* rather than a historian. In *adab*, history, like other branches of learning, subserves the purpose of the *adīb*, but it would be wrong to confuse Mas'ūdī's encyclopaedic history with *adab*. The discursiveness of *adab* is found in Mas'ūdī but this is placed within a clearly delineated historical framework. See also Miquel, *La Géographie humaine*, pp. 210–12.

3 See *Murūj*, secs. 33, 2484.

4 Cf. Eutychius, *Annales*, 1: 149, 176, 196. Mas'ūdī was familiar with this work (see *Tanbīh*, p. 154).

5 See Mas'ūdī's remarks in this regard in *Murūj*, secs. 1369, 1440. Cf. sec. 3146.

6 Rosenthal, *Muslim Historiography*, pp. 87–88.

or Ṭabarī.[1] These latter, as may be ascertained in their works, relied extensively on *isnād* so that, from the viewpoint of style, their historiography often appears as collateral to Tradition.

But recent research has shown that the sciences of historiography and Tradition "were twin, though not identical, disciplines".[2] It therefore becomes necessary not to confuse the evolution of their content or techniques, and not to read into one discipline the conclusions which issue from the other. Thus, in the matter of *isnād*, it has been shown that while in Tradition the *isnād* tended to become more rigorous with time,[3] in historiography it had a more chequered career.[4] The early *akhbāriyyūn* made little or no use of it. Later historians of the eighth and ninth centuries, under the influence of the growing rigorism in the use of *isnād* by the Traditionists, tended to display almost the same rigor themselves.[5] Finally, the trend towards continuous narrative asserts itself in the late ninth century, so that by the time that Mas'ūdī comes to write his histories, this trend has firmly entrenched itself in Islamic historiography. Attention must be focused on this third stage of development during which continuous narrative begins to make considerably less use of *isnād* and to fuse various accounts (which Ṭabarī, for example, keeps separate) into one polished whole.[6] A process of selectivity prompted Balādhurī, Dīnawarī, and Ya'qūbī to compose narrative accounts in which conflicting versions are relegated to the end of each report where they appear almost as footnotes to the main text.

The *isnād* was more or less suppressed by these historians because, to begin with, new historical themes were being explored which had

1 H.A.R. Gibb, "Ta'rīkh," *Encyclopaedia*, *Supplement*, p. 236; 'A. 'A. Dūrī, "The Iraq School of History to the Ninth Century—a Sketch," in *Historians of the Middle East*, p. 52.

2 Abbott, *Studies*, 1: 7; cf. Jawād 'Alī, "Mawārid Ta'rīkh al-Ṭabarī," *Majallat* 1 (1950): 157–58.

3 See Abbott, *Studies*, 2: 75–77; Goldziher, *Muhammedanische Studien*, 2: 226 ff. (trans. Barber and Stern, *Muslim Studies*, 2:209 ff.); Joseph Schacht, *The Origins of Muhammadan Jurisprudence* (Oxford: Clarendon Press, 1953), pp. 163–75.

4 See Abbott, *Studies*, 1: 44–45. But cf. Miquel, *La Géographie humaine*, pp. 354 ff. (to be used with caution).

5 See J. Horovitz, "Alter und Ursprung des Isnād," *Der Islam* 8 (1918): 41 ff., who discusses at length the ambiguous use of *isnād* by Ibn Isḥāq, for example.

6 See, e.g., Balādhurī, *Futūḥ*, pp. 17, 197; Ya'qūbī, *Historiae*, 2: 2.

little or no reference to Tradition.[1] This tended to accentuate even more the differences in content and method between the two fields of historiography and Tradition. Many practising historians of the ninth century must have found the *isnād* either useless or irrelevant to such topics as Indian or Byzantine history. This is clearly relevant to Mas'ūdī's works. Furthermore, the *isnād*, if Ibn 'Abd Rabbihi (d. 328/940) is to be trusted, was felt by many scholars, both early and late, to be expendable where certain branches of knowledge were concerned. Among these Ibn 'Abd Rabbihi includes historical reports and what may, for the sake of convenience, be called *adab*. The didactic character of this branch of knowledge was its own best justification and therefore did not need any external device like *isnād* to establish its authenticity.[2] In the third place, certain historical events had, by the ninth century, become so well established by multiple *isnāds* that the repetition of every single *isnād* was deemed superfluous.[3] Balādhurī, for example, frequently makes use of *qālū* followed by the synthesized account of an event and mentions the *isnād* only in controversial issues. Ya'qūbī presents a connected narrative where the *isnād* rarely appears.

All these factors are relevant to the declining role of the *isnād* in historical writing in the period when Mas'ūdī was writing his histories. One important dimension of this problem has hitherto received scant attention, that is, the influence of the *adab* style on the historiography of the late ninth and tenth centuries. The result was that *isnād*-based historiography fell, as it were, out of fashion.[4] Beginning with Jāḥiẓ who seldom used *isnād*, later literati like Ibn al-Mu'tazz came to feel that its use was cumbersome and excessive (*min al-takthīr*).[5] By the tenth century, Ibn 'Abd Rabbihi was writing as follows:

> I have dropped the *isnāds* from most reports, seeking to achieve simplicity [*istikhfāf*] and brevity [*ījāz*] and to avoid ponderous-

1 Cf. Abbott, *Studies*, 1: 9; Rosenthal, *Muslim Historiography*, pp. 133 ff.

2 Ibn 'Abd Rabbihi, '*Iqd*, 1: 3–4.

3 See e.g., Dūrī, *Baḥth*, p. 52; Maqdisī, *Bad'*, 1: 193.

4 Despite the attacks of some Mu'tazilites, neither the theory of multiple narration (*tawātur*) nor the concept of *isnād* were ever seriously questioned by the historians of the ninth and tenth century. But cf. Muhsin Mahdi, *Ibn Khaldūn's Philosophy of History* (Chicago: The University of Chicago Press, Phoenix Books, 1964), pp. 134, n. 2, and 134–37 (hereafter referred to as *Ibn Khaldūn*).

5 Ibn al-Mu'tazz, *Badī'*, p. 2.

> ness [*tathqīl*] and prolixity [*taṭwīl*]; for these are entertaining reports coupled with wise sayings and anecdotes, which neither profit from a chain of *isnād* nor suffer from the lack thereof. Some used to drop the *isnād* of Ḥadīth from a customary *sunna* and obligatory *sharī'a*. How much more reason do we have to drop it from a stray anecdote, a common proverb, an amusing report or an account whose lustre would fade if it grows long and bulky.[1]

The words *istikhfāf*, *ījāz*, *tathqīl* are technical terms often used by literary critics of the period.[2] Their use in this context by Ibn 'Abd Rabbihi serves to underline the important inroads which the *adab* style had made into literary prose. Its effect was felt in Muslim historiography in general and in the works of Mas'ūdī in particular.

With the preceding comments in mind, it will now be somewhat easier to examine the use that Mas'ūdī makes of the *isnād*. It will be observed, to begin with, that while in the majority of cases Mas'ūdī presents a composite account often preceded by phrases like "a group of scholars mentioned" or cites written sources, he also records complete *isnāds* relating to historical reports. These *isnāds* were either ones he himself had heard and cites in full, or others which he found in historical works (e.g., Ṭabarī) and copies in their entirety.[3] The *isnāds* are, almost without exception, to be found in the Islamic section of his two works. Caution must therefore be exercised before one determines Mas'ūdī's use of *isnād*. It is obviously inaccurate to claim that he did not use it.[4] One is therefore led to the conclusion that his limited use of the *isnād* in his two surviving works cannot be regarded as anything more than a stylistic peculiarity, especially in view of his own explicit statement that he had provided full *isnāds* for the same reports in previous works.[5] Therefore, and in common with the prevailing historiographical practice of his day which was outlined above, Mas'ūdī provided almost no *isnād* for historical reports where it was unobtainable or irrelevant. For the rest, his own explanation

[1] Ibn 'Abd Rabbihi, *'Iqd*, 1: 3–4.

[2] See, e.g., Qudāma ibn Ja'far, *Naqd*, pp. 37, 46, 66, 105, 118.

[3] E.g., Mas'ūdī, *Murūj*, secs. 1474, 1794, 2085, 2087, 2149, 2242, 2447, 2735-36, 2907, 3192, 3391; *Tanbīh*, pp. 254, 267, 293, 300.

[4] Cf. Jawād 'Alī, "Mawārid Ta'rīkh al-Ṭabarī," *Majallat* 2 (1951): 176.

[5] Mas'ūdī, *Murūj*, sec. 46.

for the limited use of *isnād* is essentially derived from the theory and practice of the literati of his own and of the preceding century, that is, for purposes of stylistic elegance, concision and convenience.[1]

It appears, in conclusion, that Masʿūdī was fully aware of his own contributions to historical and geographical knowledge, and he often reminds his readers of these contributions. Therefore, he particularly admired those historians who had contributed to the advancement of knowledge and, conversely, was ready to criticize other historians who had merely copied from their predecessors or had ventured into historical writing without adequate understanding of the historian's craft. His outlook on this matter is reflected in his views on literature and style, where he championed the "moderns" in their attempt to break the yoke of imitation and strove to do likewise in his own writing and literary style.

[1] E.g., Masʿūdī, *Murūj*, sec. 2482; *Tanbīh*, p. 279. The words *ījāz*, *ikhtiṣār* and *taṭwīl* are often used by Masʿūdī in this context (e.g., *Murūj*, sec. 2482; *Tanbīh*, p. 227).

2. REFLECTIONS ON HISTORICAL METHOD

Reasons for Reflecting on History

Mas'ūdi is the first major Muslim author of extant historical works to reflect, in a systematic manner, upon the value and method of history. No historian before him, so far as can be determined, had attempted to probe with the same thoroughness into the nature and principles of historical enquiry. Earlier historians, to be sure, had often striven to record the collective experience of the Muslim community and thereby to gain a greater measure of communal self-understanding. Occasionally, they made brief remarks about hisrical method. But Mas'ūdī was the first to combine his history with thoughtful reflection on its value and method, wherein both the veracity of historical reports as well as the nature of veracity itself would find their proper place. The purpose of this chapter will be to describe his reflections and to analyze the theoretical foundations upon which his ideas rest. But before attempting to do so, one must retrace, albeit in a necessarily brief manner, the steps which led Mas'ūdī to choose this particular approach to history rather than any other and to determine his reasons for this choice. One may begin by asking why Mas'ūdī chose to reflect on history in the first place. Why did he not for example follow in the footsteps of Ṭabarī, who explicitly rejected the application to history of the rational tools and presuppositions of theology and philosophy?[1]

The answer must be sought first in the important intellectual developments achieved in the fields of history, theology, and the natural sciences — developments which made it possible for the historian of Mas'ūdī's age to turn his attention to the theoretical implications

[1] Ṭabarī, *Annales*, 1: 6, 56. Ṭabarī's Tradition-oriented history is discussed in relation to other schools of historiography in Mahdi, *Ibn Khaldūn*, pp. 135–37.

of his craft. In the second place, and more significant to this study, the answer must be sought in Mas'ūdī's own conception of the value and method of history and of historical writing. It is here that one begins to discern why Mas'ūdī felt the need for a more theoretical conception of history — a feeling exemplified at its simplest level by Mas'ūdī's repeated exhortations to his reader, not merely to read but also to ponder upon what he reads.

The Background: History, Theology and the Natural Sciences

In the field of historical writing, the history of Ya'qūbī is of particular relevance to Mas'ūdī. Not only did Ya'qūbī incorporate the history of many pre-Islamic nations, but he also dealt with a range of topics which is closely reminiscent of the one to be met with in the *Murūj* and the *Tanbīh*. Philosophy, astronomy, medicine, ancient religions and chronologies are described in detail. He was probably the first Muslim historian to take almost the entire spectrum of human culture for his object of study.

Turning next to theology and its influence upon historical thought,[1] it is primarily with the Mu'tazilites that one must reckon. When Mas'ūdī was writing, their intellectual ascendancy had not yet been seriously threatened by Ash'arī and the Ash'arite school, although their political influence in the ninth and tenth centuries tended to ebb and flow, depending upon the favor of rulers and dynasties. Some Mu'tazila of the ninth century taught that the physical universe obeyed rational laws and viewed nature as a rational system. Thus each object had its particular "nature" given to it by God, and each object acted in accordance with its nature. The stone, for example, was given a certain nature so that if thrown, it flies, exhausts its power and falls.[2] Deviations from nature were regarded with suspicion and we may well assume that in the frequent cases where Mas'ūdī reports oddities in nature, the scepticism which he attributes

1 There is a concise treatment of this topic in Mahdi, *Ibn Khaldūn*, pp. 134, 136–38, 140 ff.

2 J. Obermann, "Das Problem der Kausalität bei den Arabern," *Wiener Zeitschrift* 30 (1917–18): 78–81.

to "men of research and critical inquiry" originated from Mu'tazilite circles.[1] This view of nature came to influence Mas'ūdī, as will be seen below.

More particularly, attention must be drawn to the influence which Jāḥiẓ exercised on Mas'ūdī, through the emphasis which this former placed on direct experiences (*'iyān*) in the gathering and classification of data. Recent researchers have demonstrated the central role which this concept plays in the writings of Jāḥiẓ.[2] The prominence accorded to direct experience by Mas'ūdī will be treated in greater detail below, but may be detected even in a cursory reading of Mas'ūdī's work.

The natural sciences, especially astronomy and scientific geography, had by the tenth century developed and refined their methods. Mas'ūdī's interest in these sciences is obvious. We are not concerned in this study with Mas'ūdī's scientific ideas as such but rather with the influence of certain scientific concepts on his own historical method and outlook. Thus, the early astronomers used their tables to establish more accurate dating of events,[3] and Mas'ūdī consistently preferred their calculations over those of the Traditionists. Of greater significance is the fact that Greek astronomy, which gradually replaced the Indian and Persian in the course of the ninth century in the Muslim empire, was regarded by certain Muslim scientists as more demanding of intellectual effort and less prone to "imitation" than the earlier astronomy. In the words of al-Battānī (d. ca. 287/900) Greek astronomy called for investigation (*miḥna*) and reflection (*i'tibār*).[4] This emphasis on research and experimentation, coupled with the fact that Mas'ūdī was very conversant with the works of Muslim scientists, came to influence his own conception of history's method. This influence will be elaborated further below.

Arab geography in the ninth century was animated by a similar

1 See S. Maqbul Ahmad, "al-Mas'ūdī's Contributions to Medieval Arab Geography," *Islamic Culture* 28 (1954): 275–86.

2 To begin with, by Pellat in *Le Milieu basrien*, but recently, and more pointedly, by Miquel in *La Géographie humaine*.

3 Ignatius Krachkovskii, *Tārīkh al-Adab al-Jughrāfī al-'Arabī*, trans. Ṣalāḥ al-dīn 'Uthmān Hāshim (Cairo: Lujnat al-Ta'līf, 1957), p. 71 (hereafter referred to as *Tārīkh al-Adab al-Jughrāfī*).

4 *Ibid.*, pp. 77–78, 82.

spirit of experimentation and revision of earlier theories.[1] Scientific geography, that is, physical or mathematical as opposed to descriptive,[2] was included by Fārābī as part of astronomy.[3] Great strides were made under the Caliph al-Ma'mūn in measurements of lands and seas.[4] Mas'ūdī was aware of this scientific activity and often cites these measurements as he found them in the works of Muslim geographers and astronomers.[5]

These, then, were some of the significant developments in history, theology, and the natural sciences which made it more natural for a historian like Mas'ūdī to reflect upon history as well as to write it. But these developments do not, by themselves, provide a complete answer to the question, Why did Mas'ūdī choose to think historically at all? The answer must clearly be sought in Mas'ūdī's own view of the value of history. Next, an attempt will be made to describe Mas'ūdī's reflections on historical method, to determine his criteria for verifying historical reports, and to delineate the main problems he encountered as well as his solutions to them. Finally, an account will be given of the historical principles upon which his reflections are based.

The Value of History

In the first chapter of this study, Mas'ūdī's main reasons for being dissatisfied with some earlier historians were described. It was suggested that, for Mas'ūdī, more was involved in historical writing than the amassing of data at second-hand. History in Mas'ūdī's view was an exact and comprehensive discipline — a view which was implied in his esteem for historians who had made critical use of sources or had broadened the subject matter of history.[6] It is clear,

1 Miquel, *La Géographie humaine*, p. 76, where he discusses al-Kindī.

2 For this distinction between literary and scientific geography,see Krachkovskii, *Tārīkh al-Adab al-Jughrāfī*, pp. 18 ff.; J. H. Kramers, "Geography and Commerce" in *The Legacy of Islam*, ed. Sir Thomas Walker Arnold and Alfred Guillaume (Oxford: Clarendon Press, 1931), pp. 85 ff.

3 Fārābī, *Iḥṣā'*, pp. 84–86.

4 Krachkovskii, *Tārīkh al-Adab al-Jughrāfī*, pp. 85–89.

5 *Murūj*, secs. 1365–67.

6 See chapter 1, above.

however, that in order to clarify Mas'ūdī's view of history as an exact and comprehensive discipline, some account must be given of his definition of history and its value.

Mas'ūdī tells his reader at the beginning of the *Murūj* that he decided to write his series of histories only after he had dealt at length with other "sciences": religion, law, political science and astronomy.[1] In other words, Mas'ūdī regarded history as the end for which his earlier works on diverse sciences had been the prelude. History was the repository of man's past and of all his sciences, of man's intellectual and not merely political achievements. The reasons for writing history, then, is "to preserve for the world a praiseworthy memorial and a systematic (*manẓūm*) and well-prepared science."[2]

As the collective record of all human knowledge, history for Mas'ūdī was the noblest of sciences.[3] Without this record, the principles of the sciences would be nullified and their conclusions would be lost. Thus, law, eloquence, theology, the wisdom of the sages, ethics, the art of government, and war are all derived (*yustakhraj*, *yustanbaṭ*) from history. But while the subject itself appeals to all men, to the wise as well as the ignorant, Mas'ūdī is careful to point out that only the man who had devoted himself exclusively to the pursuit of knowledge "can master this science, with certain knowledge of what it contains." History was not merely an aggregate of facts which supplies other sciences with their data. It must, according to Mas'ūdī, be carefully scrutinized and pondered upon. The wise man who contemplates the course of human events will discover the wisdom (*ḥikma*) to be found therein. That wisdom often manifests itself in patterns such as the rise and growth of states, the progress of human knowledge, and the decline of kingdoms and nations. These are topics which will be treated more fully in later chapters, but some indication of them will be given below. However, our conclusions in this regard must by necessity remain incomplete since we no longer possess Mas'ūdī's theoretical or polemical works, in which his reflections on these topics were more fully set forth.[4]

1 *Murūj*, secs. 5–6.

2 *Murūj*, sec. 7.

3 This paragraph attempts to provide a commentary on *Murūj*, sec. 989, where the value of history is described by Mas'ūdī in the fullest terms.

4 See Appendix B, below.

With all this in mind, it becomes possible to answer the question posed earlier of why Mas'ūdī chose to reflect upon history rather than follow the lead of historians who displayed little concern for the theoretical aspects of their craft. For while earlier Muslim historians had assumed that the value of history resided largely in correcting or complementing other disciplines (e.g., Tradition in Ṭabarī or *adab* in other historians),[1] Mas'udī believed that history merited contemplation for its own sake, a contemplation which would ultimately reveal the patterns beneath or, in other words, the wisdom mentioned above.

The Modes of Apprehension

The widening of historical horizons placed severe limitations on the use of *isnād* by the Muslim historian. The gradations of veracity in the *isnād* system represented for many Muslim historians before Mas'ūdī the only way of arriving at, or approximating to historical truth.[2] This system, developed according to Mas'ūdī by the jurists, was obviously inadequate in cases where the historian or *adīb*[3] attempted to delve into pre-Islamic history or to ascertain the truth regarding the customs and marvels of distant lands. Without a chain of transmitters, the historian had to rely on other criteria of veracity. This problem was ever present to Mas'ūdī, who felt the need to explain either briefly or at length his reasons for accepting or rejecting historical reports.[4]

For the sake of simplicity, Mas'ūdī's observations on historical method will be treated under two headings: the reports (*akhbār*) themselves and the proofs (*dalā'il*) employed to verify them. The reports, to begin with, are divided into three categories, necessary

[1] See, e.g., H.A.R. Gibb, "Ta'rīkh", *Encyclopaedia*, *Supplement*, p. 236.

[2] See, e.g., Ṭabarī, *Annales*, 1: 6, where he argues that knowledge of past events can only be ascertained through transmission, to the exclusion of rational deduction.

[3] Jāḥiẓ faces this problem and offers a brief solution to it in *Majmū'*, pp. 24–26 (partial translation in Rosenthal, *Technique*, pp. 57–58).

[4] See especially *Murūj*, sec. 1354, where Mas'ūdī presents the legal criteria for accepting reports but then cites an example of a case where such criteria are inadequate.

(*wājib*), impossible (*mumtani'*, *mustaḥīl*) and possible (*mumkin*, *jā'iz*).[1] These are categories devised by the intellect (*'aql*) to describe the modes of existence of objects and events of the external world and to determine the degree to which they are apprehended. Each mode of existence was ascertained by different proofs and each mode engendered its own problems for Mas'ūdī. But while the categories of necessary and impossible presented comparatively few difficulties, it was the category of possible which held the greatest interest for Mas'ūdī and prompted most of his comments on historical causation and veracity.[2] The concept of possibility plays a very important role in theology and was called the "cornerstone" (*'umda*) of the science of theology by Maimonides, referring to the teachings of the Ash-'arites.[3] The *Maqālāt* of Ash'arī attests to the importance of this concept, especially among the Mu'tazilites. For Mas'ūdī, the problem of possibility arose whenever the veracity of a certain type of historical report was called into question. This had to do mainly with oddities in the world of nature or fantastic stories of ancient times.

For Mas'ūdī, the question resolves itself into the proper definition of the concept of impossibility. He could, on the one hand, adopt the outright scepticism of men he often refers to as "men of research and critical enquiry" (*ahl al-baḥth wa al-naẓar*) and whom he frequently cites as being wary of reports of oddities.[4] He could, on the other hand, analyze the notion of impossibility in conjunction with the occurrence of certain phenomena, where experience may show that the verdict of theoretical reasoning is often inadequate or even wrong. Mas'ūdī chose the second alternative for reasons which will become clear shortly. He began by making a distinction between what he called "impossibility in intellect" (*iḥāla fī al-'aql*) and "impossibility in Divine Power" (*iḥāla fī al-qudra*). Where certain

[1] See, e.g., *Murūj*, secs. 291, 380, 1205, 1344. This three-fold division of reports corresponds to the division of the existents (*mawjūdāt*) by Fārābī and other Muslim philosophers and theologians (Fārābī, *Fuṣūl*, secs. 64–66).

[2] See, e.g., *Murūj*, secs. 288, 818, 1203.

[3] This saying of Maimonides is quoted by J. Obermann, who deals at some length with the principle of *tajwīz* in his "Das Problem der Kausalität bei den Arabern," *Wiener Zeitschrift* 30 (1917–18): 81–86. For a more detailed discussion of *tajwīz*, recourse must be had to the classical Islamic books on the sects (e.g., Ash'arī, *Maqālāt*, pp. 568–71 and *passim*).

[4] See, e.g., *Murūj*, secs. 288, 731, 1028, 1205.

phenomena are impossible for the intellect to accept, the creation of such phenomena is nevertheless possible for God.[1] But the acceptance of God's intervention in natural phenomena did not, for Mas'ūdī, entail either credulousness or acceptance of the Ash'arite theory of spontaneous creation,[2] according to which God creates accidents (*a'rāḍ*) without the mediation of a nature, as the Mu'tazila believed. At the same time, Mas'ūdī chose to transcend the harsh scepticism of certain Mu'tazilites who tended to reject out of hand all reports of oddities as impossible.[3] As a result, the distinction he drew between the two kinds of impossibility had the advantage of ascribing a few inexplicable phenomena to the activity of God. But more importantly, this distinction, by widening the scope of the possible, impelled him to undertake further research into physical phenomena instead of adhering to purely reflective or subjective criteria of possibility. With this in mind, one must now turn to the "proofs".

There were three modes of apprehension which furnished Mas'ūdī with his proofs. The first mode was apprehension by the senses, the second was apprehension by investigation, inquiry and deliberation, and the third was apprehension by primary knowledge. One may also add opinion (*ẓann*) as the fourth mode of apprehension, although it was not regarded as such by Mas'ūdī. Perhaps the most convenient way of understanding these modes is to examine in some detail the manner in which Mas'ūdī employs them in practice.

Beginning with the least complex, opinion, Mas'ūdī applied the term to denote the lowest and least certain mode of apprehension. For instance, where exact computation of the number of men involved in a certain historical event was clearly impossible, Mas'ūdī refers to the efforts of other historians to determine the indeterminable as "opinion and guessing".[4] He thus contrasts guessing (*ḥazr*) with exact

[1] *Murūj*, sec. 1344. See also *Murūj*, sec. 380.

[2] This theory had the effect of blurring the distinction, which some Mu'tazilites upheld, between the physical laws of nature and the activity of God in nature.

[3] See p. 34, note 1, above. See also Ash'arī's *Maqālāt* and Shahrastānī's *Milal* for the opinions of Mu'tazilites like Naẓẓām on *tajwīz* and the laws which govern physical phenomena.

[4] *Murūj*, sec. 3184. At issue is the number of victims of the Zanj revolt. See a similar verdict in *Tanbīh*, p. 386, concerning victims of the Qarmatians. See also *Murūj*, sec. 545, where he criticizes historians for "exaggerating" reports about Nebuchadnezzar.

attainment (*taḥṣīl*) when dealing with reports of distances supplied to him by sailors.[1] Where he gives exact figures, he frequently couples this with the phrase "comprised in a tally".[2] Where vagueness is unavoidable, he plainly states that such and such cannot be counted.[3]

Turning next to apprehension by primary knowledge (*awā'il al-'uqūl*),[4] it must be noted that, except for narration by multiple witnesses (*tawātur*), proofs which are self-evident (*badīhī*) are rarely of any use to a historian. Such proofs can serve to verify only the most self-evident facts or refute only the most self-evident errors. Multiple narration is regarded by Mas'ūdī as an example of self-evident proof, and he often uses this term in conjunction with phrases like "widely known" (*mustafīḍ*) without further need of proof. The most frequent instances of multiple narration are common knowledge, widespread acceptance by historians, or well-known verse.[5]

The first two modes, apprehension by the senses and apprehension by critical inquiry and deduction, figure very prominently in Mas'ūdī's attempts to establish historical truth. A key concept which underlies both modes of apprehension, especially apprehension through sense-perception, is the concept of "research" (*baḥth*). It is a concept which demands careful scrutiny, since it lies at the core of Mas'ūdī's reflections on history and historical reconstruction. To appreciate its significance, certain conclusions from the first chapter need to be recalled.

It will be remembered that in his use of sources and his literary affinities and style, Mas'ūdī, like the Mu'tazila, renounced imitation of authority (*taqlīd*), both explicity and implicitly. His insistence, for example, that information must be derived from its sources or

1 *Murūj*, sec. 215. See also *Murūj*, sec. 428, where he casts doubt on the number of butchers attached to an army, and sec. 653, where he remains purposely vague on the number of victims of a plague.

2 *Murūj*, sec. 461.

3 *Murūj*, sec. 445. See also *Murūj*, sec. 653. Mas'ūdī's statement in *Murūj*, sec. 87 about the number of Israelites who left Egypt, summarized by Walter J. Fischel, "Ibn Khaldūn and al-Mas'ūdī," *Al-Mas'ūdī*, ed. Ahmad and Rahman, pp. 55–56, is worthy of comment. Mas'ūdī probably took the figure of 600,000 from Exodus 12:37. But such reports he treats under the heading of *isrā'īliyyāt*, which he designates as *jā'iz*, i.e., possible to God but by no means proven. See *Murūj*, sec. 1354.

4 *Murūj*, sec. 1134.

5 See, e.g., *Murūj*, secs. 811, 1203, 1256; *Tanbīh*, pp. 170, 336.

from those who were expected to be in the best position to know the facts, is a case in point. This method of establishing truth in history and the sciences is clearly the reverse of imitation. It remains to determine, therefore, what Mas'ūdī understood by "research" and what were the problems confronting him.

As Mas'ūdī used the word, research generally denoted a mode of apprehension which may be called empirical, in contrast to rational apprehension, with which it is frequently coupled by Mas'ūdī.[1] Under the rubric of research three main modes of apprehension may be singled out. The first mode is sense-perception (*ḥiss*) and its corollary "direct experience" (*'iyān*), this latter having the connotation of visual experience. The importance which Mas'ūdī attaches to this mode of apprehension has already been indicated in the first chapter, where it was shown that the information derived from this source was regarded by Mas'ūdī as one of the chief distinctions of his work. His extensive travels and constant observations lend a tone of finality to whatever Mas'ūdī confirms or denies by direct experience.[2] Such information is necessary, that is, irrefutable. It is used by Mas'ūdī to correct the errors of his predecessors, to fill in lacunae in the accounts of other historians and, of course, to provide information on subjects hitherto untreated by other writers.[3] From time to time, Mas'ūdī invites his reader to verify for himself the information provided.[4]

This emphasis on experience leads us to the second mode of

[1] To describe these two modes of apprehension, the rational and the empirical, Mas'ūdī uses several expressions with approximately the same meaning, e.g., "intellect and research" (*'aql wa baḥth*), *Murūj*, sec. 1432; "critical inquiry and research" (*naẓar wa baḥth*), *Murūj*, secs. 731,910 and *Tanbīh*, p. 84; "intellect and investigation" (*'aql wa faḥṣ*), *Murūj*, secs. 1134, 1204; "sense-perception or inference" (*ḥiss aw istidlāl*), *Murūj*, sec. 296. Mas'ūdī uses such expressions when he wishes to confirm or deny the truth of reports by rational and empirical modes of apprehension.

[2] Examples of apprehension by *'iyān* are very numerous; see, e.g., *Murūj*, secs. 234, 296, 440, 502, 705; *Tanbīh*, pp. 49–50, 66.

[3] See his criticism of Jāḥiẓ and Ibn Khurradādhbih in *Murūj*, sec. 217 and *Murūj*, sec. 503, and his dissatisfaction with the accounts of India given by Abū al-Qāsim al-Balkhī and al-Ḥasan ibn Mūsā al-Nawbakhtī in *Murūj*, sec. 159.

[4] E.g., *Murūj*, sec. 1363, where he asserts that the people of Iraq can discover for themselves how the various seasons affect health; *Murūj*, sec. 929, where he points to the ruins of Thamūd (Petra) as proof that the bodies of its inhabitants were of normal size. See also *Murūj*, sec. 369.

'iyān, that of verification (*īqā' al-miḥna*).[1] Here the historian appears in the guise of the natural scientist, offering verifiable explanations for the occurrence of certain natural phenomena, for example, the origin of the seas, earthquakes or the magnetic properties of metals.[2] This interest in the causes of natural phenomena had an important bearing on Mas'ūdī's historical writing, to the end that he was frequently ready to suggest mathematical or physical explanations of events, based on observations for which he claimed verifiability. An interesting example is the explanation suggested for the story of the Sleepers in the Cave, based on the movement of the sun.[3] Mas'ūdī the natural scientist is at the elbow of Mas'ūdī the historian, calculating or criticizing chronologies, confirming or denying the verifiability of reports.[4]

The third mode of *'iyān* is perhaps the most difficult to understand since it is the one where the least explanation is offered by Mas'ūdī. This is apprehension by "customs and experiences" (*al-'ādāt wa al-tajārib*). Reflection on the real import of this mode of apprehension, especially when it centers on the term "custom",[5] requires that careful attention be paid to the workings of nature as described and analyzed by Mas'ūdī. As used in this context, the word "nature" (*ṭabī'a*) will mean the phenomena or the processes of the external physical world. These phenomena are clearly of consuming interest to Mas'ūdī: rivers and seas, climate and minerals, animal and plant life, the mountains and heavenly bodies, envelop man and provide a backdrop to his history as conceived by Mas'ūdī in his two works. Man is studied in his natural setting. The interaction between man and nature will be the subject of the third chapter of this study. For present purposes, however, an account will be given

1 *Murūj*, sec. 303.

2 On the origin of the seas, see *Murūj*, secs. 302–3; on earthquakes, *Tanbīh*, pp. 49–50; on magnetism, *Murūj*, sec. 816.

3 *Tanbīh*, p. 134.

4 See, e.g., *Tanbīh*, pp. 129–130, where Mas'ūdī employs calculations based on Ptolemy's own works to prove that he was not to be identified with one of the Ptolemaic rulers of Egypt; *Tanbīh*, pp. 46–47, where he takes an Abbasid wazīr to task for his failure to realize that the sun sets at different times in different countries.

5 On the importance of this term in Muslim theology and philosophy, see Louis Gardet and M.-M. Anawati, *Introduction à la théologie musulmane* (Paris: Éditions Vrin, 1948), pp. 352–53; Mahdi, *Ibn Khaldūn*, pp. 140 ff.

of Mas'ūdī's conception of nature and its workings with the specific intention of clarifying his reasons for accepting certain phenomena as natural and credible and others as supernatural and incredible.

The student of Mas'ūdī notes, to begin with, that the author's interest in the phenomena of nature is almost invariably accompanied by his suggestion of reasons or causes (*'ilal*) for these phenomena. These suggestions, frequently forceful but sometimes tentative, reveal nature as obedient to the processes of cause and effect. Thus, in a typical instance, Mas'ūdī would begin by describing the particular phenomenon in detail, then proceed to offer the various theories which were advanced to explain it together with his personal preferences or reasons for accepting one particular theory rather than another.[1] Together with this search for causes, the student of Mas'ūdī detects a belief in the orderliness and uniformity of nature. The orderliness is conveyed by the use of such terms as "arrangement" or "system".[2] Physical phenomena, the tides for instance, have their "laws" and their "dispositions." This orderliness is the work of God's wisdom, which admits of neither negligence nor error.[3] The uniformity of nature, on the other hand, is clear to anyone who reasons by analogy (*qiyās*), whereby similar causes produce similar effects and similar effects may often be the result of similar causes.[4]

The study of the laws of the nature, therefore, gives rise to the mode of apprehension which Mas'ūdī terms "customs and experience." When the "custom" of a particular thing is properly apprehended, it then becomes possible to say of certain occurrences that they move or act according to their "custom" and of other things that they are known "by custom".[5] Two questions, however, are raised in this connection. First, How and where does one study the processes of nature, and secondly, Where does one draw the line between what is "customary" and what is not? The first question will be answered

1 Examples of this procedure are too numerous to cite. Mas'ūdī's analysis of tides, for instance, may be cited as typical (see *Murūj*, sec. 259 ff.).

2 See, e.g., *Tanbīh*, p. 16.

3 *Tanbīh*, pp. 8–9, 15-16.

4 See, e.g., *Murūj*, sec. 90, where Mas'ūdī reasons that what causes the Dead Sea in the Jordan Valley to be devoid of living things may be responsible for the same effect in a lake in Persia.

5 See, e.g., *Murūj*, sec. 258 where certain winds are known "by custom" and *Murūj*, sec. 301 where the cycle of sea-rain-river-sea is described as a "custom".

briefly below but the second must be postponed until all the modes of apprehension have been analyzed, when the question of possibility will be reintroduced for fuller analysis.

In his study of nature, Mas'ūdī's reliance on Greek philosophers and scientists is pronounced. Aristotle, who is most often referred to as the "author of the *Logic*," is quoted extensively along with other Greek authorities in the various sciences. From Aristotle, Mas'ūdī derived such ideas in cosmology, meteorology and physical geography as the ether, the extent and shape of the earth, the oneness of the ocean and the physical change of land into sea and vice versa.[1] The Muslim scientists most frequently cited are Ya'qūb ibn Isḥāq al-Kindī (d. 256/870) and his pupil Aḥmad ibn al-Ṭayyib al-Sarakhsī (d. 286/899).[2] From them and from others, Mas'ūdī derived some of his ideas on the causes of the tides, the sphericity of the earth and the transmutation of metals.[3] Of more relevance to this study is the scientific method he derived from these sources which influenced his own attempts at historical reconstruction. This will be treated more fully below when we come to analyze the theoretical foundations of his historical method. But we must emphasize at this juncture that Mas'ūdī's own observations of the workings of nature are, as was shown above in discussing apprehension by sense-perception, equally important determinants of what the "custom" is where certain phenomena are concerned.

In order to conclude this analysis of the various modes of apprehension, one must now turn to apprehension by critical inquiry and deduction. The two key terms used in this context by Mas'ūdī are

1 S. Maqbul Ahmad, "al-Mas'ūdī's Contribution," *Islamic Culture* 28 (1954): 275–86.

2 Citations of Aristotle are numerous. For al-Kindī, see Brockelmann, *Geschichte*, 1: 209; Brockelmann, *Supplement*, 1: 372; for al-Sarakhsī, see Brockelmann, *Supplement*, 1: 404, and Franz Rosenthal, *Aḥmad b. aṭ-Ṭayyib as-Sarakhsī* (New Haven: The American Oriental Society, 1943). A book on the influence of the sun and the moon written by Thābit ibn Qurra (d. 288/901) was transmitted to Mas'ūdī (*Tanbīh*, p. 73) by Thābit's son, Sinān ibn Thābit (d. 331/942). For Thābit, see Brockelmann, *Geschichte*, 1: 217; Brockelmann, *Supplement*, 1: 384; for Sinān, see *Geschichte*, 1: 218; *Supplement*, 1: 386. On Mas'ūdī's indebtedness to Greek science, see S. Maqbul Ahmad, "Al-Mas'ūdī's Contribution to Medieval Arab Geography," *Islamic Culture* 27 (1953): 61-77 and 28 (1954): 275–86.

3 *Murūj*, secs. 268, 1326–28, 3312.

"reasoning by inference" (*istidlāl*) and "reasoning by analogy" (*qiyās*). By these means, Mas'ūdī infers conclusions from, and correlates the data of experience. His belief in the orderliness and uniformity of nature, as outlined above, makes the use of such reasoning all the more suitable for the understanding of phenomena. As may be expected, the place where Mas'ūdī discerns the greatest need for the use of inference and analogy is while assessing the veracity of "reports narrated by a single authority" (*akhbār al-āḥād*). These reports constitute a sizeable majority of the information which Mas'ūdī incorporates in his works. Such reports, according to Mas'ūdī, may be accepted or rejected depending upon the proofs adduced in their support.[1] But some of these reports may also be regarded as neither proved nor disproved, and Mas'ūdī is compelled to suspend judgement on their veracity (without abdicating his right, however, of historical or scientific explanation of their nature). The proofs adduced for acceptance or rejection are largely proofs of inference or analogy. A few examples will illustrate this.

There are, to begin with, numerous examples of scientific analogies which reason from the properties of certain things to the properties of others. The magnetic properties of the earth are analogous to the magnetism of certain metals, like iron.[2] The creation of the world can be inferred from the transient character of natural objects.[3] Mathematical measurements, not only of dates, but also of objects, constitute proofs from inference.[4] Genetics and chemistry supply many proofs by analogy.[5] Geographical observations can help in reasoning from the known to the unknown.[6] In the historical thinking of Mas'ūdī, these scientific proofs serve to bridge the gap between the familiar and the unfamiliar by tempering scepticism on the one hand[7] and forestalling ignorance on the other.[8] They therefore provide

1 *Murūj*, sec. 291, gives a clear statement of his views on this matter.

2 *Murūj*, secs. 1326–27.

3 *Murūj*, secs. 1431–32.

4 *Tanbīh*, pp. 129–30; *Murūj*, sec. 731.

5 *Murūj*, secs. 816, 1217, 1220. See also sec. 3290.

6 *Murūj*, secs. 203–5, 405.

7 See, e.g., p. 34, note 1, above.

8 Mas'ūdī constantly berates both the superstition of his contemporaries (*Murūj*, secs. 288 and 1204) as well as the tendency of many to reject the unfamiliar (*Murūj*, sec. 249).

Mas'ūdī with the chance of offering explanations of phenomena drawn from the diverse sciences of his age. If man cannot be abstracted from nature, then the history of man can be clarified through the study of natural processes. This conception of historical explanation will shortly become more evident when the question of possibility is analyzed.

To return to *akhbār al-āḥād.* Aside from the scientific proofs, there are other, more traditional criteria adopted by Mas'ūdī to establish or reject the veracity of these reports. Thus Mas'ūdī rejects the reports which the science of Tradition labels as *mursal* or *mujtanab*.[1] Furthermore, no credence can be put in certain *akhbār al-āḥād* which have not been adopted generally by knowledgeable historians. Much less credence can be given to reports which even biased historians, who may have been expected to include them, pass by in silence.[2] For the rest, that is, for those reports whose falsity cannot be established, the historian must look for proofs,[3] if available, from among the various kinds of proofs detailed in the preceding pages.

Nature and the Supernatural

To complete this analysis of Mas'ūdī's observations on historical method, one must now turn to the question of oddities, to a whole class of reports which pose perhaps the most intriguing problems for the historian. Here, Mas'ūdī was faced with such problems as the distinction between what is "customary" and what is "not customary" in nature, the explanation of phenomena which he acknowledges to be subject neither to cause and effect nor to the orderliness and uniformity which he detects in nature, and the definition of the realms of possibility and impossibility.

In the first place, Mas'ūdī's conception of a nature obedient to laws, while clearly influenced by Greek and particularly Aristotelean theories, was different from these latter in one important respect.

1 See *Tanbīh*, p. 290. For the technical terms *mursal* and *mujtanab*, see James Robson, "Ḥadīth," *Encyclopaedia*, ed. Gibb et al. Theodoor Willem Juynboll, "Ḥadīth," *SEI*, is also useful.

2 *Tanbīh*, p. 336.

3 *Murūj*, sec. 291. Mas'ūdī emphasized the fact that his books were bolstered with proofs (e.g., *Tanbīh*, p. 76).

Nature and natural laws were, as shown above, the work of God's creation, of God's Wisdom. An essential limitation is thus placed upon man's intellect, according to Mas'ūdī. God has an exclusive knowledge of all things (*ista'thara bi 'ilm al-ashyā'*), revealing to men what is to their good in accordance with the times and with their needs. Some things, therefore, He alone knows and has not revealed to men, so the human mind cannot fathom them.[1] This led Mas'ūdī to draw a distinction between the impossible and the inacceptable as regards certain reports of oddities.[2] No oddity, no reversal of natural custom is impossible to God. However, such reversals, if they cannot be accounted for by the mind, must be held to be inacceptable (*lā taṣiḥḥ*). Therefore, for all practical purposes, that is, for purposes of inclusion in a work which claims to be supported by "proofs," they must be rejected. Included in this category are the stories of the anthropomorphists (*ḥashwiyya*) among the Traditionists, popular fables, the Old Testament and Jewish stories (*isrā'īliyyāt*), and the literature of marvels.[3] All the same, such stories may occasionally be included, because Mas'ūdī never lost sight of the entertainment value of history and referred to these stories as "delightful".[4] Other stories are supported by cogent "proofs," e.g., *tawātur*, and yet they are clearly contrary to natural custom. With regard to them, Mas'ūdī maintains an attitude of perplexity, expressed in the proviso "God knows best" which is appended to them.[5]

What is undoubtedly of greater interest is Mas'ūdī's repeated attempts to offer "customary," that is, scientific, explanations for these oddities. This is perhaps the most significant facet of his analysis of oddities because it underlines his concern for historical research and the pursuit of natural causes. The marvels which he encountered

1 *Murūj*, sec. 816.

2 See, e.g., *Murūj*, sec. 1344, where this distinction is maintained.

3 See, e.g., *Murūj*, secs. 288, 1028, 1204–5, 1338–39, 1344, 1354. In all these places, Mas'ūdī illustrates this distinction between the impossible and the inconclusive. For the "marvels" literature of this period, see especially Carra de Vaux's interesting introduction to his translation of a "marvels" work entitled *L'Abrégé des merveilles* (Paris: Librairie Klincksieck, 1898). Carra de Vaux establishes, *inter alia*, that this work cannot be identified with Mas'ūdī's lost *Akhbār al-Zamān*. But see Dunlop, *Arab Civilization*, pp. 110 ff.

4 This is true, for example, of stories about the ghoul (*Murūj*, sec. 1196). History as entertainment was discussed in chap. 1.

5 See *Murūj*, secs. 811 and 1256.

on his travels, either by direct experience or through reports, inclined him to view nature, not with the scepticism of the theorist, but with a tolerance which was born of the experiences of the travelling scholar. Yet, as a writer, he was also aware of the critical attitudes of his audiences and it sometimes seems as if he were restraining his impulse to relate more marvels.[1]

In accepting God's intervention in nature's laws, he widened the realm of the possible. Thus, for instance, the mouse which caused the Great Dam of Ma'rib to collapse must be accepted as a historical fact, as a "moral lesson" (*'ibra*) of God.[2] The greatest of God's lessons is of course the Koran.[3] But this cannot be the only proof for Mas'ūdī. For he rejects by implication the view current among certain religious circles that all phenomena for which no analogy can be found in nature are Divine acts.[4] Certain phenomena of attraction and repulsion among animals or the magical properties of certain talismans may indeed have been "miracles" (*mu'jizāt*) originally created for the benefit of prophets now long dead, but which persisted beyond the death of the prophet in question.[5] Nevertheless, this acceptance of Divine agency did not obscure for Mas'ūdī the need for scientific research and explanation in order to keep alive what would otherwise be termed mysterious. In other words, the acceptance of mystery did not by any means negate the importance of research.

For this reason, the student of Mas'ūdī often meets with what may be termed philosophical or psychological explanations of oddities. An example of the first is the explanation offered for mythical hybrids and beasts like the *nasnās* or the *'anqā'*. These, says Mas'ūdī, may well have been animal species which nature misconceived while conveying them from potentiality (*quwwa*) to actuality (*fi'l*). They therefore remained odd and unique, a species distinct from and repulsed by the others.[6] Psychological explanations are sometimes offered to

1 This is clearly seen in *Murūj*, sec. 249.

2 *Murūj*, sec. 1256.

3 *Murūj*, secs. 1003 and 1324.

4 He records (*Murūj*, sec. 265) this view while discussing tides but gives no weight to it and proceeds with his analysis of tides, outlining one scientific theory after another.

5 *Murūj*, sec. 818.

6 *Murūj*, sec. 1344. The ghoul is explained along similar lines (*Murūj*, sec. 1199).

account for a class of reports which includes ghouls, devils and other daemonic phenomena. Mas'ūdī suggests that these may arise as a result of man's lonely journeys across the wilderness where he falls prey to "sickly thoughts and evil imaginings".[1] Such loneliness breeds fear which in turn makes man imagine voices and phantoms calling to him. Fearing death, he can no longer control his thoughts, and his imagination conjures up the impossible, such as demons and phantom voices.[2]

A more revealing example of Mas'ūdī's psychological analysis is his treatment of fortune-telling (*kahāna*). Here, according to Mas'ūdī, was a phenomenon which was amply documented in both Arabic and foreign, e.g., Greek, sources.[3] An entire chapter is devoted to this subject. The explanation, in Mas'ūdī's view, lies in a peculiar state of the soul, akin to the state of the dreamer, when man attains a perception of psychic knowledge (*al-'ilm al-nafsī*) which enables him to foretell the future.[4] Fortune-telling is associated with purity of soul, solitude, and aversion from human intercourse. It is to be found mostly among the Arabs, and its intensity is dependent upon the element of "light in the soul" (*nūr al-nafs*). Mas'ūdī also refers to it as "comparable to the miraculous" (*muqārina li al-i'jāz*) and as a "special divine gift" (*laṭīfa*).[5] This divine gift is used by Mas'ūdī to account for psychological traits found in particular tribes or nations but not others. Such, for example, is the ability to detect footprints (*qiyāfa*), a faculty common to certain Arab tribes, which Mas'ūdī witnessed.[6] In accepting the existence of differences in the psychological makeup of nations, Mas'ūdī's explanation, at least in part,[7] was based upon a divine gift.

1 *Murūj*, sec. 1203.
2 *Murūj*, sec. 1207. One is tempted to detect in this psychological analysis of phantoms Mas'ūdī's own experiences as a traveller.
3 In *Murūj*, sec. 1233, Mas'ūdī writes, "Fortune-telling has never been lacking in any nation."
4 *Murūj*, secs. 1233–49.
5 *Murūj*, sec. 1240.
6 *Murūj*, secs. 1227–28. Mas'ūdī further suggests that, aside from *qiyāfa*, certain other qualities like augury (*'iyāfa*, *zajr*) were peculiar to the Arabs. Likewise, other nations are endowed with other faculties (*Murūj*, secs. 1218–19). On Arab divination in general, see Toufic Fahd, *La Divination arabe* (Leiden: E. J. Brill, 1966).
7 Other psychological differences, caused by the physical environment, will be treated in chap. 3.

There was one other phenomenon which was of some interest to Mas'ūdī. This was the question of longevity and the immense life-span and physical size of certain individuals and nations of antiquity.[1] These reports were found in Islamic Tradition as well as Judaic sources and therefore posed a special problem of interpretation. Mas'ūdī's answer was characteristic of his search for scientific, that is, demonstrable causes. That answer seems to have been inspired by Indian theories of the cyclical revitalization of the life force in nature.[2] Mas'ūdī sets aside the scepticism of writers who rejected reports of longevity and gigantism, in the belief that their scepticism was not warranted.[3] His own observations of the remains of 'Ād convinced him of the gigantism of its inhabitants.[4] But he also sets aside the credulity of the storytellers with respect to the size of the people of Thamūd because, here again, his observations convinced him that they were of normal size.[5] It appears, therefore, that longevity and other exceptional characteristics were not common to all nations of antiquity. But those who were so endowed derived these characteristics from the fact that when nature was first created by God, it was at the "height of its power and perfection" (*nihāyat al-quwwa wa al-kamāl*).[6] In their pristine condition, nature and nature's elements (*mādda, mawādd*) produced more perfect bodies and, therefore, longevity. With the passage of time, these elements decreased and the human life-span grew progressively shorter. Earth, like mankind, has its "youth" as well as its "old age."[7]

The implications of this view of nature are of considerable interest. They suggest that, for Mas'ūdī, the laws of nature are not uniform in all periods of history, and that one cannot read the present phenomena of nature into the past or vice versa. The historian must be conversant with the changes in these laws so as to avoid an erroneously

[1] In *Tanbīh*, p. 3, Mas'ūdī states that he has treated the reason for such longevity in certain of his works. In *Murūj*, sec. 928, he specifies these works as *Kitāb al-Ru'ūs al-Sab'iyya min al-Siyāsa al-Mulūkiyya* and *Kitāb al-Zulaf.*

[2] *Murūj*, secs. 154–58.

[3] *Murūj*, sec. 1263.

[4] *Murūj*, sec. 924.

[5] *Murūj*, sec. 929.

[6] *Murūj*, secs. 1261–62.

[7] *Tanbīh*, p. 70.

sceptical attitude.[1] Here again Mas'ūdī's interest in cosmology helps to broaden his historical reasoning and to underline his emphasis on research as the true matrix of historical enquiry.

The Concept of baḥth

To complete this study of Mas'ūdī's historical method, it is necessary to draw the conclusions appropriate to it, describe the principles upon which this method rests, and attempt to trace and identify the provenance of these principles. It must first be noted that his observations on historical method described in the preceding pages are gleaned from references scattered throughout the *Murūj* and the *Tanbīh*. Mas'ūdī did not intend either of these works to be taken as a statement of his theoretical views on history. This, as will be recalled, is emphasized by his frequent caveat that the two works were works of history and not of "research and critical inquiry." This caveat, however, has been set aside in this study in the belief that Mas'ūdī provides his reader with enough clues to his thinking to justify our analysis of his reflections on history. This must be stated before we proceed to the broader analysis of the bases underlying these reflections.

It must by now be evident that the concept of research plays a fundamental role in Mas'ūdī's historical thinking. In essence, it embodies his quest for scientific causes and explanations of historical events. In conjunction with the concept of *naẓar*, of critical inquiry, Mas'ūdī clearly implies that the past is discoverable if the historian uses the proper techniques. To appreciate the boldness of this view, one must keep in mind the Prophet's prohibition against the attempts of the genealogists to go back in time beyond a certain point. The fact that Mas'ūdī quotes this prohibition[2] and then proceeds to contravene it shows that he did not blindly follow traditional limitations to historical research which used as support this kind of *ḥadīth*, which may represent a pious fear of going into the past beyond a certain point.

1 A succinct treatment of the belief among Muslim thinkers in the qualitative difference in nature's laws at different eras is given in Seyyed Hossein Nasr, *An Introduction to Islamic Cosmological Doctrines* (Cambridge, Mass.: Harvard University Press, 1964), pp. 118–21 (hereafter referred to as *Cosmological Doctrines*).

2 *Murūj*, sec. 1438.

If the past is discoverable, if the facts of history could be established or, at least, ascertained with reasonable certainty, then the historian should be satisfied neither with scepticism nor with credulousness. The scepticism which Mas'ūdī encountered came from two main sources, the Mu'tazila and the natural scientists. A common Mu'tazilite attitude to historical reports, especially those with theological significance, was to test their veracity against their own theological teachings. Thus reports which were anthropomorphic in character or tended to uphold constraint (*jabr*) were rejected as false, while other reports which supported their tenets were accepted and emphasized. Their scepticism was the result of their desire to maintain the integrity of their theological teachings.[1]

The natural scientists as reported by Mas'ūdī often cast doubt on, or corrected information relating to geographical or other data. For example, the wall which Alexander the Great reportedly built against Gog and Magog could not, according to Muḥammad ibn Kathīr al-Farghānī (d. 246/860), be as wide as was claimed.[2] The scepticism of the natural scientists may also be detected in other instances where Mas'ūdī related reports about oddities in nature, adding that "men of critical inquiry and research" expressed doubts about such phenomena.[3] Credulousness, on the other hand, could assume many forms. It could be the gross credulousness of the storyteller who amused his audiences by the recital of folk tales and legends without

[1] The clearest statement of this view is in al-Qāḍī 'Abd al-Jabbār ibn Aḥmad, *Sharḥ*, pp. 268 and 769, where he argues that reports embodying constraint (*jabr*) and anthropomorphism (*tashbīh*) are to be rejected by inference (*istidlālan*). Although the *Sharḥ* is a comparatively late source for purposes of this study (the Qāḍī died in 415/1025), this view of historical reports was also held by earlier Mu'tazilites; see, e.g., Baghdādī, *Farq*, pp. 114, 125, 128 (Naẓẓām on miracles, knowledge of past events and *tawātur*); p. 149 (Fuwaṭī on the murder of the Caliph 'Uthmān); pp. 109-10 (Abū al-Hudhayl on miracles); Baghdādī, *Uṣūl*, pp. 11–12 (Naẓẓām on *tawātur*). See also Ash'arī, *Maqālāt*, p. 226 (the Mu'tazila on prophecy and the sins of the prophets). Al-Khayyāṭ, *Intiṣār*, p. 45, defends Naẓẓām by stating that he made no distinction between reports transmitted by Muslims and non-Muslims except in matters of worship (*ta'abbud*). However, since the Mu'tazila had their own views on what true worship really was, the result would be to deny a wide variety of reports in order to uphold a certain theological position. The Qāḍī 'Abd al-Jabbār, together with most Mu'tazilites, defined and divided reports in terms of their final end, which is their use (*fā'ida*) to men who are responsible (*mukallafūn*).

[2] *Murūj*, sec. 731.

[3] E.g., *Murūj*, secs. 1205, 1263.

any regard to truth. Credulousness could also appear in the guise of imitation, of the narration of historical reports through the blind acceptance of the authority of those who transmitted them.[1] But most subtle of all is the credulousness of those who abdicated the duty of the historian by claiming that inexplicable phenomena must be ascribed to the activity of God. Instead of searching for natural causation, such writers acknowledge their impotence *ab initio*, before any attempt has been made to verify, to understand or to analyze.[2]

In rejecting the two extremes of scepticism and credulousness, Mas'ūdī was insisting upon the importance of continued research and critical inquiry into the workings of nature as a vital aid in understanding the history of man.[3] This is a view which was not expressed, so far as is presently known, by any previous historian. It is a view which describes both the method of the historian as well as the framework in which the subject is to be studied. Seen in this light, the concept of research seems to depend upon, or at least reflect, some of the basic tenets of Islamic philosophy and natural science. Research as Mas'ūdī used the term has much in common with the term "investigation" (*faḥṣ*) which is used frequently by Fārābī in his *Philosophy of Aristotle* to denote one of the methods employed by man's intellect in its search for the "causes of sensible things" (*asbāb al-ashyā' al-maḥsūsa*).[4]

Of more direct relevance to Mas'ūdī's concept of research is the method of the natural scientists. Muslim scientists did not, as a rule, devote much time to discussions of their scientific method. Their scientific works, however, sometimes included short introductions where they briefly described their method. Mas'ūdī, however, was greatly interested in this side of their work. He records, for example, a lengthy debate in the presence of the Caliph al-Wāthiq on the principles and methods of medicine.[5] Some claim that medicine is

1 Thus, Mas'ūdī's criticism of Madā'inī for merely transmitting what he heard (*Murūj*, sec. 3146) is motivated by his consistent rejection of imitation.

2 See p. 44, note 4, above. See also *Murūj*, sec. 1438.

3 It is noteworthy that the arrangement of subject matter in both the *Murūj* and the *Tanbīh* serves to highlight the importance of nature. Both works commence with a review of the sciences of nature, approximating one-fourth of each work.

4 Mahdi, *Alfarabi's Philosophy*, p. 72.

5 *Murūj*, secs. 2857-66.

a science which can be acquired only through experience (*tajriba*), others that it is a science which is derived from certain basic principles, for instance, that two contrary principles cannot coexist in the same place. Still others maintained that the method of medicine is the method of analogy and inference and medication is prescribed accordingly.

Among astronomers and mathematicians, the concept of research entailed certain attitudes towards the acquisition of knowledge which seem to have a direct bearing on Mas'ūdī's own method. It entailed, to begin with, the rejection of imitation of authority in favor of independent investigation, however exalted that ancient authority may have been. The words of Ḥabash ibn 'Abdallāh (d. ca. 220/835), the famous astronomer, are typical of this attitude:

> When al-Ma'mūn died and the observations ceased, I was inclined to consider what these men had investigated and observed of the sun and the moon, and further to investigate the other planets so that my doubts might be resolved through firm knowledge. For it is necessary for one who undertakes to ground himself thoroughly in any art or science not to be satisfied with mere imitation of authority without personal inquiry and not be content with fragmentary knowledge without comprehensive understanding.[1]

Ḥabash proceeds to state that those who wish to acquire a sure grasp of the science of astronomy must not only improve and correct the works of ancient authorities but must always be ready to amend and correct their own.

The same aversion to imitation may be found in the writings of a contemporary of Mas'ūdī, the mathematician Ibrāhīm ibn Sinān ibn Thābit ibn Qurra (d. 335/946). He finds that some of his contemporaries were so slavish in their imitation of Ptolemy and Aristotle that they went as far as rejecting mathematical calculations and even the evidence of their senses.[2] His emphasis throughout is on the necessity of independent analysis and calculation in the problems of geometry, not simply reading and imitating the works of previous

[1] A. Sayili, "The Introductory Section of Ḥabash's Astronomical tables Known as the Damascene Zīj," *Ankara Universitesi Dil ve Tarih-Cografya Fakultesi Dergisi* 13 (1955): 150.

[2] Ibrāhīm ibn Sinān, "Fī Ḥarakāt al-Shams," in *Rasā'il*, pp. 54–57.

geometricians. A corollary to this concept is the claim, frequently to be met with among Muslim scientists, that knowledge in the sciences increases constantly. Here again, the words of Ibrāhīm ibn Sinān seem to bear close resemblance to the views of Mas'ūdī:

> It is incumbent upon him who reads this book and happens to find it deficient in some respects to realize that when a man broaches a theme which few men have broached before, some deficiencies must come to the fore. The reason is that the sciences grow and increase when one man begins a study of one science and others follow who add to his efforts by correcting and amending them. Therefore, he who discovers any errors should honestly state them and should add or subtract, if this is necessary, to what he finds.[1]

A second corollary is the belief expressed by Muslim scientists that the principles of the sciences must be learned and mastered in the proper order. Thus al-Kindī, for example, warns that mathematics must be learned before philosophy, for a man might spend his entire life studying philosophy to no avail if he does not master mathematics. His only accomplishment would be his ability to narrate (*riwāya*) but not to understand philosophy.[2] Similarly, Ibrāhīm ibn Sinān argues that a man might read all the books there are on geometry and still know nothing of geometry if he does not himself work out (*yastakhrij*) and analyze the problems in that science.[3] He adds that the principles (*awā'il*) of this science are sometimes avoided by certain geometricians who prefer to use abbreviated methods and thus fall into error.[4]

Continuous observation and experience led Mas'ūdī to adopt the viewpoint of philosophy and natural science rather than of theology towards the phenomena of nature. This entailed a tolerance towards the acceptance of reports of oddities which eschewed the doctrinal commitment of certain leading figures in the Mu'tazilite school. Such tolerance was born of the belief in the continuous increase of human knowledge, in the ability of each succeeding gene-

[1] *Idem*, "Fī al-Taḥlīl wa al-Tarkīb," in *Rasā'il*, pp. 4–5.

[2] Al-Kindī, *Rasā'il*, pp. 369–70.

[3] Ibrāhīm ibn Sinān, "Fī Ḥarakāt al-Shams, " in *Rasā'il*, p. 66.

[4] *Ibid.*, p. 36.

ration of scholars to add to the sum of what was known before. And this is so, says Mas'ūdī, because of the prudence engendered by experience (*ḥanakat al-tajārib*) and the avoidance of error.[1]

In conjunction with this, Mas'ūdī held that the study of nature, broadly speaking, must be pursued with the help of principles first established by philosophy, both Indian and Greek. His reliance on Indian and Greek philosophy will be discussed in detail in later chapters. In general, however, the student of Mas'ūdī notes very frequent citations of the opinions of philosophers and scientists which are sometimes explicitly contrasted with, and preferred to, the opinions of "men who accept revelation" (*al-shar'iyyūn*).[2] Sciences such as astronomy, meteorology, geography, mineralogy, zoology, genetics and metaphysics fall under philosophy.[3] Their principles must be derived from the writings of those philosophers who were especially concerned with these particular sciences.[4] Emphasis is therefore laid upon the revival of the principles of the philosophic sciences as a means of restoring the true understanding of man and his world. These principles have either been ignored or they have acquired useless accretions and become perverted.[5] Thus, when Mas'ūdī regrets, on the one hand, the widespread ignorance of his generation and proposes,

1 *Tanbīh*, p. 76. Cf. Fārābī, *Iḥṣā'*, p. 110. See Rosenthal, *Technique*, pp. 68–69, who quotes Fārābī's interpretation of Plato's *Timaeus*, where Plato is said to have stated that all conceivable knowledge would eventually come within reach of mankind; for this, see Mahdi, *Alfarabi's Philosophy*, pp. 65–66. See also the remarks of Grunebaum, *Medieval Islam*, p. 347, n. 47. Mas'ūdī was familiar with the *Timaeus* (*Murūj*, sec. 1248).

2 In *Murūj*, sec. 203, Mas'ūdī states, on the authority of "Greek and Indian philosophers" that the sea encircles the earth. According to him, "men of revelation" dispute this point, but he pays no heed to their arguments and proceeds in *Murūj*, sec. 205, to confirm the verdict of the philosophers. In *Murūj*, sec. 1221, while discussing genetics, Mas'ūdī states that the opinions advanced are those of "ancient philosophers" and not of "jurists who reason by analogy." See also *Murūj*, secs. 1204–5.

3 *Murūj*, sec. 14, where Mas'ūdī criticizes Sinān ibn Thābit for not devoting himself to these and other "philosophic" subjects, in which Socrates, Plato and Aristotle excel. See also *Murūj*, sec. 674.

4 Examples are too numerous to be cited in full. The frequent quotations from the writings of Aristotle and other Greek authorities are evidence of Mas'ūdī's desire to emphasize the proper study of the principles of the philosophic sciences.

5 The Sabians, for example, are called the "ḥashwiyya" of the philosophers, to distinguish them, according to Mas'ūdī, from the "true" philosophers (*Murūj*, secs. 210, 1394). Mas'ūdī deplores (*Tanbīh*, pp. 13–14) the neglect of scientific

on the other, to bequeath to posterity "a systematic science" (*'ilman manẓūman*),[1] he is referring in large measure to the need for the reinstatement of those principles in their proper sphere.

The question now arises, How is history relevant to this attempt to restore the principles of the philosophic sciences? What can history "teach" the man who wishes to undertake this attempt? One such "lesson" of history only will be discussed at this juncture, since this chapter has been concerned with Mas'ūdī's historical method. This has to do with a recurrent theme in Mas'ūdī's analysis of the history of ancient nations, namely, their relapse into ignorance after an initial period of wisdom. The most important passage bearing on this theme will be translated and analyzed:

> These nations we have mentioned did not disavow their maker. They knew that Noah was a Prophet and that he fulfilled the threat of torment he made to his people. However, confused opinions (*shubah*) prevailed among them because they had forsaken research and the use of their critical faculty. Their spirits tended towards lethargy and towards the pleasures and blind imitation to which man's natural characteristics (*ṭabā'i'*) beckon.[2]

In many places, Mas'ūdī attempts to show how man, initially endowed with critical faculties of intellect, fell prey to false religions and beliefs because he forsook the use of these faculties and preferred, out of laziness, to follow a course of unquestioning obedience to tradition or to the subtleties of charlatans.[3] The evolution of the religion of India and China as described by Mas'ūdī illustrates this progressive perversion of man's intellect.[4] The contrast that Mas'ūdi draws between *shubha* on the one hand and *naẓar* on the other is one that is familiar to Muslim theologians, especially the Mu'tazilites.

principles by astronomers of his time who pay little heed to the science of spheres, stars and their movements (*'ilm al-hay'a*) and devote themselves instead to judicial astrology (*'ilm al-aḥkām*). This latter cannot be studied meaningfully without reference to the principles of the former. On the place of these sciences in the doctrine of the Ikhwān al-Ṣafā', see Nasr, *Cosmological Doctrines*, pp. 75 ff.

1 *Murūj*, sec. 7.

2 *Murūj*, sec. 1171.

3 See, e.g., *Murūj*, secs. 326, 703, 1136, 1371. In all these places *shubha* or the plural *shubah* is used to denote the relapse into idolatry. See also *Murūj*, secs. 535, 1372, 1380–81.

4 *Murūj*, sec. 1370 ff.

They too, in their writings and polemics, stressed the importance of critical inquiry and some claimed it to be the primary duty of the Muslim believer.[1] Many Mu'tazilites were, therefore, emphatic in their rejection of *taqlīd*, going so far as to call anyone who held his faith by *taqlīd* as a *fāsiq* or even a *kāfir*.[2]

Mas'ūdī's own rejection of *taqlīd* has often been alluded to in the preceding pages. It may therefore be suggested, in order to conclude this study of Mas'ūdī's historical thought, that he attempted in his reflections on historical method to bring to the fore the essential role of research and critical inquiry. Likewise, in the pages of his history, he attributed the decline of knowledge in certain nations to a decline in their capacity for independent research and critical thought. Mas'ūdī's reliance upon the method of natural science and his rehabilitation of Indian and Greek philosophy underlines his concern for the principles of the sciences which, in his view, were threatened by ignorance. This is a major theme, a universal judgement which history provides to the discerning reader.

1 The Qāḍī 'Abd al-Jabbār considers *naẓar* to be the first duty of the believer (see *Sharḥ*, p. 39). Earlier Mu'tazilites, e.g., Naẓẓām as quoted in Shahrastānī, *Milal*, 1: 79, also held this view. Al-Aṣamm specifically contrasted *shubha* with *naẓar* (Ash'arī, *Maqālāt*, p. 223).

2 See, e.g., Baghdādī, *Uṣūl*, p. 255. Of particular interest in this regard is the attack of Abū Ja'far al-Iskāfī (d. 241/855) against the *Kitāb al-'Uthmāniyya* of Jāḥiẓ. The opening sentence of al-Iskāfī's attack is a condemnation of "ignorance and imitation." (Jāḥiẓ, *Rasā'il*, p. 13). This work was known to Mas'ūdī, who held al-Iskāfī in high esteem (*Murūj*, secs. 2281–82).

3. DIVINE AND NATURAL FACTORS IN HUMAN HISTORY

Introductory Remarks

In the preceding chapter, an attempt was made to describe the main features of Mas'ūdī's reflections on history and to ascertain the reasons for his choice of a philosophic and scientific approach towards historical reconstruction. It was argued that, in his attitude towards the sciences, he strove to emphasize the proper study of the principles of these sciences by stressing the means he considered essential towards that end, namely, research and critical inquiry. Armed with the methods of *falsafa* and science, the historian can subject the events of the past as well as the phenomena of nature to a thorough examination which will eventually reveal to him and to his readers the underlying pattern and the "lessons" of the historical process.

Some of the implications of this view will be worked out in this and in succeeding chapters of the present study. This chapter will examine in particular the most important divine and natural factors influencing the course of human history. To begin with, detailed note will be taken of Mas'ūdī's account of the creation of the world, since this raises the larger problem of God's activity in history. This in turn will lead to an analysis of Mas'ūdī's views on prophecy and, by contrast, on nonrevealed religions. This will then raise the more general problem of man in his environment, of the influence of regions and climates on human development. Once the divine and the natural factors have been analyzed, an attempt will finally be made to draw general conclusions therefrom, relative to the constituent elements of human societies and the reasons for their rise, decline and fall.

The Creation of the World

Stories of the creation were recorded and transmitted in the Islamic community from the earliest times. Aside from references to creation in the Koran and Tradition, a number of Muslim storytellers and historians took an active interest in the subject, embellishing the Koranic account with others drawn mainly from the Old Testament.[1] By the middle of the tenth century, Maqdisī, a contemporary of Mas'ūdī, was writing that there were many and divergent accounts of creation and that he proposed to deal only with the most reliable of them.[2]

Mas'ūdī presents two vividly contrasting accounts of the creation of the world. The first is related on the authority of 'Abdallāh ibn al-'Abbās, famous Traditionist and cousin of the Prophet, which is in essence a reconstruction of the relevant Koranic passages, to which Mas'ūdī adds details supplied by traditional sources, like the historians Wahb ibn Munabbih (d. 110 or 114/728 or 732) and Ibn Isḥāq (d. 150/767).[3] It tells of the earth supported by the whale, "the whale in the water, the water on the stones, the stones on the back of an angel, the angel on a rock, the rock on the wind." When the whale moved, the earth quaked so God weighed it down with mountains.[4] Then follows the creation of the *jinn*, of Adam and the rebellion of Iblīs (Satan). The account is concluded by Mas'ūdī's statement that this

[1] A scholarly treatment of this subject may be found in Abbott, *Studies*, 1: 32–56, where two eighth and ninth century papyri dealing with the story of creation are carefully analyzed. See also Franz Rosenthal, "The Influence of Biblical Tradition on Muslim Historiography," in *Historians of the Middle East*, pp. 40–44; Dūrī, *Baḥth*, pp. 103–13, who emphasizes the role of Wahb ibn Munabbih (d. 110 or 114/728 or 732) in introducing coherent accounts of the creation into Muslim historiography.

[2] Maqdisī, *Bad'*, 2: 1–2. Maqdisī mentions ten such story-tellers and historians who transmitted accounts of the creation.

[3] Although Mas'ūdī mentions no source for his first account of the creation other than Ibn al-'Abbās, comparisons with more extensive accounts recorded in Ṭabarī and Maqdisī readily reveals the other sources. Thus, *Murūj*, sec. 34 may be compared to Ṭabarī, *Annales*, 1: 49–51 and Maqdisī, *Bad'*, 2: 48–49; *Murūj*, sec. 35 to Ṭabarī, *Annales*, 1: 87–88; *Murūj*, sec. 39 to Ṭabarī, *Annales*, 1: 90; *Murūj*, sec. 40 to Ṭabarī, *Annales*, 1: 92–93. The most significant, perhaps, is *Murūj*, sec. 36, a description of the seven heavens, which Maqdisī records (*Bad'*, 2: 6) as narrated by Wahb on the authority of Salmān al-Fārisī.

[4] *Murūj*, sec. 34.

version of the creation is to be found in religious and traditional sources and that he copied it as transmitted to him or as he found it in books.

This version of the creation is in no sense reflective or analytical. The same narrative may be found in one form or another in such traditional and historical authorities as Ibn Hishām, Bukhārī, Ṭabarī and others.[1] It is basically exegetic in character, serving to fill in lacunae in the Koranic story of the creation.[2] Such narratives were also cultivated by preachers to exhort their audiences and to draw appropriate moral lessons from these legends.[3] Some Muslim historians included these stories in their histories largely for their symbolic value. This, at least, seems to be the case with Maqdisī and Mas'ūdī. The former enjoins his readers to reflect on the meaning of these stories, not their literal expression; the latter appears to regard them as symbolic of God's direct creation of the world in contrast to some other accounts which maintain the eternity of the world.[4]

The second account,[5] based on a report of the Shī'ite Imām Ja'far al-Ṣādiq and going back to 'Alī ibn Abī Ṭālib, is contemplative, well structured, and charged with theological significance. God is not simply the creator of the first account but the conscious and purposeful architect of world destiny. God, it is reported, first gave the multitudes of humanity the form of fine dust (*naṣaba al-khalq fī ṣuwar ka'l-habā'*) before the creation of the heavens and the earth. Into this as yet uncreated concourse of humanity, God projected a beam of light which focused on the image of Muḥammad. Muḥammad is then addressed by God as the progenitor of a line of divinely guided men for whose sake both the creation of the world and its later history are justified. This "election" (*intikhāb*) of Muḥammad and his line which constitutes the ultimate justification of human history, was

1 See, e.g., Ibn Hishām, *Tījān*, pp. 2–13; Ṭabarī, *Annales*, 1: 19 ff.; Bukhārī, *Ṣaḥīḥ*, Book 59, *passim*. See also Ibn Qutayba, *Ma'ārif*, pp. 9–62.

2 For a discussion of such narratives in their historical setting, see Abbott, *Studies*, 1: 46–50.

3 See, e.g., Abbott, *Studies*, 1: 53, n. 9.

4 For Maqdisī's views, see especially *Bad'*, 2: 50, where he refers to these stories as "symbolization and representation" (*tamthīl wa tashbīh*). See also *Bad'*, 1: 154, 176; 2: 2, 25; 4: 173–76. Mas'ūdī sums up this account of the creation in *Murūj*, sec. 42 by implying that his intention is to symbolize the contingency (*ḥudūth*) of the world.

5 *Murūj*, secs. 43–46.

"mixed in with the reason" (*shāba bi baṣā'ir al-khalq*) of the uncreated multitudes of mankind and proclaimed on high by the angels even before the creation of Adam. This divine plan, however, was not fully unfolded when the world began. To Adam was granted only a partial vision of the truth. He was taught the "names of all things" and was an "imām" and an exemplar among the angels. But God chose to hide His full light from the course of history until the moment when He brought forth Muḥammad, who then revealed the complete truth, the inward (*bāṭin*) as well as the outward (*ẓāhir*) dimensions of the divine plan. Henceforth, Muḥammad and his line are the repositories of knowledge, the lights of heaven and earth, the proofs of God on earth (*ḥujaj rabb al-'ālamīn*). The last of the line, the Mahdī, is the saviour of the community and the final end to which the divine light was originally directed. This account raises a number of important problems, for instance Mas'ūdī's reasons for juxtaposing two versions of creation which are so radically disparate, the sources from which Mas'ūdī drew the second account, and the significance of this account for the work as a whole. The most convenient point of departure is perhaps the search for the background of this account. Once this is established, the significance of the whole can, perhaps, be more easily determined.

The main theme of 'Alī's account, that is, the divine election of Muḥammad and his line and the transmission of light, is one which bears close resemblance to the doctrine of the *Nūr Muḥammadī* ('the light of Muḥammad') as expounded by the Shī'a. This doctrine was, to quote Massignon, given "more logical coherence" by the Shī'a than by other Muslim groups.[1] A historical work on the creation from an Imāmī Shī'ite standpoint was written by a certain Yūnus ibn 'Abd al-Raḥmān of the circle of the Imām Mūsā ibn Ja'far al-Ṣādiq (d. 183/799).[2] It would not be rash to speculate that such early Imāmī Shī'ite works may well have developed this doctrine especially when one bears in mind that Shī'ite poets like Kumayt (d. 126/743) "had

1 For the doctrine of *Nūr Muḥammadī*, see Louis Massignon, "Nūr Muḥammadī," *SEI*, p. 452; Tj. de Boer, "Nūr," *SEI*, p. 451; Louis Gardet, *Dieu et la destinée de l'homme* (Paris: Éditions Vrin, 1967), p. 183. However, the doctrine as related by Ibn Hishām, *Tījān*, p. 7, on the authority of Wahb, makes no mention of the transmission of light to Muḥammad's progeny.

2 Abbott, *Studies*, 1: 37.

already sung of the light emanating through Adam via Muḥammad into the family of ʿAlī".[1]

In Masʿūdī's own times, numerous references to this doctrine are found in Imāmī Shīʿite works on law and theology.[2] There can be little doubt that Masʿūdī derived this account of the creation from these sources. What is admittedly harder to ascertain at this juncture is his reason for recording two disparate accounts of the creation where one would normally have expected either a single coherent account or many accounts held loosely together. Such, at least, seems to have been the practice of Masʿūdī's immediate predecessors.[3] Given, therefore, a Shīʿite source for this story of the creation, one must address himself to the question of Masʿūdī's motive for including it alongside a more traditional and less contemplative account. Reflection on the significance of this story leads to the conclusion that the story possesses a deeper meaning, for it postulates a certain relationship between God and mankind which is not provided by the first account. It is as if the first account, with its frequent Koranic quotations, were merely the *ẓāhir*, the outward account of the creation, while the second, ʿAlī's account, is the *bāṭin*, the inward interpretation of that event.[4]

1 Tj. de Boer, "Nūr," *SEI*, p. 451.

2 Kulaynī (d. 329/941) mentions several versions of this story of the creation (see, e.g., *Kāfī*, 1: 194 ff., 389 ff., 438 ff.). Ibn Bābawayh (d. 381/991 or 992), records this doctrine in his *Maʿānī*, pp. 15, 55, 56, 108–10, 351; cf. *idem*, *Tawḥīd*, pp. 83, 109–10 and, especially, 263. Ibn Abī al-Ḥadīd (d. 656/1258), possibly because of his Muʿtazilite views, rejected as "legends" (*khurāfāt*) the stories of the creation which referred to the whale, the stones, and so forth (cf. *Sharḥ*, 1: 90). For similar reasons, perhaps, he makes no mention of the doctrine of *Nūr Muḥammadī*. Non-Shīʿite authors like Maqdisī describe this doctrine as Shīʿite (see *Bad'*, 1: 150). The doctrine was central to Ismāʿīlī theology as well (see Massignon, "Nūr Muḥammadī"; Abū Yaʿqūb al-Sijistānī, *Ithbāt*, pp. 181 ff.). Shahrastānī, *Milal*, 1: 291–92, says the doctrine was espoused by the Kāmiliyya, an extreme Shīʿa (*ghulāt*) group.

3 E.g., Yaʿqūbī and Ṭabarī. In Yaʿqūbī's case, we do not possess the full text which must have included the creation, but the story of Adam is single and coherent. Ṭabarī, as is customary throughout his history, records numerous reports on the creation narrated by various chains of authorities.

4 Such interpretation (*ta'wīl*) is, of course, very frequent in Imāmī Shīʿite theological and legal texts of Masʿūdī's times. Of particular relevance in this context are the interpretations provided by the various Imāms regarding Koranic texts dealing with the creation; see, e.g., Kulaynī, *Kāfī*, 1: 129 ff., 194–95; Ibn Bābawayh, *Tawḥīd*, pp. 106 ff. Numerous other examples can be cited.

This divine plan, that is, the election of Muḥammad and his line, was not revealed all at once with the creation of the world. Instead, God chose to conceal this plan until Muḥammad was able to reveal it in all its temporal and eternal, inward and outward manifestations. It may be assumed, therefore, that the pre-Islamic era is one to which the full truth as embodied in God's plan was not accessible. Thus, whereas innate human reason has attested, *ab aeterno*, to the election of Muḥammad and his line, God so disposed mankind that it did not gain complete knowledge until a certain moment in history finally arrived. Seen in this light, the history of the world would therefore be a history of the progress of mankind towards the attainment of final revelation.

This much at least can be deduced from an analysis of this Shī'ite-inspired account of the creation. The full implications of this view of the historical relationship between God and mankind will be elaborated below. But before concluding this section, it is necessary to revert briefly to the question posed above, viz., the reason for the contrast between the two stories of the creation. It is suggested, in answer, that Mas'ūdī viewed God not as the mere Creator of the first account but as the Divine Source of guidance of mankind, as the Originator of a line of prophets and Imāms whose task it is to provide this guidance referred to in 'Alī's account.

Prophecy and Prophets

It is in his treatment of prophets and prophecy that Mas'ūdī illustrates most clearly God's activity in history, that is, what was referred to above as the divine plan. In the first place, the line of prophets or their stewards (*awṣiyā'*) which stretches from Adam to Muḥammad, is uninterrupted. In the early stages of this prophetic line Mas'ūdī contrives to follow 'Alī's account of the creation very closely. Thus, when Adam grieves after his fall, God comforts him with the announcement that from his seed a light will issue (i.e., Muḥammad) who will be the seal of the prophets and whose progeny, the Imāms, will fill the world with their call (*da'wa*) and bring that world to its end.[1] Mas'ūdī further speaks of a covenant (*waṣiyya*)

[1] *Murūj*, sec. 55.

and a light being passed from one era to the next until God delivers the light to 'Abd al-Muṭṭalib, grandfather of Muḥammad.[1] With respect, therefore, to Old Testament and Koranic prophets, no significant problems are raised by Mas'ūdī's presentation. It may be difficult to ascertain the exact transmission of the covenant or of the the light from one prophet to another, but Mas'ūdī asserts that they were indeed transmitted. In the main, Mas'ūdī treats these prophets as preachers of God's unity sent by God to remind their fellow men of God's oneness and retribution. A more difficult problem is the claim advanced in the Alid account of the creation concerning the very foundation of prophecy and the election of Muḥammad and his line. For it will be remembered that God is said to have "mixed this in" with the reason of mankind. If, as has hitherto been assumed, Mas'ūdī intended this account to provide a legitimate explanation for the origin and nature of prophecy — if, in other words, Mas'ūdī believed that prophecy had its foundation in reason — how did he account for the history of nations which ostensibly had no prophets?

The nations of the earth, according to Mas'ūdī, trace their genealogies to the children and grandchildren of Noah who dispersed to the four corners of the earth after the flood.[2] In the earliest periods, Mas'ūdī asserts that they retained their belief in prophecy, acknowledging at least the prophethood of Noah as well as the unity of the Creator.[3] In later periods, a few wise rulers, even as far away as China,

[1] *Murūj*, sec. 58. Mas'ūdī carries the story of Hebrew kings and prophets down to the Babylonian captivity. His authorities, including the Koran and the Old Testament and Muslim historians like Ṭabarī and Ibn Qutayba, can be ascertained by use of Pellat's notes to his edition of the Arabic text. Where the transmission of light is concerned, Mas'ūdī uses the phrase "and the light shining in his forehead" for almost every prophet up to Noah (*Murūj*, sec. 63), and then drops it thereafter. This does not mean that the light suddenly ended, especially when Mas'ūdī explicitly asserts the contrary in *Murūj*, secs. 58, 60. The most probable explanation is that the repetition of the phrase about the transmission of light for each prophet or steward would have been stylistically cumbersome, for he takes up the phrase again when describing 'Abd al-Muṭṭalib (*Murūj*, sec. 1127). For a detailed discussion of the views on prophecy among Muslim scholars and sects, see Gardet, *Dieu et la destinée de l'homme*, pp. 148–228.

[2] *Murūj*, sec. 66. The Flood will be treated at greater length in chap. 4, below.

[3] *Murūj*, sec. 1171.

believed in all the major prophets down to Muḥammad.[1] Such cases, however, are exceptional. No era according to Mas'ūdī was bereft of a prophet or his steward. Most nations, however, derived their laws not from a divine revelation through a prophet but rather through reason and the wisdom of kings and sages. These latter provided their peoples with "rational duties" (*farā'iḍ 'aqliyya*) by which they could regulate their life.[2]

Seen in its totality, the pre-Islamic era of world history is one where the full truth of the divine plan is accessible but hidden. The vast majority of humanity lives without the benefit of divine prophecy. The most advanced nations approximated to the truth by having their own rational duties; the rest lived a life which Mas'ūdī describes as "ignorant" (*jāhiliyya*). But as the time of Muḥammad draws nearer, the perception of God's plan becomes clearer to a few. In the pre-Islamic Arabian peninsula, destined to be the home of final revelation, the religious perception of men was more acute than anywhere else on earth. Prophets in the period between Jesus and Muḥammad become increasingly aware of the momentous event of the coming of Muḥammad. They await his coming and sing his praises.[3] A progress or at least a quickening in the process of revelation through prophets is discernible as the divine plan unfolds towards its full and final disclosure. Inasmuch as these Arabian prophets had an increasingly clearer vision of the final end to which divine revelation was tending, they may be said to have been endowed with a progressively greater share of truth. This much, at least, can be surmised from Mas'ūdī's account.

Reason and revelation are, in 'Alī's account of the creation, "mixed together," but we have seen that in the pre-Islamic era they follow separate ways. At no moment does God forsake the world; at no time is the world left without the guidance of an intermediary, a prophet or his steward. On the other hand, the arts and the sciences of many nations arise and develop without prophetic inspiration. The

1 This, surely, is the import of the story of the Quraysh merchant who wandered into China and had a long conversation with a Chinese king on prophecy (*Murūj*, secs. 342–50). Cf. the story of the Caliph Abū Bakr's ambassador to the Emperor of Byzantium in Dīnawarī, *Akhbār*, pp. 21–22.

2 Typical are the examples of India and China (*Murūj*, secs. 152–61, 321).

3 *Murūj*, secs. 122–51, where Mas'ūdī describes the period between Jesus and Muḥammad. The center of the historical stage is occupied by Arabian prophets.

wisdom of India and China, the arts and sciences of these nations, are fashioned out by reason without the aid of prophets, and their wise men are able to deduce the principles of social organization without the benefit of a revealed law. This is why Mas'ūdī begins the *Murūj* with an account of the prophets from Adam to Muḥammad and then turns immediately to India, the land of "virtue and wisdom."[1] The history of revelation is complemented by the history of reason. Prophecy has its counterpart in human wisdom.

Before bringing this account of the creation of the world to a close, it may be pointed out that Mas'ūdī's reader is presented here with a problem of interpretation. The difficulty lies in reconciling what is evidently a theological or theosophical account of God's activity in history with Mas'ūdī's emphasis, as outlined in chapter 2, on scientific criteria for establishing historical veracity and on the importance of research. The explanation lies in a common Muslim medieval attitude to reason and revelation, more precisely to a professed acknowledgment of God's unceasing activity in history but alongside a parallel belief in the natural laws of the physical universe. Shī'ism, both Twelver and Ismā'īlī, was particularly prone to this theosophical-scientific view of the world, probably because of the need to prove the continuous presence of divinely inspired *imāms*. The Letters of the Brethren of Purity (*Rasā'il Ikhwān al-Ṣafā'*) is perhaps the best example of this cosmology.

Natural Religion: Reason and Revelation

The nonrevealed or "natural religions" (*al-milal al-ṭabī'iyya*), as he calls them, were of consuming interest to Mas'ūdī. The copious information provided on them in the *Murūj* and the *Tanbīh* and the thoroughness with which Mas'ūdī examined all forms of nonrevealed or natural religion are evidence of his interest.[2] The assessment of the accuracy or otherwise of this information, however, lies beyond the scope of the present study. Rather, an attempt will be made to explore some of the implications of his treatment of the various forms of natural

1 *Murūj*, sec. 152 ff.

2 Mas'ūdī's lost *Kitāb al-Ru'ūs al-Sab'iyya fī Anwā' al-Siyāsāt al-Madaniyya wa Milalihā al-Ṭabī'iyya* dealt in part, as he himself informs us, with the influence of the heavenly bodies as set forth in nonrevealed religions (*Murūj*, sec. 1223).

or nonrevealed religions with the aim of determining how Mas'ūdī defined and described nonrevealed religions, and what bearing this had on the relationship of God to mankind, which constitutes the theme of this chapter.

To begin with, the student of Mas'ūdī detects a certain uniformity or pattern in the treatment of natural religions. Most forms of natural religion had similar beginnings and developed similar features. We have seen that in the immediate post-diluvian period, the nations of the earth worshipped God and believed in the prophets. However, Mas'ūdī's study of the subject disclosed to him an almost universal process of decline or regression into idol worship. This decline began with anthropomorphism, with the belief that God and the angels were bodies. This led to idol worship, to the worship of idols and statues which these nations held to resemble God. When some sages convinced them that the heavenly bodies were the nearest visible and living bodies to God, they converted to star worship and then to idols which were in the shape and number of the heavenly bodies. With time, only the idols themselves were worshipped and they forsook the worship of stars until the advent of Būdāsaf who reintroduced the worship of heavenly bodies. The deities worshipped as symbols and representations of the seven major heavenly bodies (the sun and moon and the five planets) differed from one nation to another, but idol worship was common to all of them.[1] Seven great houses of worship were built in honor of the seven heavenly bodies.[2] Thus, according to Mas'ūdī, there was a considerable degree of uniformity in natural religion.[3]

To this idol worship which centered upon the heavenly bodies, Mas'ūdī gave the name Sabianism (*al-Ṣābi'a* or *al-Ḥanīfiyya*). Both names are somewhat confusing, the latter perhaps even more than the former, until one remembers that Sabianism is used by Mas'ūdī as the general term for star worship in the ancient world of whom the Sabians of Ḥarrān are only one sect. When Mas'ūdī wishes to designate these

[1] The evolution of nonrevealed religions is explained in *Murūj*, sec. 1370 ff. See also, *Tanbīh*, p. 84; *Murūj*, secs. 75, 535, for some of the more important references to such religions.

[2] Their locations are given in *Murūj*, sec. 137 ff.

[3] E.g., he compares the religion of China, Shamanism, to the idol worship of pre-Islamic Arabia (*Murūj*, sec. 325).

latter, he almost always appends "of Ḥarrān" to their name.[1] As for the word "Ḥanīfiyya," this was recognized by Mas'ūdī as a loan word from Syriac where it was applied to the Sabians and has nothing to do with the Koranic use of the term.[2]

The Sabians of Ḥarrān were of special interest to Mas'ūdī. He recognized in their religion an admixture of Greek philosophy which, however, he designated as literalist (*ḥashwiyya*), and distinguished this from true philosophy as practiced by the wise men of Greece.[3] The Sabians built temples to the First Cause (*al-'illa al-ūlā*) and to the Intellect (*al-'aql*), but Mas'ūdī could not determine whether they meant the First or the Second Intellect.[4] Their philosophic tradition was, in the main, a continuation of the philosophy of Pythagoras and Thales,[5] what Mas'ūdī called the "first philosophy" (*al-falsafa al-ūlā*). Their theory of prophecy was based not upon revelation but upon the purity of soul achieved by the "prophets", chief among whom they honored Agathodemon and Hermes.[6] Aside from the Sabians, Mas'ūdī also devoted some attention to the pre-Zoroastrian fire worship of ancient Persia as well as to Zoroastrianism and its offshoots, Mazdakism and Manichaeanism.[7]

[1] Mas'ūdī applies the word Ṣābi'a to the ancient religions of China, Persia, Egypt, Greece and Rome (*Tanbīh*, pp. 161–62). Yves Marquet in his important article, "Sabéens et Iḫwān al-Ṣafā'", *Studia Islamica* 24 (1966): 35–80 and 25 (1966): 77–109, writes that Mas'ūdī's use of the word was wide and vague. Marquet fails to note that Mas'ūdī's use of the word stemmed from his belief in a uniform star worship among the ancient nations, of which the Sabians of Ḥarrān of his own day were the most important remnants.

[2] See, in particular, Frants Buhl, "Ḥanīf," *SEI*, pp. 132–33, where Mas'ūdī's use of the word is discussed.

[3] *Murūj*, sec. 1394.

[4] *Murūj*, sec. 1389. Mas'ūdī refers his reader to Aristotle and his commentators for a definition of the First and Second Intellect.

[5] *Tanbīh*, pp. 116, 162. According to Mas'ūdī, the Pythagorean tradition was represented among Muslim philosophers by Abū Bakr Muḥammad ibn Zakariyyā al-Rāzī (*Tanbīh*, p. 162).

[6] *Tanbīh*, p. 19; *Murūj*, sec. 1234. For a discussion of the views of Maimonides on Sabianism, see Leo Strauss's introductory essay in Maimonides, *Guide of the Perplexed*, trans. by Shlomo Pines (Chicago: The University of Chicago Press, 1963), pp. xxxiv ff.

[7] For fire worship, see *Murūj*, secs. 1399–1402. For Zoroastrianism, see *Tanbīh*, pp. 90–94 and *Murūj*, sec. 547. For Mazdakism, see *Tanbīh*, pp. 101-2. For Manichaeanism, see *Tanbīh*, p. 135.

Throughout Mas'ūdī's examination of the various forms of non-revealed religions there run certain themes which are of importance to the central issue of this chapter. To begin with, the lapse into idol worship is viewed by Mas'ūdī as an aberration of the mind. Man falls prey to idol worship through a failure of his reason which can lead him, when it functions properly, to knowledge of God. Thus, idol worship is introduced to pre-Islamic Arabia by a Meccan prince who imported an idol from Syria and copied Syrian idolatry. Fire worship is begun in Persia by a king who is intrigued by the explanation offered by its worshippers.[1] In these and many other cases, Mas'ūdī speaks of confused opinions and myths (*khurāfāt*), of ignorance and weakness of opinions.[2] The purveyors of various forms of idolatry are spoken of as charlatans who prey on men's minds with "ornate speech"[3] and lead them astray.

However, certain wise kings and sages of antiquity were able to transcend the bounds of idolatry and to worship God as the sole creator. Mas'ūdī tells us that "intelligent" men regarded the idols merely as symbols of God's worship, whereas the ignorant associated the idols with the Deity and worshipped them both.[4] Hence, the discourse of kings like Anūshirwān and Ardashīr reproduced by Mas'ūdī is of value in illustrating the highest degree of wisdom and piety that natural religion could attain to without the aid of revelation. It would, therefore, be instructive at this point to ask how Mas'ūdī treated this body of wisdom and religious beliefs, and to determine why and in what respect his treatment differed from that of other Muslim historians. These beliefs comprise, in the main, certain beliefs about God as well as rational duties which are imposed by legislator-kings or sages. Together, they constitute for Mas'ūdī a religion (*dīn, diyāna*).[5] The beliefs about God are that He is one, just, wise and the creator of the world. The rational duties aim at the regulation of conduct.

[1] *Murūj*, secs. 1372, 1399.

[2] See, e.g., *Murūj*, secs. 212, 326, 535, 617, 703, 1371, 1384. In the case of the Meccan prince and the Persian king, Mas'ūdī seems to be chastising *taqlīd*, the bane of independent reasoning.

[3] This phrase occurs several times in connection with false prophets and charlatans; see, e.g., *Murūj*, secs. 212, 326, 1380.

[4] E.g., *Murūj*, sec. 325, where Mas'ūdī writes about the idol worship of China.

[5] *Murūj*, sec. 321.

Sages and legislator-kings aimed to instil fear of God and thus prescribed punishments for sins, prayers to God, justice in treating men according to their deserts, asceticism and the curbing of bodily desires, honesty in speech and in fulfillment of promises and kindness to kinsmen and neighbors.[1]

Certain common religious and ethical ideas recur constantly in the speeches or discourse of these ancient kings and sages. The most recurrent of these ideas is the belief in justice which is viewed as the most universal of the ethical values which God has instituted among mankind. The Indian philosopher, the Persian priest and the Chinese king are all cognizant of the supremacy of justice, for it is the moral expression of the wisdom with which God constructed the world, the ethical counterpart of the divine wisdom. To recognize God's wisdom entails the recognition of justice as the supreme principle of morality and the mainstay of the social order.[2] In consequence, kingship (*mulk*) must be supported by religion (*dīn*), while religion is itself built upon justice, obedience and fear of God.[3] From these basic religious and ethical beliefs other virtues are deduced. Ardashīr the Sassanid promises clemency to his subjects, praises God for His bounties and enjoins his people to the ascetic life.[4] An Indian philosopher tells Alexander that wisdom brings man nearest to the Creator; that no human act resembles the acts of God more closely than man's charity to his fellow men.[5] Honesty, generosity, keeping faith, prudence and courage are virtues which must govern human relations as well as the relations between a king and his subjects.[6] It is then that prosperity (*'amāra*, *'umrān*) comes to a kingdom and its people.[7]

These, then, are the highest religious and ethical beliefs that nonrevealed religion can produce. They are the fruits of reason

[1] See, e.g., such passages as *Murūj*, secs. 158, 532, 626, 628.

[2] See *Murūj*, secs. 320, 597, 694.

[3] See *Murūj*, secs. 586, 597, 628, 694. See also the interesting discourse of Indian sages in *Murūj*, secs. 157–59.

[4] See *Murūj*, secs. 577, 587. See also *Murūj*, sec. 616.

[5] *Murūj*, sec. 694.

[6] *Murūj*, secs. 583, 626.

[7] *Murūj*, secs. 597, 631.

unaided by revelation.[1] Mas'ūdī regarded these beliefs not merely as interesting expressions of the human spirit, but as aids to the understanding of pre-Islamic as well as Islamic history. By following these principles, as will be seen below, ancient societies flourished. By neglecting them, they fell to ruin. This was the moral of the story of the pagan world.[2]

To summarize this discussion of Mas'ūdī's views on prophecy and nonrevealed religions, something must be said of Mas'ūdī's treatment of the problem as compared to the treatment accorded to this subject by other Muslim historians. Mas'ūdī's account differed from the accounts of his predecessors in at least three important respects. In the first place, Muslim historians before Mas'ūdī had not formulated a clear conception either of the content of pre-Islamic prophetic revelation or of the nature of nonrevealed religion. With respect to revelation, some historians followed the Koran and turned pre-Islamic prophets into what may be termed proto-Muslims. In other words, they put into the mouth of these prophets an Islamic vocabulary and made them perform Islamic rites like pilgrimage, almsgiving and fasting. With respect to nonrevealed religions, these historians were more vague. Some turned even virtuous kings and sages into proto-Muslims while others were either uninterested in pre-Islamic religions or blatantly hostile. In the second place, no predecessor or contemporary historian, with the possible exception of Maqdisī, had conceived of anything which resembled Mas'ūdī's formulation of the historical development of reason and revelation, a development which, as was seen above, had been presaged in 'Alī's account of the creation of the world. In other words, they failed to take sufficient note of the religious history of nations which had no access to revelation but which nevertheless developed natural religions based on reason. In the third place, the story of Hebrew prophets, to take one example, had already been histori-

[1] This rationalism has its counterpart among the prophets in the story of Abraham (*Murūj*, sec. 76) who, according to Mas'ūdī, arrived at his knowledge of God through inference (*istidlālan*). However, Abraham, unlike pagan sages, later received revelation from God. Note how Mas'ūdī affirms that right reason leads logically to the worship of God.

[2] Mas'ūdī makes the neglect of these virtues to be the cause of ruin of ancient kingdoms. See, e.g., *Murūj*, secs. 595 ff., 604 ff., 618, 646.

cized in the Old Testament, and Muslim historians frequently quoted from the Torah. Nevertheless, some historians either ignored the Torah or added a large quantity of extraneous material which often turned these prophets into proto-Muslims.

It is against this background[1] that Mas'ūdī's views on prophecy and nonrevealed religions must be assessed. When Mas'ūdī's own views, together with this background, are kept in mind, it becomes clear that Mas'ūdī treated the problems raised by prophecy and nonrevealed or natural religions within a conceptual framework more clearly defined than that of his predecessors. If the history of prophecy showed a gradual progress in revelation, there was no need to turn any pre-Islamic prophet into a proto-Muslim. Likewise, since reason alone could lead to knowledge of God as well as the formulation of rational duties, there was no need for him to turn any virtuous sage

[1] It must first be remembered that the Koran puts an Islamic vocabulary into the mouth of several prophets. Certain historians followed the Koran in this respect and added non-Koranic stories of prophets practicing Islamic rites. Ibn Qutayba, for example, records that Adam fasted in the month of Ramaḍān (*Ma'ārif*, p. 24; see also pp. 19, 20, 23). For a similar practice among other historians, see Ibn Hishām, *Tījān*, pp. 2–54, *passim*; Ṭabarī, *Annales*, 1; Ya'qūbī, *Historiae*, 1: 3. The whole question is, of course, a vexing one and hinges upon the exact definition of the revelation possessed by these prophets which the Koran calls Islām. In any case, these historians leave little doubt that the revelation possessed by these prophets was almost identical to the Islām of Muḥammad. But such was not the case with other historians, like Dīnawarī, Maqdisī and Mas'ūdī. Dīnawarī is far less inclined to turn these prophets into proto-Muslims. Maqdisī's views are nearer to Mas'ūdī's. Thus he keeps an open mind about the Islām of these prophets and there is little or no proto-Muslim speech or conduct among them. He even suggests that the religion of Abraham was rational and instinctive (*fiṭrī*), needing no revelation (*sama'*); see *Bad'*, 3: 50 (see also 3: 3, 9–10, 47).

Much of the proto-Islamic speech and conduct of these prophets is derived by these historians from the accounts of Wahb ibn Munabbih. Ibn Qutayba, for example, quotes the Old Testament extensively but also adds much material from Wahb. Mas'ūdī's account, on the other hand, relies almost exclusively on the Old and New Testaments and, consequently, avoids turning these prophets into proto-Muslims. So much for proto-Islam among prophets. In the case of ancient nations possessing no revelation, Ṭabarī, for example, puts an Islamic vocabulary into the mouth of kings (see, e.g., *Annales*, 1: 179, 228, 436 ff., and 2: 612–13). So, curiously enough, does Dīnawarī (see *Akhbār*, pp. 35, 37, 44, 61, 77–80). On the other hand, hostility to nonrevealed religions can be detected, e.g., in Ya'qūbī, *Historiae*, 1: 179, where he states that he does not propose to record the offensive (*mustabsha'a*) religious beliefs of the Persians, and in Maqdisī, *Bad'*, 3: 210, where the Greek kings are simply described as unbelievers (*kuffār*).

or king into a proto-Muslim. By consulting the written and other sources of the various religions and nations, Mas'ūdī was able to do historical justice to prophecy and paganism while fitting their history into his pattern of reason and revelation.

Nature and Society

Thus far, attention has been drawn to some of the most important divine factors influencing the course of human history. It has been argued here that Mas'ūdī's understanding of the role which reason and revelation play in human affairs, together with his interest in defining that role, permitted him to write about the pre-Islamic era without doing violence to its history as he was able to ascertain it from its sources. But Mas'ūdī was cognizant of other, geographical and climatic factors which played an equally important part in shaping man's history. Such things as man's natural environment, his habitat and the influence of climate are of great importance in shaping his intelligence and, in consequence, a given society's degree of civilization. Therefore, since Mas'ūdī believed that there was a correlation between man's reason and his natural environment, his account of man's perception of the divine as outlined above must be complemented by an examination of his views on those natural factors which help or hinder the progress of human reason. These factors will now be studied in detail. The object however, will not be to explore Mas'ūdī's geography and cosmography as such but rather to determine the nature of the relationship of these sciences to the course of human history.

The universe of Mas'ūdī is the Ptolemaic one or, perhaps more accurately, the Indian-Ptolemaic, for Mas'ūdī believed that Ptolemy derived his *Almagest* from Indian sources.[1] The earth rests in the midst of nine concentric spheres (*aflāk*), seven of which have one planet (*kawkab*) each.[2] The four elements which make up the first seven

[1] *Murūj*, sec. 153; a comprehensive discussion of Mas'ūdī's indebtedness to Ptolemy will be found in S. Maqbul Ahmad, "Al-Mas'ūdī's Contributions to Medieval Arab Geography," *Islamic Culture* 27 (1953): 61-77. See also S. M. Ziauddin Alavi, "Al-Mas'ūdī's Conception of the Relationship between Man and Environment," *Al-Mas'ūdī*, ed. Ahmad and Rahman, pp. 93–96; also S. M. Ali, "Some Geographic Ideas of al-Mas'ūdī," *ibid.*, pp. 84–92. See also J. H. Kramers, "Geography and Commerce," in *The Legacy of Islam*, pp. 87–88.

[2] *Tanbīh*, pp. 7 ff.; *Murūj*, secs. 197 ff., 1326–27.

spheres are arranged in ascending order as earth, water, air and fire, and each is present in the other in potency.[1] The mineral, plant and animal life which constitutes the sublunary region is connected with the elements of the higher regions of this order. This universe of elements and spheres exercises a marked influence on man, by shaping and influencing his environment.[2] The order of this universe is a sign of God's creative wisdom.

The earth itself witnesses a constant activity of ebb and flow, of lands becoming seas and seas receding to form lands.[3] But the movement is not eternal, for there runs through it all a conception of a physical universe running down, so to speak, of a steady decrease in the matter of the universe, of a nature which is less and less capable of turning potentiality into perfect actuality.

This is how Mas'ūdī states the problem:

> We have mentioned in our previous works and in certain parts of this work what the ancients asserted concerning the reason for long and short life spans and the great size of bodies at the beginning of the world and their gradual decrease in the course of the ages, and that when God first made His creation the nature which God gave as a mould for the bodies was at its highest degree of quantity, power and perfection.
>
> When nature is perfectly potent (*tāmmat al-quwwa*), the human life span is longer and bodies are stronger since the blow of sudden death occurs when the powers of nature dissolve. Thus, when that power was at its most perfect, life spans were longer and bodies stronger and more numerous. The world of creation when it first began, was perfect in age but it has decreased little by little because matter has decreased, so that bodies and life spans have decreased because of this decrease in matter (*mādda*). Hence the end of nature (*nihāyat al-ṭabī'a*) will result in the utmost decrease in bodies and life spans.[4]

1 *Tanbīh*, p. 9. But see Rosenthal, *Technique*, pp. 68–69 and Grunebaum, *Medieval Islam*, p. 331.

2 Mas'ūdī held that the effect of the sun and the moon on the sublunary region was greater than that of the other heavenly bodies (see, e.g., *Murūj*, sec. 1319; *Tanbīh*, pp. 72–73).

3 In *Tanbīh*, p. 3, Mas'ūdī says that he has treated this subject in earlier books. See also *Tanbīh*, p. 111; *Murūj*, sec. 213.

4 *Murūj*, secs. 1261–62. Ibn Khaldūn rejected this theory: see Mahdi, *Ibn Khaldūn*, p. 255.

This passage clearly illustrates Mas'ūdī's conception of a universe which began in perfection but which will ultimately lose all its matter. Elsewhere, he argues that since the universe constantly witnesses things coming into being and others ceasing to be, the universe itself must finally come to an end, to nothing.[1] Mas'ūdī, therefore, rejects the Indian notion of an eternal universe and of matter being ceaselessly transformed from the complex to the simple and back to the complex again.

The inhabited earth is divided into seven latitudinal regions, all of which lie north of the equator. It is also divided longitudinally into east and west. The regions lying to the extreme north are far from the sun and therefore cold and snow-bound. The regions lying to the extreme south, near the equator, are severely affected by the sun and the heat.[2] The temperature of the air and the change of seasons, the dryness and the humidity, the elevation of the land, the heat and the cold, the movement of the winds affect the temperament, the physical characteristics, the moral character and the reason of man.[3] The most temperate of regions is the fourth whose climate, by virtue of its temperance, produces the most perfect bodies and the most perfect minds. This region, called also the region of Babylon (*iqlīm bābil*), has Iraq as its center. Iraq, therefore, enjoys the most moderate of climates, the purest water and air, the most fertile land. In consequence, it is the historical home of the most virtuous, the wisest and the most temperate of men.[4] Even revelation, as we shall see below, could occur only in temperate zones. Geographical factors, therefore, are chiefly responsible for determining man's physical as well as mental and cultural attributes. The arts and sciences developed by the great nations of antiquity could not have arisen if these nations had inhabited intemperate regions of the earth. "The laws of each nation," Mas'ūdī writes, "were determined by their modes of worship, the quarters from which they derived their

1 *Murūj*, secs. 1430–32.

2 *Tanbīh*, pp. 22 ff.; *Murūj*, secs. 187 ff., 1332.

3 Mas'ūdī asserts (*Murūj*, sec. 369) that he discussed this topic in his *Kitāb al-Qaḍāyā wa al-Tajārib*.

4 *Murūj*, secs. 978, 983, 987; *Tanbīh*, pp. 34 ff.

livelihood, their natural characteristics which were innate in them and the other nations bordering them".[1]

It remains to sketch in brief the manner in which Mas'ūdī incorporated these theories of environment into his treatment of ancient nations.[2] Among the nations that he especially esteemed were the Indians, the Persians and the Chinese. In each case, Mas'ūdī takes care to emphasize that the temperance of their air, the lightness of their water and the mildness of their diet accompanied and made possible their high level of civilized life, their arts and sciences and their institutions.[3] The nomadic Arabs, too, are said by Mas'ūdī to have preferred the life of the desert rather than of the mountains or the cities, since the mountainous regions with their variations of terrain breed instability of character, while the air and water of the cities collects dirt and is conducive to disease. Their nobility, courage, and agility of mind were developed through their nomadic existence.

Further examination of this issue would go beyond the purposes of this study. But before turning to the broader question of human society, it may be useful to take stock of Mas'ūdī's thoughts on the problem of the divine and the natural factors which impinge upon human events. It will be noted, to begin with, that these two forces which mould human events are largely interdependent. Mas'ūdī regards the physical universe as the creation of God and its laws as a sign of God's wisdom. When one considers the great nations of the past as well as the line of prophecy, one cannot dissociate them from their natural habitat. The most temperate of climates is, perforce, the home of the most elevated achievements of reason and of revelation.

[1] *Tanbīh*, p. 84. This may well be an echo of the Koranic verse "and for every nation We decreed a mode of worship" (*wa li kulli ummatin ja'alnā mansakan*), Koran 22:33.

[2] It should be borne in mind that the effect of climate on history was recognized by the earliest historians and scientists of Greece. See, e.g., Arnold J. Toynbee, *Greek Historical Thought* (New York: Mentor Books, 1964), pp. 143–46. The influence of Hippocrates on Mas'ūdī's ideas is quite marked (see, e.g., *Murūj*, secs. 1360–64, 2860). For a full discussion of the opinions of Greek geographers on the influence of climate, see J. Oliver Thomson, *History of Ancient Geography* (Cambridge: Cambridge University Press, 1948), pp. 106 ff.

[3] See, e.g., *Murūj*, secs. 169–70, 382–83, 388, 980–81. For other nations, see *Murūj*, secs. 1110, 1337, 1361; *Tanbīh*, pp. 22 ff. Numerous other examples may be cited.

Religion and Kingship

In order to complete this examination of Mas'ūdī's views on the divine and the natural in human history, one must deal at greater length with certain basic concepts which have been alluded to above. In particular, attention will be drawn to Mas'ūdī's treatment of society rather than of the individual. Certain salient features of their growth and decline will be studied with a view to determining the causes of progress as well as of decline. One may profitably begin by examining a problem which seems to have occupied Mas'ūdī in no small measure: the question of the relationship between religion, whether natural or revealed, and kingship. There can be little doubt that it was a problem to which he devoted much thought in his other writings, now lost. In the lengthy introduction of the *Tanbīh*, he writes:

> We mentioned in these books . . . for what reason kingship cannot do without religion in the same way that religion cannot do without kingship and neither can be firmly established without the other and why this must necessarily be so and for what cause. We also stated how evils (*āfāt*) afflict kingship, states disappear and laws and religions are obliterated; the evils, also, which occur in kingship and religion internally as well as the external evils which oppose them; how religion and kingship may be protected and how each can be remedied with the help of the other if it is stricken internally or by external afflictions; what is the objective of the remedy and its nature; the indicators (*amārāt*) of prosperity (*iqbāl*) in states; the governance of countries, religions and armies in their various classes . . . [1]

The relationship between religion and the secular authority constitutes a theme of considerable importance in at least one major Muslim historian after Mas'ūdī.[2] The fact that Mas'ūdī did not treat this question directly in his extant works need not deter the student of his thought from examining and attempting to reconstruct what indirect information he does provide,[3] which comes largely in the course of his discussion of kingship, both ancient and modern.

[1] *Tanbīh*, pp. 3–4.

[2] See Mahdi, *Ibn Khaldūn*, chap. 5 and *passim*.

[3] E.g., Grunebaum, *Medieval Islam*, p. 339, n. 39, where he states, as regards the relationship of *dīn* to *mulk*, "Unfortunately, we do not know Mas'ūdī's solutions."

Mas'ūdī's account of the earliest kings of India and Persia is predicated upon the rational necessity of kingship. Reason, in other words, has led men to recognize its necessity because, in the first place, man by nature is envious, unjust and aggressive, and an evil man can only be deterred by fear of a more powerful force which could punish or restrain him. In the second place, as ancient men contemplated the modes of living organisms and especially the constitution of the human body and the soul, they came to the view that it was the heart which ordered and arranged the various powers and sensations. The body would function properly as long as the heart did so but once this chief principal was corrupted, the rest fell into decay. This body, this microcosm (*al-'ālam al-ṣaghīr*), was for them a symbol of the social order. Men therefore sought out a king who would be just to them and would institute social regulations (*aḥkām*) arrived at by the intellect.[1]

Having indicated the rational necessity of kingship, Mas'ūdī proceeds to describe its usefulness. He does so, in the main, by ascribing to ancient kings a primary role in introducing the various arts, sciences and skills to their nations. These kings formulated the laws which governed their societies, built great cities, dug canals, mined the earth for minerals, established the rules of warfare, taught their countrymen the various kinds of crafts, discovered the principles of science and acted, in short, as the teachers of their community.[2] For this reason they were endowed, according to Mas'ūdī, with a high nobility of character and with exceptional intelligence and foresight.[3]

Now the relationship between kingship and religion is revealed by Mas'ūdī in the short speeches or asides delivered by the kings or wise men of ancient nations. In its most general terms, this relationship is stated to be essential to the well-being of the social order. As reason

[1] *Murūj*, sec. 531, where Mas'ūdī describes the founding of Persian monarchy. See also *Murūj*, sec. 152. Nations with weak kings or without kings at all are themselves weak and ineffectual; see, e.g., *Murūj*, secs. 482, 557.

[2] See, e.g., *Murūj*, secs. 62, 70, 75, 152, 316, 517, 522, 527. In most cases, these kings were founders of dynasties.

[3] These qualities are described in detail, according to Mas'ūdī, in his lost *Kitāb al-Zulaf* (*Murūj*, sec. 630). But some of them may be surmised from his account or the great kings of antiquity as in *Murūj*, secs. 160–64, 320, 509, 531–32, 577 ff.

decrees the necessity of kingship, so kingship stands in need of religion. A typical instance of this is the account given of a king of China who told his subjects that he proposed to institute a religion (*diyāna*) which would hold them together and regulate their lives, for without law (*sharī'a*) and order, corruption would set in. He therefore ordained for them a religious-legal polity (*siyāsa shar'iyya*) and rational duties. He further instituted prayers to draw them to their Creator and decreed punishments (*ḥudūd*) for adultery, sacrifices for the temple and general rules to order and arrange their affairs.[1] Similarly, a Persian sage informs his king that kingship needs a law (*sharī'a*), that law needs a king, that a king needs men, that men need money, that money needs prosperity, and that prosperity needs justice. Justice is the balance (*mīzān*) which God instituted between Himself and His creation. Religion and kingship are twins and cannot do without each other. Religion is the basis of kingship and the king is its guardian. That which has no basis is certain to collapse and that which has no guardian is certain to be lost.[2]

For Mas'ūdī, the most important element of social well-being was a religion which embodied rational laws and regulations.[3] Nations that did not have the benefit of revelation were nevertheless able, in varying degrees, to forge their own rational laws by which they ordered their social life. The most important constituent of these rational laws and regulations is the principle of justice.[4] Justice implied a hierarchical society, a society arranged in ranks, where the rights of all members are protected, the strong as well as the weak, and where the piety, clemency and generosity of the king engenders material prosperity for the nation.[5] This, it appears, is what Mas'ūdī meant by the "internal" factors affecting the strength of kingdoms. Where justice

1 *Murūj*, secs. 320–21; see also *Murūj*, secs. 584–86.

2 *Murūj*, secs. 586, 597.

3 See, e.g., *Murūj*, sec. 329, where the kingdom of China is said to have flourished until the moment when order (*niẓām*), laws (*sharā'i'*) and regulations (*aḥkām*) fell into decay. See also n. 1, above.

4 *Murūj*, secs. 320, 532, 577, 597, 626, 631.

5 For the hierarchical ordering of ancient societies, see, e.g., *Murūj*, secs. 164, 176, 444, 578, 581–82. For justice defined as the piety, generosity and clemency of the ruler, see *Murūj*, secs. 577, 616, 628.

prevails, a kingdom flourishes. Where a king is impious and unjust, the kingdom falls into ruin.[1]

There are also other "external" factors which can affect the well-being of kingdoms. The most recurrent, historically speaking and as defined by the kings and sages of antiquity, is the rise of clever contenders for power with the subsequent breakup of the kingdom into smaller units each ruled by an aspirant to the throne.[2] This breakup of kingdoms usually begins when a king has been unable to maintain internal justice because of weakness or impiety. Rebellions break out and central authority is broken. But such rebellions seem to be preceded in most cases by the decay of religion and law or, more exactly, by the breakup in the alliance between kingship and religion. Thus, a religion which is tenuously upheld leads to the weakening of social bonds and governmental authority and the subsequent rise of splinter kingdoms, civil war and material decay. For Mas'ūdī, the maintenance of social cohesion (*jam' al-kalima, ḍamm al-shaml*) is one of the most important effects of a religion.[3]

To Mas'ūdī, this necessary interdependence of religion and royal power was a characteristic not merely of ancient nations but of modern states existing in his own day. In several passages of the *Murūj* and the *Tanbīh*, Mas'ūdī points sorrowfully to the example of Islam, diagnosing the ills of the Caliphate and the breakup of the Islamic empire as a consequence of the neglect of religion and the absence of justice. Iraq, his native land, the historic home of the world's greatest nations as he so frequently described it, lay in ruins. The injustice of the various dynasties had resulted in the desolation of a land once fertile and prosperous.[4]

Justice, then, was the most important single principle and determinant of social well-being. In many of the great nations of antiquity, it brought in its wake a large measure of material prosperity (*'umrān*). For Mas'ūdī, this latter was chiefly associated with successful

1 This is the verdict of *Murūj*, secs. 179–83, 329, 595, 632. Numerous other instances may also be cited.

2 See, e.g., *Murūj*, secs. 329 ff., 504; *Tanbīh*, pp. 87, 400.

3 See *Murūj*, secs. 321, 504, 571.

4 See the long passage in *Tanbīh*, pp. 40–41, where the injustice of the Turks and the Daylam is blamed for the desolation of Iraq. For the breakup of the Caliphate, see *Murūj*, sec. 504 and *Tanbīh*, p. 400.

cultivation of land and the building of cities.[1] Conversely, the decline of states was often indicated by desolate lands and ruined cities. It may therefore be surmised that when Mas'ūdī speaks of the "indicators of prosperity," he means a regime of justice, proper cultivation and flourishing cities.

But what of other nations, ancient or contemporary? A few nations possessed neither a king nor a religious law and therefore posed a special problem for the historian, even though Mas'ūdī does not provide enough detailed information on them. To these nations, Mas'ūdī applied the term "ignorant nations" or "ignorant cities" (*umam jāhiliyya, mudun jāhiliyya*). By this Mas'ūdī meant basically two things: nations and cities without a king or without a religion and religious laws or without both.[2] These nations are described as pagan (*kuffār*) and possess no knowledge of God. They were also leaderless and therefore had no central authority such as a king, religion or religious laws to regulate their affairs. Apart from the fact that such nations or cities tended to be weak and to fall prey to better-organized and more powerful neighbors, Mas'ūdī also points out that what customs or practices they lived by were irrational or strange. Some, for example, bury the wife alive with her dead husband, others insist that no bachelor can die unmarried and thus marry him off after his death.[3] Lacking in revelation and unaided by reason largely owing to their natural habitat, such nations illustrate vividly the chaos engendered in a society by want of a ruler or a religion.

The Sources of Mas'ūdī's Views

To conclude this chapter, an attempt will be made to trace the provenance of some of the ideas set forth by Mas'ūdī in the preceding pages. Broadly speaking, three main topics were dealt with: (1) divine

[1] See *Murūj*, secs. 152–53, 237, 312, 316, 522, 527, 584, 597, 626.

[2] For the basic definitions of the word "jāhiliyya," see *Murūj*, secs. 445, 455, 499, 905. In one place (*Murūj*, sec. 451) a judge of a city is said to pronounce judgement in accordance with the "code of ignorance" (*ḥukm al-jāhiliyya*), which Mas'ūdī defines as "rational questions" (*qaḍāyā 'aqliyya*). Here the word is distinguished from *shar'*, i.e., law in either its revealed or rightly rational manifestations as it existed either among the people of revelation or among the great pagan nations.

[3] *Murūj*, secs. 445, 449, 483.

factors influencing the course of human events, (2) man's natural environment and his relations thereto, and (3) certain principles that determine the progress of human societies.

The election of Muḥammad and his progeny by God and the "mixing" of this with human reason was shown to be derived largely from Shī'ite sources. The doctrine of the transmission of light presupposes a continuous process of revelation which, in one sense, goes beyond Muḥammad. Mas'ūdī's treatment of the Imāms will be dealt with in later chapters, but it may tentatively be suggested at this point that Mas'ūdī shared the Twelver-Imāmī view that the world could not exist for a moment without a "proof," i. e., an Imām. This increasing availability of divine truth as embodied in successive revelations to prophets and in divine guidance in the post-Muḥammadan era to the Imāms, was a characteristic feature of the history of revelations.

In his treatment of man's natural environment, Mas'ūdī's reliance on Greek authorities is pronounced. Extensive citations from the works of Aristotle, Hippocrates and others serve to underline this reliance. In many instances, Mas'ūdī was able to verify this information from his own observations of the geography and climate of the nations and regions of the world. In this manner, Mas'ūdī was able to integrate the history of ancient nations into its geographical and climatic setting and to use this latter in order to throw light on the former.

With respect to the principles which guide human societies, especially the principle of justice and the alliance between religion and kingship, the determination of sources is a more difficult undertaking. To begin with, the principle of justice which constitutes the mainstay of the social order in ancient nations implies, as was seen above,[1] a society arranged in ranks where the rights of all citizens are protected by a wise and pious king. This conception of justice has much in common with Platonic political theories as interpreted by Muslim philosophers, especially Fārābī. The *Fuṣūl* of Fārābī, in particular, presents interesting parallels to this conception. There, Fārābī holds that justice consists in the division of the good things shared by the people in a city where the good things are defined as security, wealth, honor,

[1] See p. 76, n. 5, above.

dignities and so forth. It further implies that each citizen should possess a portion of these good things according to his deserts. Justice, then, preserves and protects the division of the good things in society, while injustice consists in the deprivation of these good things or their improper division.[1]

The alliance between religion and kingship which Mas'ūdī contends was responsible for the rise of great nations of antiquity, finds a parallel also in the political writings of Fārābī. There, too, the first chief of the city combines virtues which Mas'ūdī ascribes historically to the great founders of dynasties.[2] The role of this first chief in moulding and instructing the community is reflected in Mas'ūdī's account of the role of great kings like Anūshirwān, Ardashīr and others. The student of Mas'ūdī cannot escape the conclusion that in these important features of his description of the principles governing the progress of human societies, Mas'ūdī attempted to illustrate by historical example certain tenets of Shī'ism on the one hand and of the political philosophy of Fārābī on the other. This will become even more evident in the fourth chapter.

1 See Fārābī, *Fuṣūl*, secs. 57, 58. The Mu'tazilite conception of justice is theological rather than political in nature. While Mas'ūdī's view of justice is in certain respects akin to that of the Mu'tazila, the role which Mas'ūdī assigns to justice in the preservation of human societies clearly owes more to the Platonic-Fārābian tradition of political philosophy.

2 See Fārābī, *Fuṣūl*, sec. 43; *idem*, *Milla*, p. 46 and *passim*.

4. THE ANCIENT NATIONS

The Ancient Nations and Islam

In the preceding chapter, some of Mas'ūdī's views on God's activity in history and on nature and human society were outlined and analyzed. With reference to human societies, it was shown that Mas'ūdī's researches revealed to him the existence of certain principles which govern the progress of nations as well as their decline, chief among which are the principle of justice and the alliance between kingship and religion. This chapter will be devoted chiefly to a detailed examination of ancient nations in an attempt to illustrate more fully the conclusions of the preceding chapter and also to pose and attempt to answer other questions which were not touched upon earlier. We will begin, therefore, by examining the problem of the ancient nations as a whole and then proceed to study each nation individually. Further, an attempt will be made to describe the predominant characteristics of each nation and their significance to world history in general and to Islam in particular. Finally, in seeking to define the significance of the characteristics of these nations to Islam, we will examine Mas'ūdī's views on the transmission of knowledge in general, and on progress, both moral and intellectual, in particular. For in order to understand the relationship of pre-Islamic history to Islam, we must attempt to describe Mas'ūdī's views on knowledge and its transmission from one nation to another. Mas'ūdī believed, as we shall see below, that many ancient nations excelled in certain arts and sciences which were of significance to the Muslim community. The contributions of these nations to the Islamic community were at times explicitly described by Mas'ūdī and at other times were hinted at or implied. For this reason, we must note here that our conclusions on some points are, perforce, tentative since we no longer possess Mas'ūdī's theoretical works in which these problems were more explicitly treated.

Beginning in the ninth century A.D., Islamic historiography had, as one of its main concerns, the problem of the relationship of the pre-Islamic era to the Islamic and vice versa. The Muslim historian was faced with the spectacle of many great nations, ancient as well as contemporaneous, who rose to heights of glory without their having an Islamic heritage. The significance of their history for Islam is an old problem in Islamic historical thinking, but it acquired a sense of urgency during the ninth century and beyond.[1] It is a major problem in the histories of Masʿūdī.

It is generally agreed that Wahb ibn Munabbih was the first Muslim historian to introduce in a systematic and extensive manner the stories of other nations as a prelude to Islamic history proper.[2] But there is little indication in Wahb's fragments as they survive in later histories that he dealt with the significance of their history for Islam. It seems, rather, that it was the literati of the eighth and ninth centuries, men like Ibn al-Muqaffaʿ and Jāḥiẓ, who first brought the question of the contributions of ancient nations into sharp focus. Ibn al-Muqaffaʿ and, more particularly, Jāḥiẓ attempt repeatedly to define the relationship between the Arab Islamic community on the one hand and the wisdom of other nations on the other. Jāḥiẓ is considered by some to have been the greatest precursor of the doctrine of Eternal Wisdom which held that "the wisdom of all nations found its way into Arabic literature in a slow process of transmission from nation to nation and from generation to generation".[3] This theme will be developed in the course of this chapter.

The way towards incorporating this theme into historiography seems, then, to have been prepared by *adab* works. Of Masʿūdī's predecessors in the ninth and tenth centuries, the three historians who strove to incorporate the most sizeable accounts of pre-Islamic history into their works were Dīnawarī, Ṭabarī and Yaʿqūbī. But Dīnawarī, despite his extensive knowledge of Persian and Byzantine history, had

1 There is a brief but suggestive treatment of this question in Rosenthal, *Technique*, pp. 69–72.

2 See Dūrī, *Baḥth*, p. 26.

3 Rosenthal, *Technique*, p. 71. Rosenthal discusses at some length the question of the interdependence of civilizations as commented upon by the literati of the eighth and ninth centuries. To the references cited by Rosenthal, one may add Jāḥiẓ, *Bayān*, 1: 152–53, 360; 3: 24 ff.; *Majmūʿ*, pp. 100–101; *Rasāʾil*, ed. Hārūn, 1: 67–73; Tawḥīdī, *Imtāʿ*, 1:70–96.

little to say about Chinese or Indian history and even less about other nations. Ṭabarī was greatly interested in Persian history, which he interwove with biblical and, later, pre-Islamic Arab history. But he deliberately excluded the history of other nations on the grounds that their kingship was not continuous and so their history could not be accurately ascertained.[1] Ya'qūbī made what was perhaps the most ambitious attempt by including the history of all the great nations of antiquity known to him. But Ya'qūbī did not describe the significance of their history for Islam in precise terms, although the detailed description of these contributions, particularly of India and Greece, to geography, astronomy, medicine, philosophy, political theory, ethics and so forth is in itself an acknowledgement of the importance of this body of pre-Islamic wisdom. According to Ya'qūbī, the importance of these contributions lay in the fact that wisdom originated with these nations and all who aspired to the mastery of one of these sciences had perforce to consult their books and build upon the foundations that they had established.[2] For Ṭabarī, on the other hand, the chief value of the study of ancient nations was didactic. By studying their history, one gained a deeper insight into the workings of God, how He exalted the virtuous and humbled the evil.[3]

An examination of Mas'ūdī's treatment of ancient nations may well start, therefore, by an attempt to describe his views on the significance of the history of these nations to Islam. What did these nations contribute to world history in general and to Islam in particular

1 Ṭabarī, *Annales*, 1:353; see also 1:148, where Ṭabarī justifies his choice of Persian history in ascertaining and checking ancient chronology by the fact that their kingdom was the longest-lasting of all. Maqdisī, *Bad'*, 3:208, states that scholars in his days did not bother to record Indian, Byzantine and Chinese history because accurate histories were not available.

2 See, e.g., *Historiae*, 1:105, where Ya'qūbī asserts that Indian wisdom was the progenitor of all later wisdom, and 1:107, where he gives a resumé of the medical works of Hippocrates which "students of medicine are obliged to study."

3 The struggle between the righteous and the unrighteous is, for Ṭabarī, the "moral" of the story of the pre-Islamic era; see *Annales*, 1: 2–7. In this, he was undoubtedly following the koranic treatment of the same theme, where mankind is urged to ponder upon the virtuous or the evil of past generations. In Ṭabarī, this theme is most often illustrated by the stories of the conflicts between prophets and kings, e.g., Abraham vs. Nimrod, Joseph vs. Pharaoh, etc. But one must add that Ṭabarī's extensive treatment of Persian history stemmed also from his belief that the community (*umma*) of Muḥammad was heir to the Persian empire (*Annales*, 1: 353).

and what value could be derived from studying their history? The second question has been answered partly in chapter 2, where it was shown that, for Mas'ūdī, the value of history in general lay in its preservation of past knowledge, and partly in chapter 3, where it was shown that certain abiding principles, like the workings of justice, could be gleaned from a scrutiny of the past. The first question, however, entails a more specific examination of the predominant characteristics and contributions of these nations as shown in Mas'ūdī's account of their history. But in order to assess that contribution properly, one must begin by describing the genealogy of ancient nations with specific reference to the problems that Mas'ūdī encountered in attempting to reconcile that genealogy with biblical and koranic accounts.

Genealogy of Ancient Nations

Mas'ūdī begins his *Murūj* with a detailed account of the descent of mankind from Adam, placing close reliance on the biblical account. Thus he copies faithfully the ages of the various patriarchs and prophets, although he occasionally follows Ibn Qutayba in minor details of parentage and descent.[1] But the more universal interest in the genealogy of nations is evident from the scattered remarks that Mas'ūdī appends to this biblical material. References are made to the fact that a given nation, the Indians or the Slavs for instance, is descended from a certain biblical figure.[2] Mas'ūdī is attempting to link non-biblical nations to the main biblical genealogy. This, however raises a perplexing problem of interpretation. That problem, stated simply, is the following. According to both the biblical and the koranic accounts, the whole of mankind perished in the Flood and the only survivors were Noah and his three sons and their wives,who peopled

[1] Charles Pellat's footnotes to the first volume of his edition of the *Murūj* detail the biblical and other sources of Mas'ūdī's account of the descent of the children of Adam. The important Shī'ite element which Mas'ūdī introduced into the account of the creation and the later biblical history has been described in chap. 3. There is a cursory treatment of the biblical material in Islamic historiography in Franz Rosenthal, "The Influence of the Biblical Tradition on Muslim Historiography," *Historians of the Middle East*, pp. 40–45. But Rosenthal does not mention the important additions which Muslim historians made to the biblical tradition concerning the descent of nations.

[2] E.g., *Murūj*, secs. 61, 63.

the earth again after the Flood.[1] Therefore, it is evident that to recognize the claim of any nation to descent from a figure in the pre-Noah era would be to go against the biblical-koranic account.[2] However, Mas'ūdī was not the first Muslim historian to realize that certain nations made precisely that claim to descent from a prediluvian figure. Some Persians, for example, claimed that their ancestor, Jayūmarth (or Kayūmarth), was Adam, that their descent from him was uninterrupted and that the Flood either did not take place or did not reach Persia.[3] Such a problem, it is true, apparently did not perplex many historians,[4] but it was an important one for a historian like Mas'ūdī, who had made a detailed study of the history of a great number of ancient nations and had found conflicting traditions of descent.

The vague manner in which Mas'ūdī introduces his various references to the Flood is itself somewhat suspicious. It is true that he nowhere denies explicitly the occurrence of the Flood, but he does cast doubt on its universality in three ways. In the first place, he reports without comment that certain nations trace their ancestry from prediluvian personages, as was described above.[5] In the second place, he expresses unusual scepticism with regard to the koranic verses about the descent of all mankind from the progeny of Noah.[6] Finally, and most revealingly, he casts doubt on the universality of the Flood in many passages of the *Murūj* and the *Tanbīh*. There is, for example, the speech of the king of China who tells a Muslim traveller that the

[1] See Genesis 7: 23 and Koran 37: 76. Mas'ūdī adds to Noah's family forty men and forty women which he most likely copied from Ibn Qutayba, *Ma'ārif*, p. 23, where Ibn Qutayba is quoting Wahb.

[2] This is forcibly stated, for example, in Ṭabarī, *Annales*, 1: 199–200. See also Ṭabarī, *Tafsīr*, 23: 38–39.

[3] A detailed discussion of this claim may be found in Ṭabarī, *Annales*, 1:147 ff., where Ṭabarī concludes that Jayūmarth was a descendant of Noah. (See also *Annales*, 1: 199.)

[4] Thus, e.g., Ibn Qutayba, Ya'qūbī and Maqdisī chose to ignore Persian claims to a prediluvian descent. It may be noted in passing that Christian historians of the period described Kayūmarth as a descendant of Sām, son of Noah. See, e.g., Agapius (Maḥbūb) ibn Qusṭanṭīn al-Manbijī, *'Unwān*, p. 104.

[5] See p. 84, n. 2, above.

[6] To the koranic verse "and We made his progeny those who survived," Mas'ūdī appends the sceptical comment, "And God knows best about its interpretation." (*Murūj*, sec. 66).

Chinese and the Indians have no knowledge of a universal flood.[1] There is the report that the Persians, too, have no record of a universal flood, to which Mas'ūdī appends a noncommittal remark, "and God knows best about this".[2] There is the report about the ancient Egyptians where Mas'ūdī, by dint of personal observation of human remains, is ready to believe that their "flood" was in fact a widespread plague.[3] There is, finally, a report about the origins of the seas included in the midst of the Flood story to the effect that the salty water of the seas is a remnant of the Flood which had overtaken the "disobedient" portions of the earth.[4] This theory however is ignored when Mas'ūdī comes to treat of the origin of the seas in a more scientific manner.[5]

We know from at least one source that such doubts were occasionally expressed in the fourth/tenth century and that some denied even the occurrence of the Flood.[6] In the case of Mas'ūdī, two tentative reasons for his doubt may be suggested. The first was his belief that the various nations were best conversant with their own history.[7] Therefore, if the histories of certain nations, the Persians or the Indians for example, contained no record of "momentous events"[8] like the Flood, their histories must be taken seriously. The second reason for Mas'ūdī's scepticism is perhaps more suggestive. Mas'ūdī follows Aristotle's *Meteorology* closely and quotes it copiously in his treatment of physical phenomena like the seas, winds, rivers, and their origin and flux. Aristotle affirms that the great changes of lands into seas and vice versa or of fertile lands into infertile do not occur at all times and do not affect all regions of the earth at once. Thus, he states that the Flood

1 *Murūj*, sec. 345; cf. *Tanbīh*, p. 201 and *Murūj*, sec. 1103. The passage in *Murūj*, sec. 314, e.g., strongly implies the existence of a prediluvian Indian nation.

2 *Murūj*, sec. 530; cf. *Tanbīh*, p. 197.

3 *Murūj*, sec. 813.

4 *Murūj*, sec. 65.

5 *Murūj*, sec. 299 ff. Mas'ūdī himself subscribes to the view that there is a constant flux of land becoming sea and vice versa (cf. *Tanbīh*, pp. 3, 70). In this, he is following Aristotle's view. See Casimir Petraitis, ed., *The Arabic Version of Aristotle's Meteorology* (Beirut: Dar el-Machreq, 1967), pp. 46 ff. (hereafter referred to as Aristotle, *Arabic Meteorology*). In general, Mas'ūdī's account of the seas in *Murūj*, sec. 299 ff. relies heavily on Aristotle, *Arabic Meteorology*, pp. 50–60.

6 Maqdisī, *Bad'*, 3: 17–19.

7 For a detailed treatment of this view, see chap. 1. See also *Tanbīh*, pp. 196 ff.

8 This is the phrase used by the Chinese king to his Muslim visitor in *Murūj*, sec. 345.

of Deucalion affected Greece alone, and even certain parts of Greece, not the whole Greek mainland.[1] It is suggested that this view may well have influenced the scepticism that Mas'ūdī displays regarding the universality of the biblical-koranic Flood.

But Mas'ūdī, while seeming to doubt the universality of the Flood, does not appear to deny its occurrence. There are lengthy accounts of the genealogy of nations and their descent from the three sons of Noah, which appear to belie the scepticism outlined above. Mas'ūdī's genealogies differ in certain important details from the genealogies to be found in Muslim and Christian historians of the period.[2] There were, according to Mas'ūdī, two divisions of the earth: the first instituted by Noah and the second after the destruction of the Tower of Babylon, bringing sudden diversity of languages and the subsequent dispersal of the sons of Sām, Ḥām and Yāfith. The descendants of Noah had, until the destruction of the Tower of Babylon, lived in one geographical area and had been united by one language and one kingdom.[3] Thereafter, the various descendants of each son

[1] Aristotle, *Arabic Meteorology*, pp. 48–49. See also Plato's *Timaeus*, in Plato, *The Dialogues of Plato*, trans. by Benjamin Jowett, 3rd ed. (Oxford: Clarendon Press, 1892), 3: 442–44.

[2] Mas'ūdī's account may be compared with Ya'qūbī, *Historiae*, 1:13, 17. But where Mas'ūdī implies that most of mankind lived in the region of Babylon after the first division of the earth, Ya'qūbī contrives to bring the dispersed nations back to Babylon so that they can be dispersed once more when the Tower is destroyed. In this respect, Mas'ūdī keeps more closely to the biblical account, where Sām and Yāfith (Japhet) dwell together after the first division of the earth (Genesis 9:27) and where the sudden diversity of languages and the final dispersal come to the whole of mankind, who were then one people dwelling in one place (Genesis 2). See also Eutychius, *Annales*, 1:16–18, and Manbijī, *'Unwān*, pp. 18, 21–22, who follow the biblical version. Maqdisī, *Bad'*, 3:26 ff., mentions only the first division of the earth but does not, surprisingly enough, record the dispersal after the destruction of the Tower. Ibn Qutayba, *Ma'ārif*, pp. 24 ff., relying largely on Wahb, mentions only the first division of the earth which led immediately to dispersal. The diversity of languages occurred in Babylon and presumably spread miraculously among the dispersed nations. Ṭabarī, *Annales*, 1: 211 ff., records many accounts, but generally speaking, offers the same version as Ibn Qutayba.

[3] The first division of the earth did not, it seems, result in any vast dispersal, for Mas'ūdī records that, until the destruction of the Tower of Babylon, the sons of Sām and Yāfith dwelt together in Babylon (*Murūj*, sec. 67), and only the sons of Ḥām seem to have left that region. In *Murūj*, sec. 70, he writes that the second and final dispersal took place from Babylon. The common language prior to the destruction of the Tower was Syriac (*Siryānī*) as in *Murūj*, sec. 530 and *Tanbīh*,

of Noah began to leave their original abode and to disperse all over the earth.[1] The problem, however, is one of reconciling this with the scepticism expressed about the universality of the Flood. But this conflict of genealogies is not satisfactorily resolved by Mas'ūdī, who records the biblical theory of the descent of *all* mankind from the sons of Noah, while expressing doubts about the universality of the Flood. One reason that may be suggested for the unresolved genealogical contradictions and ambiguities in Mas'ūdī and other historians is the ambiguity of the biblical account itself, on which are based, directly or indirectly, the versions offered by the Muslim historians.[2] Mas'ūdī is aware that discrepancies exist between the "revealed" and the "nonrevealed" accounts of the beginnings of the world.[3] He therefore records the "revealed" accounts as he was able to ascertain them, and also the scepticism which accompanied his researches into the earliest history of the earth and its peoples.

The Seven Ancient Nations

One common feature of the earliest history of nations, namely the lapse into idolatry, has already been discussed in chapter 3. An attempt must now be made to describe other common features of that history and to detail the characteristics of each nation before reverting to the problem, raised earlier in this chapter, of the significance of their history to Islam.

The first common feature that one detects in the history of these earliest nations is the transition from nomadic to sedentary life, with the subsequent growth of the arts and crafts and of science and philo-

p. 79, and Nimrod is spoken of as the ruler of all mankind at that time (*Murūj*, secs. 522–23).

1 *Murūj*, sec. 1141 ff.

2 For a complete discussion of the historical and genealogical problems associated with individuals or nations as they are presented in Genesis 6 and 7, see the authoritative commentary of Ephraim A. Speiser in the *Anchor Bible* (New York: Doubleday, 1964), 1: 51–56, 58–59, 61–63, 65–73, 75–76. The different versions of these events to be found in Muslim historians (see n. 2, p. 87, above) reflect different interpretations of the ambiguous biblical text.

3 *Tanbīh*, p. 77. The most complete genealogical information on the nations which dispersed after the destruction of the Tower may be found in *Murūj*, sec. 1141 ff. But short genealogical data are provided in the introduction to the history of each nation as set forth in the *Murūj*.

sophy among them.[1] Mas'ūdī appears to regard this transition with favor, despite the praise which he bestows on the life of the nomadic Arabs. Cities were built, the land was mined for precious minerals, the principles of astronomy were discovered and ancient sages formulated the fundamental questions of theology and philosophy. Furthermore, men were able to lay down the rules of statecraft and of warfare.[2] These were the achievements of nations which led a sedentary life, while other nations, which continued a greater or lesser degree of nomadic existence, had little to offer of arts or sciences. Here, the natural environment, described in the preceding chapter, was an important contributing factor to the development of these arts and sciences. Another common feature of these nations was the fact that they held a certain body of wisdom in common. In each of the seven great nations of antiquity, to be discussed in detail below, seven sages met at various times to discuss the transient character of states and religions, the nature of the world, the creation of mankind and the end to which this life is directed.[3]

Before examining the ancient nations and their significance to world history, we must attempt to define briefly how Mas'ūdī, generally speaking, defined a nation. The concept of a nation for him is largely linguistic. Language is the most important constituent of a nation.[4] Land is a minor factor since certain nations, the Turks for instance, split and migrated but still retained their nationhood. A unitary kingdom is also of minor importance since some nations, e.g. the Persians, were living in politically fragmented kingdoms but were still described as Persian. Physical and other characteristics played an important role in the earliest times but we hear less of this in later periods. In other words,while certain factors like land and a unitary kingdom were important in the early period of world history,they ceased to have much importance thereafter, while language remained

[1] *Murūj*, secs. 1102, 1150, 1166.

[2] *Murūj*, secs. 152, 158, 320–21, 522, 527 and *passim*.

[3] *Tanbīh*, pp. 84–85. The legend of the Seven Sages is old and of Mesopotamian origin. For a detailed discussion of this legend, see O. Barkowski, "Sieben Weise," *Pauly-Wissowa Real-Encyclopädie*, tier 2, vol. 4, pp. 2242–46 and, more recently, Erica Reiner, "The Etiological Myth of the 'Seven Sages'", *Orientalia* 30 (1961): 1–11.

[4] See, e.g., the discussion of the "nationality" of such figures as Abraham, Ishmael and Qaḥṭān in *Tanbīh*, pp. 80-81.

the most important single constituent of nationhood. The most important and powerful of these earliest nations were,according to Mas'ūdī, seven in number. They arose in the period after the dispersal which followed the destruction of the Tower of Babylon and were distinguished by three things: their physical characteristics, their natural customs and their languages.[1] In the order in which Mas'ūdī deals with them in the *Tanbīh*,[2] they are: (1) the Persians, (2) the Chaldeans, (3) the Greeks, (4) the Egyptians, (5) the Turks, (6) the Indians, and (7) the Chinese. Each of these nations comprised subdivisions, but each was, at one time, united in one kingdom and spoke one language. Each nation excelled in a particular art or science. Each must now be examined in detail.

The Persians

Of all ancient histories, Persian history was perhaps the most familiar to Muslim historians of the ninth and tenth centuries. These historians were struck by the long and rich Persian heritage and some even regarded Muslim history as an extension of Persian history and the Muslim empire as a successor to the Persian.[3] Mas'ūdī himself travelled extensively in Persia and was able to use Persian sources, both written and oral.[4] He transcribed faithfully what he had learned of Persian history, accepting the Persian version of their own history rather than any other, in conformity with his normal practice.[5]

Mas'ūdī dealt at great length with Persian history. He gave full accounts of the genealogy of the race,[6] the successive kings and

[1] *Tanbīh*, p. 77.

[2] *Ibid.* The classification of the most important ancient nations into seven is un known to Muslim historiography before Mas'ūdī. The most frequent classification was four: the Byzantines, the Arabs, the Persians and the Indians (see, e.g., Jāḥiẓ, *Bayān*, 1: 384; Tawḥīdī, *Imtā'*, 1: 70). It appears that this classification is Greek in origin; see Dionysius of Halicarnassus, *The Roman Antiquities*, trans. by Earnest Cary (Cambridge: Loeb Classical Library for Harvard University Press, 1937), I, Book I, 2–3. This classification was later adopted by Ṣā'id (d. 462/1069) in his *Ṭabaqāt al-Umam*, pp. 5–7: see the translation of this work by Régis Blachère, *K. Ṭabaqāt al-Umam* (Paris: Larose, 1935), p. 31 and n. 2.

[3] See p. 83, n. 1 and n. 3, above.

[4] See *Tanbīh*, pp. 106, 110; *Murūj*, sec. 571.

[5] *Tanbīh*, p. 105.

[6] E.g., *Murūj*, secs. 563–67.

dynasties,[1] the various religions[2] and representative samples of Persian wisdom as expressed by kings and sages.[3] But Mas'ūdī also believed that each of the seven ancient nations embodied a certain principle, excelling in certain arts and sciences which distinguished them from other nations.[4]

The ancient Persian dynasties had occupied, according to Mas'ūdī, the most temperate of the seven geographical zones into which the earth is divided. They had therefore been recognized by the other ancient nations as preeminent in glory and power. As successors to the kings of Babylon, the first Persian dynasty institutionalized the monarchic principle and perfected the art of government and of statecraft. It is primarily in this sphere that the Persians excelled. This was both a theoretical and a practical excellence, for their preeminence in government stemmed from the greatness of their empire as well as from the political wisdom which sustained that greatness. The Persian government was organized in seven classes of ministers, priests, governors and so forth. The king's court was also organized in castes, each of which possessed distinct powers and privileges.[5] It was an empire of cities,with power centralized in the hands of the king, so that the character of the particular monarch was of great importance in influencing the course of events for good or ill. At the height of its power, the Persian empire enjoyed great material prosperity, order in its administration and the allegiance of many kings of other nations.

What is even more impressive than the formal edifice of the empire in Mas'ūdī's account is the political wisdom which was evolved by Persian statecraft. The principle of justice and the alliance between kingship and religion, discussed in chapter 3, were principles which

[1] *Murūj*, sec. 530 ff.; *Tanbīh*, pp. 85 ff. On his Sassanian genealogy only, see G. Morrison, "The Sassanian Genealogy in Mas'ūdī," *Al-Mas'ūdī*, ed. Ahmad and Rahman, pp. 42–43.

[2] E.g., *Murūj*, secs. 547–48, 1434–37; *Tanbīh*, pp. 90–91.

[3] *Murūj*, secs. 577, 580, 584–86, 597, 628; *Tanbīh*, p. 87.

[4] For a typical statement of this view, see *Murūj*, secs. 395–97 (see also sec. 344); *Tanbīh*, p. 77. The idea that each ancient nation had made its own particular contribution to culture did not originate with Mas'ūdī; see, e.g., Jāḥiẓ, *Rasā'il*, ed. Hārūn, 1: 67 ff.

[5] *Murūj*, secs. 583, 585; *Tanbīh*, pp. 103–4.

were first enunciated by Persian kings. But other principles of government were also developed which contributed to the well-being of the kingdom. Prosperity, for example, was in large measure due to the building of cities, equitable taxation and the constant care for agriculture and maintenance of canals, roads, frontier posts and so forth.[1] Piety and morality were held to be ideal qualities of the ruler and indispensable in his relations with his subjects.[2] In fact, the greatest of ancient Persian kings were depicted by Mas'ūdī as epitomes of the Platonic philosopher-king. Ardashīr, for example, was a disciple of Plato according to Mas'ūdī, who describes his words and deeds in terms reminiscent of Plato's ideal ruler.[3] Mas'ūdī further detected a common body of wisdom among both the ancient Persians and the Greek philosophers as regards the ideal qualities of kingship and the principles which should guide the conduct of kings.[4]

In sum, Mas'ūdī held that Persian excellence lay in the field of statecraft. This assessment did not originate with Mas'ūdī, since earlier historians and literati had often made the same assessment.[5] But Mas'ūdī's handling of this theme was undertaken within a more explicit frame of reference, namely, one which viewed the sum total of world history as composed of the individual contributions of seven great ancient nations. Furthermore, the view that the greatest of Persian monarchs were guided by Platonic political ideals strongly suggests the existence of a common body of wisdom of which many of these ancient nations partook. This particular theme will become more evident as we proceed.

[1] E.g., *Tanbīh*, p. 39; *Murūj*, sec. 627.

[2] Certain virtuous kings were said to have performed the pilgrimage to Mecca (*Murūj*, secs. 573–74). See also *Murūj*, sec. 628.

[3] See *Murūj*, sec. 585 and *Tanbīh*, p. 100, for Ardashīr's contacts with a Platonist ascetic. Ardashīr's preoccupation with justice on the one hand and the classes into which he divided his subjects on the other was no doubt meant to suggest a Platonic influence on Ardashīr. See also *Tanbīh*, p. 87, where an advice of Ardashīr is compared to an opinion of Aristotle.

[4] See, e.g., *Murūj*, sec. 630; *Tanbīh*, p. 87. Ibn Khaldūn held a similar opinion of the Persian monarchy (see Mahdi, *Ibn Khaldūn*, p. 249). On the popular wisdom literature of the Orient and its relationship to the Greek, see Mahdi, *Ibn Khaldūn*, p. 158, n. 4. Mas'ūdī unfortunately refers his readers to some of his lost works for a fuller treatment of this theme.

[5] See, e.g., Dīnawarī, *Akhbār*, p. 47, on Ardashīr as a model whom other kings emulated; Jāḥiẓ, *Rasā'il*, ed. Hārūn, 1: 67, on the Persians as excelling in kingship; Ṭabarī, *Annales*, 1: 148, for a similar verdict on Persian monarchy.

The Chaldeans

In Mas'ūdī's account, the Chaldeans were a group of nations who preceded the Persians in time and whose home was Iraq, Syria, Diyār Muḍar, Diyār Rabī'a and the Arabian peninsula. The word "Chaldeans" as used by Mas'ūdī was a collective noun referring to several nations, all of whom were, at one time, united in one kingdom and spoke one language, Syriac.[1] These nations included the Babylonians, the Ninevites, the Assyrians, the Arameans, the Ardawān, the Jarāmiqa, the Nabateans of Iraq and the people of the Sawād.[2] Mas'ūdī also refers at times to this national group as the Syrians (*al-Siryān*) or the Nabateans (*al-Nabaṭ*), to the end that Chaldeans, Syrians and Nabateans are termed synonyms.[3]

But Mas'ūdī encountered serious problems in the reconstruction of their history. The antiquity of their history, the fact that the Koran states that the nations which followed Noah are known only to God, and their gradual conquest and absorption by the Persians, were recognized by Mas'ūdī as factors which hampered the proper ascertainment of their history.[4] The king list which he sets down in the *Murūj* was in all likelihood based upon the list in Ya'qūbī,[5] although Mas'ūdī adds certain details not found in Ya'qūbī and refers his reader to a more extensive treatment of their history in his other, now lost works.

Despite these difficulties of historical reconstruction, Mas'ūdī describes their particular excellence in some detail. Thus, they were the first nation to establish a monarchy after the Flood. They were also the earliest builders of cities and roads and the earliest nation to practice proper husbandry. In Iraq, they were the first to dig

[1] *Tanbīh*, p. 79.

[2] *Tanbīh*, p. 78. The ancient Arabs and the Hebrews also belong to this national group. Krachkovskii, *Tārīkh al-adab al-Jughrāfī*, pp. 182–83, credits Mas'ūdī with developing the conception of a Semitic race.

[3] *Tanbīh*, p. 184.

[4] *Tanbīh*, pp. 94, 105–6. See also *Tanbīh*, pp. 37–38, where Mas'ūdī states that most Nabateans after Islam traced their ancestry to the Persians.

[5] For the lists in *Murūj*, secs. 509, 517, 520, 523 ff., see Ya'qūbī, *Historiae*, 1: 90–92. For the verdict on the Chaldean nation in *Murūj*, sec. 527, see Ya'qūbī, *Historiae*, 1: 92. See also the note to sec. 509 in Pellat's revised translation, *Les Prairies d'or* (Paris: Société Asiatique, 1962), 1.

canals. They also began the mining of iron, copper and lead, and were the first to establish the rules of warfare and of battle formations. They commenced the investigation of the properties of light and color from which they evolved fire worship and astrology. In sum, these were the first builders, the first notable farmers, and the first astrologers.[1]

The Greeks

The heritage of Greece in science and philosophy is more in evidence in the works of Mas'ūdī than that of any other ancient nation. Mas'ūdī had a very extensive knowledge of Greek works in the various branches of science and quotes these works frequently in his extant writings. In consequence, the Greek contribution to world history in general and to Islam in particular was more explicitly spelled out than were the contributions of other nations. This will become apparent shortly.

Comprised within the national group called the Greeks (*al-Yūnān*) by Mas'ūdī, there were, aside from the ancient classical Greeks, the Romans, the Byzantines, the Slavs, and the Franks. Like the other seven nations of antiquity, the Greek nation was at one time a single kingdom and spoke a single language. Mas'ūdī details at some length the various ancestors of this composite nation.[2] Perhaps the most important of these legendary ancestors is Yūnān, ancestor of the classical Greeks. Regarding his life, two facts are of particular significance. The first is his supposed testament to his son,[3] in which he urges him

[1] *Murūj*, secs. 75, 527, 528. For the confused state of information on Babylon in Muslim historians, see G. Awad, "Bābil", *Encyclopaedia*, ed. Gibb et al., 1: 846. On the tradition of Nabateans as the first farmers, see M. Plessner, "Der Inhalt der Nabatäischen Landwirtschaft," *Zeitschrift für Semitistik* 6 (1928): 27–56, which describes the contents of *K. al-Filāḥa al-Nabaṭiyya* attributed to Ibn Waḥshiyya. On this matter, see Toufic Fahd, "Ibn Waḥshiyya," *Encyclopaedia*, ed. Gibb et al., 3: 963–65.

[2] For the properly Greek ancestry, see *Murūj*, secs. 664–65, 670; *Tanbīh*, p. 115; for the Roman, see *Murūj*, secs. 715–16; for the Slavs and Franks, see *Murūj*, sec. 905 ff. An assessment of Mas'ūdī's information on the Slavs is given in E. M. Murzaev, "The Significance of al-Mas'ūdī for the works of Russian and Soviet geographers," *Al-Mas'ūdī*, ed. Ahmad and Rahman, pp. 14–19, and Tadeusz Lewicki, "Al-Mas'ūdī on the Slavs," *ibid.*, pp. 11–13.

[3] *Murūj*, sec. 667.

not to forsake the way of the intellect. This advice seems to underline what was most characteristic of the Greek contribution to world history. The second is the belief that Yūnān was the brother of Qaḥṭān, ancestor of the Arabs, an opinion which Mas'ūdī attributes to "careful scholars of antiquity" and to the philosopher al-Kindī.[1] The attempt, albeit tentative, to establish a relationship between these two figures suggests an awareness of a cultural affinity between their descendants which will be investigated further below.

The most sizeable historical information on this composite nation is given for the classical Greeks, the Romans and the Byzantines, although a Frankish king list has also been commented upon by modern scholars.[2] Classical Greek political history begins for Mas'ūdī with Philip of Macedon, while Roman history begins with Julius Caesar and is carried on by Byzantium. In greatness and glory of empire, the Greek dominion was second only to the Persian.[3] The conquests of Alexander are recorded at length, as are the reigns of the Roman and Byzantine emperors. But the political history of this nation was obviously of secondary importance to Mas'ūdī when measured against its scientific contributions.[4]

This contribution is made almost entirely by classical Greece and is chiefly represented by its wisdom or philosophy. Genuine philosophy, according to Mas'ūdī, is Greek while other nations, the Sabians of Ḥarrān for example, are merely its vulgar exponents.[5] Mas'ūdī believed that the Greeks were the chief authorities on a considerable number of sciences, and his own copious reliance on the works of Aristotle attests to this fact. We have also indicated in chapter 2

1 *Murūj*, secs. 665–66; *Tanbīh*, p. 115.

2 For an assessment of the Frankish king list in *Murūj*, sec. 914 ff., see Bernard Lewis, "Mas'ūdī on the Kings of the Franks," *Al-Mas'ūdī*, ed. Ahmad and Rahman, pp. 7–10; *idem*, "The Use by Muslim Historians of non-Muslim Sources," *Historians of the Middle East*, pp. 180–91.

3 *Tanbīh*, pp. 6–7.

4 Jawād 'Alī argues in "Mawārid Ta'rīkh al-Ṭabarī," *Majallat* 2 (1951):174, 176, 189, that Mas'ūdī obtained his information on Greek and Roman history from "Christians he met on his travels,"but that he did not mention his sources. This, however, is not entirely accurate, since he explicitly states (*Murūj*, sec. 733) that his sources for Greek and Roman history were the "books of the Melkite Christians." Chief among these, he singles out Eutychius and al-Manbijī (*Tanbīh*, p. 154).

5 *Murūj*, secs. 210, 1394.

how Mas'ūdī strove to emphasize the importance of the proper study of the principles of these sciences, which he believed were being distorted or neglected by some of his contemporaries.[1] This belief in the necessity of a revival of the Greek sciences was no doubt accentuated by his low opinion of the general state of knowledge in his own days.[2] The achievements of the Greeks in the various sciences and the demonstrations they adduced were, thus, of lasting value.[3]

Mas'ūdī does not specify the sciences in which the Greeks had made the most significant contributions. In the absence of explicit statements, one must seek out his meaning and purpose in other ways. Thus when he takes Sinān ibn Thābit to task for treating subjects of which he knew little, Mas'ūdī writes:

> If he had devoted himself to his own science of which he is sole master, like the science of Euclid, the *lineae secantes* (*muqaṭṭa'āt*), the *Almagest* and the Circles (*mudawwarāt*); and if he had begun by explaining the opinions of Socrates, Plato and Aristotle, treating the heavenly systems, meteorological phenomena, natural temperaments, relations, compositions, conclusions, premises and compound syllogisms, how natural things are distinguished from supernatural, substances, figures and measurement of forms and other problems of philosophy, he would have avoided superficiality and would have produced something more worthy of his own skill.[4]

In this passage, Mas'ūdī implies that for sciences like geometry, meteorology, astronomy, logic, and physics, the Greek philosophers were the customary authorities. To this list, one may add other sciences like music, medicine, political philosophy, geography, zoology,

[1] See, e.g., *Tanbīh*, pp. 13–14.

[2] This subject will be treated further at the end of this chapter.

[3] See, e.g., the brief statement in *Murūj*, sec. 674. A complete résumé of the Greek contribution to the various sciences may be found in *Tanbīh*, pp. 115–22. S.M. Stern has shown in *Al-Mas'ūdī*, ed. Ahmad and Rahman, pp. 28–41, that Mas'ūdī must have used *al-Madīna al-Fāḍila* of Fārābī and, perhaps, other works of Fārābī as well.

[4] *Murūj*, sec. 14. The translation of this passage is based in part on that of Aloys Sprenger, *El-Mas'ūdī's Historical Encyclopaedia* (London: Oriental Translation Fund No. 54, 1841), p. 25.

cosmology and psychology.[1] In all of these sciences, Mas'ūdī cites Greek works as some of his most important sources.

These sciences, considered as a whole, were not, strictly speaking, the product of Greek wisdom alone. Other nations, like the Persians or the Indians, were often cited alongside the Greeks as the originators of certain sciences or scientific opinions. This is expressed in phrases like "the Greek and Indian sages state", implying the existence of a common fount of wisdom.[2] But apart from a passage in which Mas'ūdī states that Ptolemy's *Almagest* was derived ultimately from the Indian *Siddhanta*,[3] it remains true to say that there are almost no direct quotations from scientific works which are not Greek. Thus, Mas'ūdī refers to specific Greek (and Islamic) works on the sciences, but there are no significant references to specific Persian, Indian or Chaldean scientific sources. This is somewhat baffling if one considers Mas'ūdī's belief in a pristine body of wisdom held in common by these nations. It is not exclusively a question of survival, for Mas'ūdī does refer in general terms to the scientific opinions of non-Greek nations.[4] Mas'ūdī does not provide a direct answer to this problem and the answer can only be surmised from his treatment of the Greek cultural achievement as a whole.

It appears that while at an early stage of their history, these ancient nations did possess a common wisdom, the Greek excellence in the sciences (paralleled, e.g., by the Persian excellence in government as outlined above) made them the greatest repositories of these sciences, so that Mas'ūdī affirmed that wisdom (*ḥikma*) *was* Greek.

[1] For music, see *Murūj*, sec. 742; for medicine, see *Murūj*, secs. 1320–22, 1363; for political philosophy, see *Murūj*, sec. 630; *Tanbīh*, p. 87; for geography, see *Murūj*, secs. 203–5; for zoology, see *Murūj*, sec. 866; for cosmology, see *Tanbīh*, pp. 8 ff.; for psychology, see *Murūj*, secs. 1247–48. This, of course, is only a partial listing.

[2] See, e.g., *Murūj*, secs. 203, 630, 1319, 1429; *Tanbīh*, pp. 8, 77, 222. This did not mean that the ancient nations held identical scientific opinions, since Mas'ūdī often points out differences in their views (see, e.g., *Murūj*, sec. 866; *Tanbīh*, pp. 33, 71). It means rather that they shared a common scientific heritage.

[3] *Murūj*, sec. 153; see Ya'qūbī, *Historiae*, 1:92, for a similar view. Curiously enough, Manbijī, '*Unwān*, p. 99, asserts that Ptolemy's *Almagest* was derived from the Chaldeans.

[4] See n. 2, above. For the gradual triumph of Greek geographical sciences over the Indian-Persian in Muslim culture, see Krachkovskii, *Tārīkh al-adab al-Jughrāfī*, pp. 77 ff.

The Greeks seem to have absorbed the scientific heritage of other nations and then to have developed that heritage to its highest level in the ancient world. To this, one may add the survival of their writings and their translation into Arabic.

Mas'ūdī strove to establish a cultural affinity between this Greek heritage and his own Islamic one, and to imply that Arab-Muslim science was the heir to the philosophic heritage of Greece. The suggestion that Yūnān was the brother of Qaḥṭān has already been mentioned as a symbol of this relationship. More important is the care which Mas'ūdī takes in quoting his Greek sources and the attempt to revive their proper study. Mas'ūdī believed that Christianity, when it triumphed in the Byzantine empire, had all but obliterated Greek wisdom.[1] That wisdom, however, survived with the Greek sages whence it passed into the heritage of Islam.[2]

The Egyptians

The generic name which Mas'ūdī applies to the composite nation of whom the Egyptians were the most famous members is Lūbiya or Libya, in origin a Greek name which referred to the whole continent of Africa.[3] This is also the sense in which Mas'ūdī applied this term, including among this nation the Egyptians, the black tribes of the south, and the inhabitants of the *Maghrib*.[4] Like the other seven nations, this one also was once a single realm with a single language. Much information is provided by Mas'ūdī on this nation, most of which concerning, not the ancient unitary nation, but the present diverse nations and tribes which once constituted that nation. Egypt is described at greater length than the other nations and detailed historical and geographical information is furnished, supplemented

[1] *Murūj*, sec. 741. Mas'ūdī probably derived this view from Fārābī's lost work on the history of philosophy: see Ibn Abī Uṣaybi'a, *'Uyūn*, 2: 134–35, and Max Meyerhof, "Min al-Iskandariyya ilā Baghdād," trans. by 'Abd al-Raḥmān Badawī, *al-Turāth al-Yūnānī fī al-Haḍāra al-Islāmiyya*, 2nd ed. (Cairo: Maktabat al-Nahḍa, 1946), pp. 44–45. Cf. a similar view of Jāḥiẓ, *Thalāth Rasā'il*, pp. 16–17.

[2] *Murūj*, sec. 707.

[3] Thomson, *History of Ancient Geography*, p. 12. See also the extract from al-Battānī in Krachkovskii, *Tārīkh al-adab al-Jughrāfī*, p. 108.

[4] *Tanbīh*, p. 83.

by the personal observation and research of the author. A brief summary of this information will be given below together with an assessment of the predominant characteristics of this nation.

A traditional genealogy is provided for both Egypt and the other nations, but a king list is provided only for Egypt.[1] In addition, Mas'ūdī displays a greater interest in the flora, fauna and minerals of Africa than in the political or social conditions prevailing there. This suggests that much of the information must have been gleaned from merchants, who would be more interested in the physical resources of the various tribes and nations than in their history or social and political institutions.[2] Egypt, however, is an exception. As a resident of Egypt in the period when he composed both the *Murūj* and the *Tanbīh*, Mas'ūdī knew the country intimately and was interested in all things Egyptian.

Historically speaking, Mas'ūdī was aware of a chasm which divided the ancient Egyptians from his own contemporaries. The ancient nation whose achievements (the Pyramids and temples) were still visible, could no longer be studied because its language had long since disappeared and none could be found to interpret its inscriptions.[3] In order to dramatize this distance in time, Mas'ūdī employs the artistic device of choosing the story of an old Copt who is said to have visited Aḥmad ibn Ṭūlūn, the ruler of Egypt, and to have recounted to him at length the antiquities and *mirabilia* of Egypt. The old Copt's account occupies several pages,[4] and there is no indication that Mas'ūdī regarded it as anything but a true historical narrative. The Copt's account deals, first, with the ancient towns of Egypt and the topography of the region, much different from what it was in Mas'ūdī's day but conforming to his belief that lands and seas constantly merged into each other. He then describes the Pyramids and other antiquities and gives an account of the black tribes of the south. The history of the various dikes, bridges and canals is also given in full, presumably to satisfy the curiosity of Ibn Ṭūlūn.

1 For the genealogies, see *Murūj*, secs. 806–7, 844. The Egyptian king list is in *Murūj*, sec. 808 ff.

2 The commercial character of much of the information on Africa is quite evident from passages like *Murūj*, secs. 845, 847, 875, 879, 887, 895, 898–99.

3 *Murūj*, secs. 814, 826.

4 *Murūj*, secs. 787–803.

To this narrative of the old Copt, Mas'ūdī appends much information relating to the Nile and its irrigation canals, the Nilometers and animal life in the river.[1] A whole chapter is devoted to Alexandria, its foundation by Alexander, its monuments and the magical properties thereof.[2] For the black nations of the interior, Mas'ūdī is on less certain ground.[3] Much of his information deals with the curious animals of Africa, the giraffe, the elephant and so forth. The blacks of the interior are said to be a people of eloquence and piety but possessing no law to guide their lives.[4] The minerals and precious stones of Africa are described at length and much of the information seems, again, to be of a commercial character.

Mas'ūdī describes the ancient Libyan nation as preeminent in the arts of astrology and magic.[5] The inscriptions on their temples are regarded as talismans by which they were able to repel the attacks of their enemies. An aura of mystery surrounds that nation so that its temples, monuments and treasures seem to be surrounded by magical powers which still defy the curiosity or greed of modern men. The story of the Umayyad Governor, 'Abd al-'Azīz ibn Marwān, and his unsuccessful attempt to recover an ancient treasure is a case in point.[6] Another mysterious monument is the lighthouse of Alexandria which was built as an observation tower and whose mirror afforded a view of approaching ships. Inside the lighthouse was a labyrinth known only to a few and in which many often perished.[7] The mystery of the land was apparent even in Alexander's days when the conqueror had to have recourse to magic and supernatural powers in order to counteract the mystery of the land.[8]

Mas'ūdī was confronted with a nation which seemed incomprehensible and mysterious. In describing ancient Egypt, he strove to offer natural and scientific explanations for the magical powers that

[1] *Murūj*, secs. 775–81.
[2] *Murūj*, secs. 827–43.
[3] *Murūj*, sec. 844 ff.
[4] *Murūj*, sec. 872.
[5] *Murūj*, sec. 813.
[6] *Murūj*, secs. 823–24.
[7] *Murūj*, secs 836–41.
[8] *Murūj*, sec. 834.

he believed were commanded by that nation. It seemed to Mas'ūdī that these magical phenomena and powerful talismans could be interpreted as the result of the magnetic properties of certain metals and elements. He took care to record, while describing the magic of Egypt, the magnetic forces of attraction and repulsion which he himself had observed on his travels, for example, the fact that certain towns were, because of their magnetic properties, free from snakes and scorpions. Certain chemical reactions are also cited by Mas'ūdī as examples of the transmutation of elements.[1] He therefore seems to be suggesting that the magical powers of that ancient nation find their parallel in certain magnetic and chemical reactions familiar to the scholars of his own age. In other words, the magic of the ancient "Libyan" nation, especially as it existed in Egypt, was the product, not so much of mystery or the occult, but rather of the ability of that nation to understand and harness the forces of nature. This ability was the peculiar and most characteristic achievement of that ancient nation.

The Turks

Of the seven nations of antiquity, the Turks were, in Mas'ūdī's account, the least important, if one judges by the information provided on them and the description of their history. In addition, that information is scattered and disorganized so that it is difficult to reconstruct in a meaningful manner. There is little doubt that Mas'ūdī entertained a low view of the Turks, mainly because their habitat lay in a northern climatic zone which was not conducive to the growth of arts and sciences.[2] Furthermore, the nomadic life of most Turkish tribes precluded the development of the arts and sciences which were normally associated with cities.

The Turkish nation comprised various tribes among which Mas'ūdī lists the Kharlukhiyya, the Ghuzz, the Kaymāk, the Tughuzghuz and the Khazar.[3] In addition to these eastern Turks, Mas'ūdī mentions certain western Turkish tribes who were once part of the

1 *Murūj*, secs. 815–18.

2 For the influence of climate on the Turks, see *Tanbīh*, pp. 23–24; *Murūj*, secs. 369, 1337, 1361.

3 *Tanbīh*, p. 83. Other tribes are also mentioned in *Murūj*, sec. 313.

eastern stock and later broke with them and moved westward.[1] The most important of these latter are the Bajnay, the Bajghird, the Bajnāk and the Nawkarda.[2] But all these tribes once constituted one nation and spoke one language. Mas'ūdī asserts that they trace their descent to Yāfith, son of Noah. The leading tribe of ancient times was the Kharlukhiyya of Farghāna whose king, the Khāqān, once ruled over the entire Turkish nation.[3] But no king list is provided for that ancient nation and the information about the Turks concerns mainly those Turkish tribes, both eastern and western, which were contemporaneous with Mas'ūdī. Much of that information is, again, commercial in nature, and these nations are often seen through the eyes of Muslim colonies living among them or travellers and merchants frequenting their regions.[4]

The predominant characteristic of this nation is its warlike spirit.[5] This verdict on the Turks is one which was common in *adab* works.[6] Mas'ūdī does not, in this respect, add much to the prevailing opinion on the Turks. He is, however, conscious of the fact that much of the information provided on the various Turkish kingdoms, both eastern and western, was lacking in other works of history and geography.[7]

The Indians

In the tenth century, the question as to which ancient nation was the originator of the sciences was debated with vigor by the champions of the various claimants to this honor. Certain scholars, among whom one must include Mas'ūdī, held that India was the first home

[1] *Tanbīh*, pp. 180–81. The history of this breakup is discussed at length, according to Mas'ūdī, in his lost *K. Funūn al-Ma'ārif.*

[2] *Murūj*, sec. 493.

[3] *Murūj*, sec. 313. Mas'ūdī says that he discussed the causes of the breakup of this unitary Turkish kingdom in his lost *K. al-Awsaṭ.*

[4] See, e.g., *Murūj*, secs. 450, 476, 481, 500.

[5] See *Murūj*, secs. 311–55 and 422–508 and *passim.*

[6] See, e.g., Jāḥiẓ, *Rasā'il*, ed. Hārūn, 1: 55, 70–71, on the military virtues of the Turks.

[7] This is strongly implied in his criticism of Ibn Khurradādhbih in *Murūj*, sec. 503.

of the sciences.[1] Before treating Mas'ūdī's views on this subject, however, a short account must be given of his description of India.

Mas'ūdī brings to his portrait of India a sense of intimacy gained from personal travel. Where his description of other ancient nations was often historical and dealt with nations long since dead, the Indian passages are vibrant and authoritative.[2] In India, Mas'ūdī discovered an ancient nation which still practiced many of the customs assumed to have been in existence from the beginning. The past could often be corroborated by the present.[3]

Mas'ūdī's account of the kings of India has already received adequate treatment elsewhere and need not detain us here.[4] The customary genealogy of the nation is provided together with the view, expressed with regard to all the other nations, that India was once a single kingdom with a single language.[5] The reservations that Mas'ūdī entertained concerning the descent of the Indian nation from Noah have already been described above. Political history and genealogy, however, enjoy less prominence in Mas'ūdī than the social institutions, the customs, the geography and, most important of all, the wisdom of India.

Mas'ūdī records that India was the first home of "virtue and wisdom." Possessing no direct revelation but retaining a memory of the descent of Adam from paradise to India, they were able to discover, thanks to the wisdom of their first king, the Great Brahmin (*Barhamn*), the principles of astrology and astronomy, the effect of the stars on animal creation, and the existence of the First Principle (*al-mabda' al-awwal*) from whom all other existents derive their being by emanation.[6] They also evolved a cyclical theory of an eternal world perpetually subject to certain precisely determined cycles, whose

[1] References to these views are cited by Rosenthal, *Technique*, pp. 73–74. It is interesting to add here that Jāḥiẓ implicitly recognizes the prior claims of India in *Rasā'il*, ed. Hārūn, 1: 223-24. This view was also held by Yaḥyā ibn 'Adī, as cited by Rosenthal, *Technique*, p. 73, n. 5.

[2] See, e.g., his criticism of two other writers on India in *Murūj*, sec. 159, and of Jāḥiẓ in *Tanbīh*, p. 55.

[3] E.g., *Murūj*, sec. 184.

[4] See the summary, analysis and footnotes in S. Maqbul Ahmad, "Al-Mas'ūd on the Kings of India," *Al-Mas'ūdī*, ed. Ahmad and Rahman, pp. 97–112.

[5] See *Murūj*, sec. 1169; *Tanbīh*, p. 83.

[6] *Murūj*, sec. 152. See also *Murūj*, secs. 395, 1200.

rotation determines the strength or weakness of the forces of nature.[1] In theology, Mas'ūdī recounts the topics discussed by the Seven Sages of India, which encompass the Creator's relationship to his creatures, the wisdom or otherwise of creation itself, whether God derives any gain from his creation and so forth. These topics are stated in the form of short statements or questions. Unfortunately, Mas'ūdī does not deal with the solutions arrived at except to state that the Indians were divided thereafter into seventy sects as a result of the diverse theologies of the Seven Sages.[2]

The astronomy and theology of the Indians are described in terms which reinforce Mas'ūdī's own view that the theology and sciences of later nations derived ultimately from India. The worship of the stars was carried from India to Persia by Būdāsaf.[3] The description of the world as an emanation from the bounty of the First Principle (*fā'iḍ 'alayhā bi jūdihi*) recalls Neo-Platonist ideas. The principles of astronomy were set froth in works like the *Sind Hind* (*Siddhanta*) from which all later astronomy was derived.[4] The theological disputations of the Seven Sages are phrased in terms which suggest that they antedated typical problems of Islamic theology.[5] Their chemical theories concerning attraction, difference and repulsion are echoed in Mas'ūdī's own analysis of certain natural phenomena.[6]

As the originators of wisdom, the Indians were a good illustration of a nation that had achieved a high degree of wisdom through the use of reason without the aid of revelation. This manifests itself even in their moral codes, where laws prohibiting fornication and drunkenness were prescribed rationally, not revealed by a prophet.[7] The principle of justice, which has figured prominently in our study of

[1] *Murūj*, secs. 154–56; *Tanbīh*, pp. 220–22.

[2] *Murūj*, secs. 158–59.

[3] *Murūj*, sec. 1371. This seems to contradict the common view that Būdāsaf journeyed from Persia to India. See David Pingree, *The Thousands of Abū Ma'shar* (London: The Warburg Institute, 1968), pp. 4–5, 16, 19. Mas'ūdī apparently intended to emphasize India's primacy in astrology.

[4] *Murūj*, sec. 153.

[5] Some of the problems raised in *Murūj*, sec. 158, may be compared to certain salient problems of Muslim theology as set forth in Ash'arī, *Maqālāt*, pp. 155–56, 251, and *passim*.

[6] *Murūj*, sec. 866. Cf. *Murūj*, secs. 815-16.

[7] *Murūj*, secs. 177–78.

ancient views on government and society, is succinctly enunciated by an Indian philosopher who was sent to meet Alexander the Great. The philosopher further enjoins Alexander to be merciful to his subjects, to shun the things of the flesh and to remember that the soul can only be purified by philosophy.[1]

Indian society as observed by Mas'ūdī was organized in a caste system which was a counterpart of the hierarchical structure of the world. For in this latter structure, the various stars create the various forms of life and are themselves controlled by the sun which is described as the Great Ruler (*al-mudabbir al-a'ẓam*).[2] This structure, as was seen above, ultimately derives its existence from the First Principle by emanation. The game of chess, invented by the Indians, is a microcosm of this cosmology and of the hierarchy of the social structure.[3] Like the various pieces of the chess-board whose moves do not vary, the kings, priests, judges, and ministers are all drawn from specific and unchanging castes.[4] Their customs and national temperament were permeated by a deep asceticism, a complete lack of interest in the things of this world. This is the moral of the stories which Mas'ūdī narrates concerning the lowliest of funeral processions as well as the most renowned of kings. Death holds no terror for their souls and is often sought as an escape from this world or as a means of forestalling the torment of the afterlife.[6] This may be presumed to be a result of their emphasis on the purity of the soul as is evident in the teachings of their philosophers and sages.

Finally, Mas'ūdī provides copious information of a zoological and commercial nature on the various Indian kingdoms of his day. He strove to determine and record the relative military strength of the various kings as well as their disposition towards the Muslims living among them. The various animals and their habits are described in detail, as are the minerals and other commercial commodities of India.[6] Such information, it may be argued, was designed for the

[1] *Murūj*, sec. 694.
[2] *Murūj*, sec. 152.
[3] *Murūj*, secs. 164–65.
[4] *Murūj*, sec. 176.
[5] *Murūj*, secs. 511, 513, 515–16.
[6] *Murūj*, sec. 413 ff.

use of Muslim merchants and princes who might be interested in trade or conquest. But even if one assumes that this was Mas'ūdī's purpose in describing these contemporary Indian kingdoms, it was certainly of minor importance compared to his historical and scholarly interest in Indian wisdom.

In sum, Mas'ūdī held that India was the first home of philosophy and science, both natural and divine. This was what distinguished them from other nations in world history.

The Chinese

The account which Mas'ūdī gives of China does not suggest that he ever visited it, for that account does not possess the same intimacy of detail or personal recollections often to be met with in his description of India. He was, nevertheless, interested in the history of China, basing his narrative on written as well as oral reports. Mas'ūdī states that the Chinese are descended from 'Āmūr, son of Yāfith, son of Noah. They are related in stock to the Turks and to certain Indian tribes, forming part of the group of nations which journeyed to the east and far east.[1] Their capital city was Yānṣū and their ancient kingdom, in conformity with Mas'ūdī's theory of the seven ancient nations, was once unitary and governed by a king to whom the entire nation paid allegiance.[2] A short king list is given for this unitary kingdom and their ancient kings are said to have lived hundreds of years.

In religion the Chinese worshipped idols and stars, although dualist religions are also said to have penetrated among them. Their idol worship is compared by Mas'ūdī to the idol worship of pre-Islamic Arabia. Mas'ūdī tells of a great and wise king called Tūtāl who consciously set about the task of creating a religion for his people in the belief that kingship could not last without religion. That religion was ultimately deist, but it included the worship of stars and royal ancestors cast in the form of statues. Their ancestor worship plays an important part in their religion. But the wise among them

[1] *Murūj*, secs. 311-12, 315. The Chinese are described as "cousins" of the Turks (*Murūj*, sec. 318).

[2] *Murūj*, sec. 315; *Tanbīh*, p. 84.

were able to perceive that idol worship was a mere means towards the worship of God.[1] Mas'ūdī particularly admired its ethical teachings which were based on reason. A recent king of China even had knowledge of prophecy and showed a travelling Muslim a book in which were drawn pictures of the prophets.[2] Prophecy and revelation, however, formed no part of the ancient religion which Mas'ūdī regarded as in essence comparable to other religions of the seven nations of antiquity.

The Chinese considered themselves supreme in the art of government. Mas'ūdī concurs with this view,[3] although he clearly does not emphasize that excellence in government as much as he emphasizes the Persian. Their great kings governed according to the dictates of reason and justice and were noted for their beneficence towards their subjects. But in the year 264 A.H., a revolt spread throughout China which broke up the kingdom into small and warring principalities, which Mas'ūdī compared to the contemporary state of the Muslim empire. The king was powerless and the order of earlier days was lost.[4] However, stories of merchants travelling in China still tell of the justice of their kings and their hospitality to strangers. Chinese society was organized, according to Mas'ūdī, along tribal lines which may be compared to Arab tribalism. Like the Arabs, they are avidly interested in genealogies.[5] Members of clans are enjoined to marry from outside their clan, as this is considered to produce healthier progeny. As a nation, Mas'ūdī often described them as interested in commerce and foreign trade, whose wares were eagerly sought after by other nations.[6]

Aside from their renown in the art of government, perhaps the most distinctive feature of the Chinese is the superb quality of their craftsmanship. Their artistry and delicate workmanship are singled out by Mas'ūdī as especially noteworthy. Their painters and sculptors possessed exceptional gifts and some of their masterpieces are

[1] *Murūj*, sec. 325. See also *Murūj*, secs. 321–24.

[2] *Murūj*, sec. 345.

[3] *Ibid.* See also *Murūj*, sec. 327.

[4] The revolt and its aftermath are described in *Murūj*, secs. 329–35.

[5] *Murūj*, sec. 328.

[6] See, e.g., *Murūj*, sec. 319.

described in detail. This is what distinguished China from other ancient nations.[1]

Before turning to more general problems arising out of Mas'ūdī's account of the seven ancient nations, we shall now attempt to summarize that account and define its salient features. Mas'ūdī seems to have taken greater interest in what may, broadly speaking, be termed the culture of these nations than in their political history. He viewed each nation as excelling in certain arts and crafts which distinguished its history as a whole from that of other nations. Thus, the Indians and Greeks excelled in philosophy and wisdom, the Persians and Chinese in statecraft, the Turks in warfare, the Chaldeans in agriculture and the Egyptians in magic and the occult. His account of each nation's history seeks to bring out its predominant national character as reflected in its religion, customs, laws and social institutions.

Patterns in the History of Ancient Nations

It remains for us to examine the more general issues arising from this survey of Mas'ūdī's treatment of ancient nations. There is, to begin with, the question of the significance of the history of these nations to Islam. Furthermore, the history of these nations follows certain discernible patterns of rise, decline and fall, of the progress of knowledge, of religious development and so forth. It must, however, be emphasized that the evidence is fragmentary and often ambiguous. But there is little doubt that the larger questions of the historical evolution of nations did occupy Mas'ūdī's attention in his other works, now lost;[2] and enough remains in his two surviving works to warrant the attempt to reconstruct his thinking on these larger issues. The conclusions arrived at below must therefore be regarded as tentative and probable rather than final. The discovery of one or more of his lost books which deal with patterns of historical development may well modify some of the conclusions reached below.

[1] Chinese artistry is described in *Murūj*, sec. 353, where a charming story is told about a Chinese painter. See also *Murūj*, secs. 319–20, 323, for descriptions of Chinese architecture.

[2] See, e.g., *Tanbīh*, pp. 2–4.

With this in mind, we will now turn to the question of the significance of their contributions to world history. This is a problem which we have met with previously in one form or another. It has been shown, for example, that Greek natural science was, for Mas'ūdī, the basis for all subsequent science. In a somewhat larger sense, Mas'ūdī speaks often of the arts and sciences of one nation being absorbed or taken over by another, so that Chaldean wisdom, for example, passed into Persian and Greek into Roman.[1] The original wisdom possessed by the seven nations had many features in common, but with the passage of time, other nations came into being and a diversity of laws, languages, and religions emerged.[2] But Mas'ūdī makes it clear that each of the seven ancient nations developed a distinctive excellence in an art or a science. His own dependence on Greco-Indian science demonstrates the relevance of that science to a Muslim scholar. The same is true of his extensive quotations from the political wisdom of Persian kings. The Sassanid empire, for example, was often regarded as a model for rulers by Muslim scholars.[3]

Furthermore, Mas'ūdī viewed the transmission of knowledge from the pre-Islamic era to Islam as both necessary and desirable. The quotation from 'Alī ibn Abī Ṭālib ("wisdom is the elusive desire of the believer; seek your desire even among the polytheists") is cited approvingly by Mas'ūdī, alongside another saying of the Persian sage Buzurjmihr ("I have taken from everything that which is best in it, even from the dog, the cat, the pig and the raven.") Buzurjmihr goes on to relate the virtues that he learned from each of these animals, namely, loyalty, cajolery, efficiency and vigilance respectively.[4] It is significant that the very first tradition related from the Prophet Muḥammad is, "I have been granted all the gifts of speech," followed by, "In me all discourse has been instilled," which Mas'ūdī takes to mean that the Prophet was the quintessence of all wisdom and eloquence.[5]

These statements, together with Mas'ūdī's interest in the history

1 *Tanbīh*, p. 7; *Murūj*, secs. 522, 707–8.

2 *Tanbīh*, p. 84.

3 See Erwin Isak Jakob Rosenthal, *Political Thought in Medieval Islam* (Cambridge: Cambridge University Press, 1958), pp. 75 ff.

4 *Murūj*, sec. 2848.

5 *Murūj*, sec. 1500.

of ancient nations, imply that the wisdom of these nations was a matter of considerable significance to Islam. To explore this further, one must also seek to determine what Mas'ūdī's attitude was to the transmission of knowledge and to the larger question of intellectual progress. Does the history of ancient nations demonstrate a cumulative advance in knowledge? Is this advance continuous or is it occasionally interrupted? Does Islamic culture itself continue this line? Does this progress include the progress of morality or of political institutions? Within the realm of knowledge itself, can progress be detected in all branches of science or is it confined to some and not others? The answer to these questions would constitute a summary of the findings of this chapter.

The Problem of Progress

To facilitate our enquiry, the problem of progress must be carefully defined.[1] In Mas'ūdī, one may divide progress into three main categories, physical, moral and intellectual. In the second place, belief in progress ought to be viewed, not merely as the belief that the present has surpassed the past, but also that the future holds still further advances.[2]

As regards physical progress, it has already been shown in chapter 3 that Mas'ūdī held that, at its origin, nature, or the external physical world, was endowed with the greatest matter and power. Men had more perfect bodies and lived longer than they did in his day. Mas'ūdī does not hesitate to accept reports of longevity, not only for biblical patriarchs but also for certain ancient kings of pagan dynasties.[3] The matter of the universe was constantly decreasing, so that less and less perfect bodies were created, and nature was less and less able to actualize its potential. Men were no longer capable of executing the same physical feats as before. The great monuments of antiquity were the work of men who surpassed Mas'ūdī's

1 Our analysis of Mas'ūdī's views on progress has benefitted considerably from Ludwig Edelstein, *The Idea of Progress in Classical Antiquity* (Baltimore: The Johns Hopkins Press, 1967), (hereafter referred to as *Idea of Progress*).

2 Edelstein, *Idea of Progress*, pp. xi, 31–32.

3 See, e.g., *Murūj*, secs. 157, 162, 316, 534, 926.

contemporaries in physical strength.[1] The end of the world, as was shown in chapter 3, would find nature at its lowest point of matter and power. Such physical decline, however, bears no relationship to progress in morality or in the arts and sciences.

As regards the progress of morality, Mas'ūdī's views are more difficult to ascertain. He certainly lamented the morality of the men of his own times, but there is no indication to suggest either that matters were different in the past or that they would change in the future.[2] The most revealing passage in this regard is meant to suggest that the world has always been a world of mixed blessings, of happiness and sorrow, riches and poverty, bliss and disaster, life and death, pleasure and pain. This passage, clearly the expression of Mas'ūdī's own feelings, echoes the sentiments of the Sassanian king, Ardashīr, and must be construed as a general comment on the instability of life and fickleness of humanity.[3] This being so, it cannot be shown that Mas'ūdī regarded men as either more moral or less so than they were in the past.

In the realm of politics, it was shown in chapter 3 that ancient nations were, like living organisms, subject to disease and decay, both internal and external. At the beginning, most of the seven ancient nations witnessed periods of glory and prosperity, induced largely by wise kings. But with the lapse of time, the mainstay of the social and political order, viz., the principle of justice and the alliance between kingship and religion, begin to decay. Revolts break out and unitary kingdoms are divided into small and warring principalities, which Mas'ūdī often likens to the state of the Muslim empire of his own day. The fatal tendency towards political fragmentation and the subsequent loss of order is the common experience of all unitary kingdoms. In comparing the political history of Islam to that of other ancient nations, Mas'ūdī is, again, implicitly denying any progress in political life and institutions.[4] The Abbasid Caliphs of his own day,

[1] See, e.g., *Murūj*, secs. 792 and 814, where the building of the Pyramids is discussed.

[2] Edelstein, *Idea of Progress*, pp. 52–53, argues that belief in moral decay was not incompatible with belief in intellectual progress.

[3] For Masūdī's views, see *Murūj*, secs. 584, 2958.

[4] Here again, belief in the inevitability of political decay need not be incompatible with belief in the progress of knowledge.

like the Chinese kings of the past, are powerless to enforce their authority and can exact only nominal loyalty from their supposed vassals. Even the wisest of Caliphs, ʿAlī, was unable to command the obedience of his followers.[1] The prosperity of certain regions could easily be whittled away by unjust rulers of the present.[2] There is, therefore, no guarantee that the social and political fabric of any kingdom could be free from "disease."

But perhaps the most interesting aspect of progress is that which concerns the progress of knowledge. For purposes of convenience, one may revive the duality of reason and revelation, which was found to be of service in the previous chapter in the analysis of the past. In other words, by knowledge is meant both knowledge of God and knowledge of all other things. For the sake of clarification, some unavoidable repetition of earlier conclusions must ensue.

In chapter 3 it was argued that revelation through prophets followed a continuous and uninterrupted line. As the time for Muḥammad drew near, the religious perception of men, especially in pre-Islamic Arabia, grew more acute. Following the Alid account of the creation, one must assume, not only a greater manifestation of divine truth as between past and present, but also a continuous manifestation of that truth as carried forward by the Shīʿite Imāms.[3] There is little doubt, therefore, that from the point of view of revelation, Masʿūdī believed in the increasing availability of truth from the creation onwards. The lapse into idolatry among the ancient nations does not alter this fact.

As regards the sciences practiced by the ancient nations, the problem is more complex. Masʿūdī undoubtedly believed that the Greeks had taken over and refined the natural sciences of their predecessors. They had succeeded in enriching and transmitting their heritage of wisdom, but Christianity proceeded to wipe out all traces of that ancient wisdom until it was recovered and revised by the

1 See, e.g., *Tanbīh*, p. 400, for Masʿūdī's description of contemporary Caliphs; *Murūj*, sec. 335, for the king of China. Masʿūdī compares his own age, politically speaking, with the age of Mulūk al-Ṭawāʾif, the interregnum between first and second Persians, i.e., the Achaemenid and the Sassanian empires. For ʿAlī, see *Murūj*, sec. 1695.

2 Iraq, according to Masʿūdī, is a case in point: see *Tanbīh*, pp. 40–41.

3 The Shīʿite Imāms will be discussed in chap. 5.

Muslims.[1] But while knowledge may suffer such temporary setbacks, Mas'ūdī undoubtedly believed that it not only has increased but will continue to increase in the future. Mas'ūdī makes this amply clear in a passage which has been alluded to before and which, because of its importance, must now be cited in full:

> And although our own age is posterior to that of authors who have gone before and our own days far removed from theirs, let us hope that we do not lag behind them in the works we wish to write or ends we aim to accomplish. And while they possess the advantage of precedence, we have the merit of emulation. Ideas and intentions may also be shared in common. It may be that the latter is a better author and a more accomplished writer by reason of the prudence engendered by experience, the fear of close imitation and the vigilance against falling into error. Because of this, sciences progress without end. The last discovers what the first has missed. This progress continues without any circumscribed or definite end. God has attested to this fact as follows, "surpassing everyone who has knowledge is another who knows".[2]

This passage is unequivocal in its advocacy of intellectual progress. If we recall at this juncture Mas'ūdī's own predilection for the "moderns" as opposed to the "ancients" in the realm of *adab*, his belief in intellectual progress becomes even more evident. He does, it is true, rely heavily on the Greeks, especially Aristotle, for much of his information in the natural sciences. But he also takes Muslim scientists for his authorities in such fields as astronomy.[3] His own personal observations of the geography, zoology and botany of the lands he visited enabled him to correct the data of earlier writers. Thus, his estimate of his own contributions to knowledge is perhaps the strongest evidence for his belief in intellectual advancement.

[1] For the role of Christianity, see *Murūj*, secs. 707, 741.

[2] *Tanbīh*, p. 76.

[3] His Muslim authorities for astronomy are cited in *Murūj*,sec. 1328. The cartography of the earth, e.g., as he saw it in the *al-Ṣūra al-Ma'mūniyya*, was pronounced superior to all earlier representations of the earth, including those of Ptolemy and of Marinus of Tyre (*Tanbīh*, p. 33). On the *Ṣūra*, see Krachkovskii, *Tārīkh al-adab al-Jughrāfī*, pp. 86–87.

5. THE PRE-ISLAMIC ARABS AND ISLAM

General Problems

The subject matter of this chapter is the treatment of Islamic history in Mas'ūdī. Islamic history occupies somewhat more than half of the *Murūj* and a little less than half of the *Tanbīh*. A few words must therefore be offered in justification of the comparatively brief treatment accorded to the Islamic part of Mas'ūdī's works in this study. The reason for this is that the present study has been chiefly concerned with Mas'ūdī's historical method and thought. In the Islamic portions of his works, Mas'ūdī uses a chronological framework for the Prophet's life and the reigns of the Caliphs who followed. In contrast to his treatment of the ancient nations, Mas'ūdī's account of the rise of Islam and of the Umayyad and Abbasid Caliphates is largely political and literary in nature. A disparity becomes immediately apparent between his cultural account of earlier nations and the political character of his Islamic history which is dynastic/annalistic in form. In order to understand this disparity, one must first bear in mind that it was not peculiar to Mas'ūdī's histories but is also found in Ya'qūbī and Maqdisī, both of whom were approximate contemporaries of Mas'ūdī and wrote histories with a similar structure.

In explanation of this disparity, it may be argued that the bulk of Arabic-Islamic history had grown enormously by the 4th/10th century. By the time of Mas'ūdī, history had become deeply involved in the theological and legal disputes of the Muslim community. History was often the only guide to the veracity of a legal or theological viewpoint and many of the major sects of Islam had diverged from the rest of the community as a result of essentially historical disputes. The Shī'ites, for example, argued for the claims of 'Alī and his progeny largely in historical contexts like the supposed delegation of authority by the Prophet to 'Alī at Ghadīr Khumm. It is therefore no accident that many of the most prominent Muslim historians of the 3rd/9th and 4th/10th centuries (e.g., Ibn Isḥāq, Wāqidī, Dīnawarī, Ṭabarī, Ya'qūbī) were accused of holding pro-Alid views or sentiments. For the Muslim historian, Muslim history was of immediate relevance to the legal and theological disputes of the community. An annalistic or dynastic treatment was often the most exact way of recording events and it would be in this fashion that the Muslim historian would best serve the needs of his colleagues: the jurists, theologians and Traditionists. Balādhurī's *Futūḥ al-Buldān* is a good example of historiography coming to the aid of jurists and administrators. This is also true of Mas'ūdī and Maqdisī.[1]

In any event, observations on historical theory and method in the Islamic section are rare and brief. The chief interest of the Islamic history part for the purposes of this study is not so much the theoretical reflections but rather the ethical and theological judgements expressed or implied. In the Islamic portion, Mas'ūdī was dealing with historical persons and events of direct, and often vital concern to his society. Many of these events were still hotly contested in his own day. The strongholds of Sunni Islam in Egypt, Syria and Iraq were being threatened by Shī'ite movements like the Qarmatians and the Fatimids, movements which traced their ultimate origin to the political and theological struggles of the early Muslim community. The ethical judgements pronounced by Mas'ūdī on early Muslim history throw light on Mas'ūdī's religious and theological sympathies. This subject has, of late, excited the interest of some modern scholars. Mas'ūdī has been variously described as a Mu'tazilite, a Neo-Platonist, and even as an Ismā'īlī.[2] Our purpose in this chapter is to shed some light on this problem through the close examination of his ethical verdicts on the persons and events of Islamic history. It is our belief that the

1 Echoes of this may be found in *Murūj*, secs. 15, 1436, 1468, 1481–82, 1502, 1510. See Maqdisī, *Bad'*, 4: 209; 5: 120.

2 S. Maqbul Ahmad affirms in a tone of finality that Mas'ūdī was a Mu'tazilite in his "Al-Mas'ūdī's Contributions to Medieval Arab Geography," *Islamic Culture* 27 (1953): 61–77; Carra de Vaux, in the introduction to his translation of the *Tanbīh*, entitled *Le Livre de L'Avertissement et de la Revision* (Paris: Société Asiatique, 1897), p. VII, maintains that Mas'ūdī strongly implied that Neo-Platonism was his own philosophy; Miquel, *La Géographie humaine*, pp. 202 ff., argues, on flimsy evidence, that Mas'ūdī was an Ismā'īlī. But more of this below.

attribution of certain rigid doctrinal positions to Mas'ūdī obscures rather than clarifies his many-sided intellectual interests and his over-all achievements as a historian.

Pre-Islamic Arabia

Mas'ūdī's views on the rise of Islam and of the Islamic empire must be examined against the background of pre-Islamic Arabia. While a discussion of the history of the pre-Islamic Arabs belongs more properly to the previous chapter, alongside the other ancient nations, their history bears a special relationship to Islamic history proper, since Mas'ūdī regarded their history largely as a process of religious preparation for the advent of Muḥammad. Hence, an account will be given here of that history and that relationship as a prelude to Islamic revelation.

Mas'ūdī provides a full and intricate genealogy of Arab tribes. Three main tribal groups are distinguished: the extinct Arabs, the Yamanī Arabs, and the Nizārī Arabs. All three groups are descended from Sām, son of Noah, but through different sons.[1] The term 'Arab' is applied to these three by virtue of their habitat (viz., the Arabian Peninsula) but chiefly by virtue of their language. Their arrival in the Arabian Peninsula began after their gradual dispersal from Babylon.[2] On the whole, Mas'ūdī's genealogies differ little from those to be found in other Muslim historians.

The problem of language, however, was a vexing one. Which of these three Arab groups was the first to speak Arabic? The Nizārī and Yamanī groups vigorously upheld their own claims to this honor. The Nizārīs held that Ishmael, son of Abraham, was given the language by God while the Yamanīs contended that Ishmael learned the language from a Yamanī tribe living in Mecca.[3] This conflict of claims masked a deeper social and political conflict between the two groups. Mas'ūdī, while granting that Ya'rub ibn Qaḥṭān, the ancestor of the Yamanīs,

1 For Arab genealogy, see *Murūj*, sec. 995 (Yamanī Arabs); *Murūj*, secs. 1091–92 (Nizārī Arabs); *Murūj*, sec. 953 (Extinct Arabs). Genealogies are provided in other places also.

2 Their dispersal is described in *Murūj*, sec. 1142 ff.

3 Conflicting claims are set forth in *Tanbīh*, pp. 79–83 and, especially, *Murūj*, secs. 996–99.

was the first to speak Arabic,[1] believes that Ishmael too was granted this honor by God, independently of his association with the Yamanīs.[2] In this instance of factional disputes and in others where Shu'ūbī (anti-Arab) claims were advanced by various groups,[3] Mas'ūdī sought to restrain what he thought were exaggerated or irrational claims of factionalism.

The political and social history of the pre-Islamic Arabs is treated at greater length and detail than that of any other ancient nation. A wealth of information on them was available from which the historian could select. Mas'ūdī treated their various dynasties independently and did not, like Ṭabarī, weave their history into Persian history. Separate chapters are devoted to the kingdoms of Yaman, Ḥīra and Ghassān. Detailed king lists are furnished with copious anecdotes about the kings and their relations with the great powers of their day.[4] Verse, both ancient and modern, is frequently cited to amplify historical incidents. Legends involving demons and jinn are carefully controlled: Mas'ūdī professes, in theory, to accept stories related by Muslim authorities and tradition but expresses in practice a thorough scepticism towards the fables of pre-Islamic Arabia.[5]

These Arab groups were devoid of any particular distinction in the arts or sciences. For most of them, the desert was their habitat and nomadism their way of life. But here, paradoxically, lay their greatest source of strength: their intensely spiritual life. Their nomadism was, according to Mas'ūdī, a conscious choice. He reports that their

[1] *Murūj*, sec. 71.

[2] *Murūj*, secs. 996–97. Both Ṭabarī (*Annales*, 1: 215) and Ibn Qutayba (*Ma'ārif*, p. 34) assert that Ishmael acquired the Arabic language through his residence in Mecca and his association with Jurhum, an extinct Arab tribe. But Ya'qūbī (*Historiae*, 1: 252), like Mas'ūdī, denies this and claims that Ishmael was divinely inspired to speak Arabic.

[3] See, e.g., *Murūj*, secs. 955–56, where Mas'ūdī takes certain Mu'tazilites to task for their specious argument that the Nabateans are superior to the Arabs. His remarks in *Murūj*, secs. 957–59 are intended to deflate those who take excessive pride in their ancestry.

[4] For the political history of the Yamanī dynasty, see *Murūj*, sec. 1000 ff.; for the kings of Ḥīra, see *Murūj*, sec. 1036 ff.; for the kings of Ghassān, see *Murūj*, sec. 1076 ff.

[5] Typical of his scepticism towards stories about the jinn are his remarks in *Murūj*, secs. 1161–62. See also *Murūj*, secs. 1204–5. Ya'qūbī seems more prepared to accept stories involving the jinn (see *Historiae*, 1: 221).

earliest leaders, having examined the two modes of life, the urban and the nomadic, deliberately chose the latter. Their reason was that cities and buildings confine human beings both physically and mentally. They repress man's noble and free desires, whereas the open spaces and open air sharpen men's minds and promote their health. Hence these Arabs, according to Mas'ūdī, were the healthiest, the most noble, the most generous and the most perspicacious of men.[1] This is the first of the spiritual characteristics of pre-Islamic Arabs.

In the second place, Mas'ūdī lays a great deal of emphasis on the ability of the Arabs as soothsayers (*kuhhān*; *kahāna*). Six chapters are devoted to this and parallel themes in the *Murūj*, all of which underline the concern of the Arabs with the nature and properties of the soul, the afterlife, the supernatural, demons, jinn, divination, augury and so forth.[2] To Mas'ūdī, this spiritual power (*al-quwwa al-rūḥāniyya*) was present to some extent in all peoples of the world but was manifested most conspicuously among the Arabs.[3] Their noble souls and clear spiritual vision granted them a spiritual light (*nūr rūḥānī*) with which they were able to transcend the confines of their senses and to gain insight into the occult.[4] Mas'ūdī cites many examples of their ability to foretell the future, explaining this as a result of their free nomadic life and their unencumbered physical existence.[5]

This sensitivity to matters spiritual made them the ideal recipients of final revelation. Mas'ūdī speaks of the omens[6] that presaged the advent of Muḥammad and of the many pre-Islamic Arabs who foretold his coming and believed in his mission.[7] Since the Arabs were more attuned to the omens of nature than any other people of ancient times, he argued, they were readily able to interpret their significance. In addition, most Arabs, because of their purity of soul (*ṣafā' al-nafs*), were monotheists,[8] and others were Christians, Jews, Magians, animists and so forth. To them, many prophets were sent.

1 *Murūj*, secs. 1108–12.
2 *Murūj*, secs. 1190–1280.
3 *Murūj*, sec. 1240.
4 *Ibid.* See also *Murūj*, sec. 1218.
5 E.g., *Murūj*, secs. 1025, 1190–93, 1227.
6 *Murūj*, sec. 1206; *Tanbīh*, pp. 227–28.
7 *Murūj*, sec. 131 ff.
8 *Murūj*, sec. 1140.

One, Khālid ibn Sinān al-ʿAbsī, miraculously rescued Arabia from Magianism and foretold the coming of Muḥammad.[1] Others, like Ri'āb al-Shannī or Asʿad Abū Karib al-Ḥimyarī, were divinely inspired to announce the advent of Muḥammad.[2] Still others were designated by Muḥammad himself as prophets or messengers and praised for their virtue and wisdom.[3] Many were pious ascetics who recognized Muḥammad when they met him as the Prophet whom they had been expecting. All these Masʿūdī calls "the people of the Interval" (*ahl al-fatra*), that is, the interval between Jesus and Muḥammad, and most of them were Arabs.

The Prophet's Life

The account of the Prophet Muḥammad's life in the *Murūj* bears little stylistic resemblance to anything that comes before or after it. The chief dates and events of his life are recorded in a manner which resembles a catalog of information rather than a narrative. The facts of his birth, his mission, his expeditions and so forth are given, but without elaboration. Masʿūdī deliberately chose to present the Prophet's life in this manner, since he refers to this body of information as an epitome (*jawāmiʿ*) which would satisfy the scholar or student who seeks concise information.[4] The primary purpose of Masʿūdī, one must assume, is to provide accurate historical facts for religious scholars. This impression is strengthened by the fact that in some places Masʿūdī alludes to the conflict of jurists over a particular historical fact which later gave rise to diverse legal interpretations.[5] One may also assume that Masʿūdī strove not to duplicate what he had written elsewhere about Muḥammad and was thus content to record the highlights of his career in a concise manner, including such information as he had omitted in his other works.[6]

[1] For Khālid, see *Murūj*, sec. 131.

[2] For Ri'āb and Asʿad, see *Murūj*, secs. 133 and 134 respectively.

[3] E.g., *Murūj*, secs. 135–37.

[4] *Murūj*, secs. 1481–82.

[5] See, e.g., *Murūj*, sec. 1468; *Tanbīh*, p. 266.

[6] The account of Muḥammad's life in the *Tanbīh* consists largely of a detailed description of the Prophet's expeditions. References to fuller accounts of the *Sīra* in his other works are given in *Tanbīh*, pp. 227–28, 261, 271, 272, 279. In the *Murūj*, Masʿūdī cites his other books treating of the *Sīra* in secs. 1441, 1445, 1460, 1463, 1467, 1476, 1498, 1509.

The most interesting theological problem in the career of Muḥammad is his relationship to ʿAlī ibn Abī Ṭālib. The figure of ʿAlī shadows that of Muḥammad as does no other Companion. There is, to begin with, the question of ʿAlī's "sinlessness" (*ʿiṣma*), that is, whether he was an unbeliever before his conversion or followed the Prophet at every stage of his religious development.[1] There is also the question of the priority of ʿAlī's conversion: whether he was the first Muslim, and his age at the time of his conversion.[2] Masʿūdī's answers betray a strong Alid sympathy in this regard. Only Shīʿite views are expounded at this point, the first asserting that ʿAlī was sinless from the beginning and the second that he was the first convert. Masʿūdī refers his readers to some books of his which deal at greater length with this topic. He then adds "and then Abū Bakr embraced Islam".[3] Masʿūdī's sympathies in this regard are reinforced in other passages where he records both the incident at Ghadīr Khumm as well as the Prophet's remark to ʿAlī ("Are you not satisfied to be for me what Aaron was for Moses?") as historical facts.[4] Masʿūdī further rejects emphatically the claim of certain writers that ʿAlī was converted at a very early age, which he describes as an attempt to disparage his conversion as that of a small and gullible child.[5] In sum, ʿAlī's career is woven conspicuously into the fabric of the Prophet's life. He is the closest Muslim to the Prophet and his natural successor.

The First Four Caliphs

In his treatment of the first four Caliphs of Islam, Masʿūdī endeavored to underline further the primacy of ʿAlī and his rejection by the community, or at least by certain important segments of the community. To account for this rejection of the most obvious successor

[1] *Murūj*, sec. 1462 ff.

[2] *Tanbīh*, pp. 231, 297.

[3] *Murūj*, secs. 1462–63.

[4] On Ghadīr Khumm, see *Tanbīh*, pp. 255–56. On the tradition about Aaron and Moses, see *Tanbīh*, p. 271. Both these traditions, which Masʿūdī relates, were taken by Shīʿite authorities of the tenth century as tantamount to an explicit delegation (*naṣṣ*) specifying the succession of ʿAlī as Imām of the community (see, e.g., Ibn Bābawayh, *Maʿānī*, pp. 67–79). For Ghadīr Khumm, see Laura Veccia Vaglieri, "Ghadīr Khumm," *Encyclopaedia*, ed. Gibb et al., 2: 993–94.

[5] *Tanbīh*, p. 231.

to the Prophet, Mas'ūdī arranged his narrative in a manner which ascribed ignoble motives to some of the leading personalities of that age. Hypocrisy and ambition were rife, and among the multitudes there was deep-seated ignorance and stupidity. Allegiance was paid to personalities rather than principles. 'Alī's Caliphate, which signalled the final triumph of legitimacy, was opposed by evil men who finally succeeded in wresting authority away from its rightful possessors. Throughout these turbulent times, 'Alī himself was blameless in word and deed, gathering around him the Prophet's most pious Companions. The narrative of Mas'ūdī will now serve to illustrate and amplify these preliminary observations.

Mas'ūdī deals briefly with the reign of Abū Bakr, the first Caliph;[1] he describes him as an ascetic, contemptuous of the luxury of this world. Brief examples are cited of his sayings and of the main events of his Caliphate, the new conquests and the wars of apostasy (*al-ridda*). But the figure of 'Alī still dominates the period. Abū Bakr, according to Mas'ūdī, acknowledged the primacy of 'Alī but accepted the Caliphate for fear of a civil war. He is therefore made to be uncertain of the legitimacy of his own position.[2] Abū Bakr's conduct towards Fāṭima, daughter of the Prophet, filled him with remorse, and 'Alī and the Hāshimites, for their part, offered their allegiance to Abū Bakr only after the death of Fāṭima.[3]

The Caliphate of 'Umar is treated at greater length.[4] He is described as a humble but very strict and pious Muslim, simple in his manner of life. His governors and army commanders emulate his example. But the bulk of information on this Caliphate is taken up in stories of the conquests in Mesopotamia and exploits of brave warriors. 'Alī takes no active part in this reign except where Mas'ūdī

1 *Murūj*, secs. 1510–23; *Tanbīh*, pp. 284–88.

2 *Murūj*, secs. 1517–18. There is a well-known tradition, possibly emanating from Anṣārī circles, that Abū Bakr's election was a "chance event" (*falta*); for this see, e.g., Bukhārī, *Ṣaḥīḥ*, 4: 304–5. Mas'ūdī's account conveys a parallel impression, namely, that Abū Bakr's election was fortuitous. Shī'ite tradition also records a similar view of 'Alī's on Abū Bakr (see, e.g., Ibn Bābawayh, *Ma'ānī*, pp. 360–61).

3 *Murūj*, sec. 1517; *Tanbīh*, p. 288.

4 *Murūj*, secs. 1524–75; *Tanbīh*, pp. 288–91.

defends his claim to have been the first to suggest the adoption of the Hijra as the beginning of the Islamic era.[1]

With the Caliphate of 'Uthmān, however, a new note of hostility is distinctly detectible. Beginning with his sons, Mas'ūdī describes many of them as either physically disfigured or morally depraved.[2] 'Uthmān himself is depicted as a spend-thrift and a lover of luxury and wealth.[3] His governors and some of his contemporaries followed his example and became possessed of vast fortunes. Mas'ūdī makes the contrast with the Caliphate of 'Umar explicit by commenting, "Nothing like this took place in the days of 'Umar ibn al-Khaṭṭāb when morality was clearly upheld and the way of life was simple".[4] Mas'ūdī further cites examples of drunken governors, of the ill-treatment of Companions of the Prophet, of nepotism and of the sinister Abū Sufyān conspiring to make the rule hereditary in the house of the Umayyads.[5] All the while, 'Alī stands aloof, displeasing the Caliph on occasion for disobeying his unjust orders,[6] but taking no part whatever in the movement which finally culminated in the murder of 'Uthmān. In fact, 'Alī is reported to have been sent to meet the rebels outside Medina and to have reasoned with them and turned them away until they discovered 'Uthmān's treachery and returned. 'Alī is also said to have sent his two sons to guard the Caliph's palace when under siege and to have beaten them when they failed to protect 'Uthmān from his murderers.[7] Mas'ūdī not only absolves 'Alī of all guilt and complicity in the murder but attempts to show how 'Alī defended a Caliph whom he clearly considered unsuitable for his post and unjust in many of his dealings.

With the Caliphate of 'Alī, Mas'ūdī's Alid sympathies become even more explicit. Opposition to 'Alī grows rapidly and is centered upon men whose motives Mas'ūdī depicts as ignoble. There is, for

[1] *Tanbīh*, p. 290.

[2] *Murūj*, sec. 1577.

[3] *Murūj*, sec. 1578.

[4] *Murūj*, sec. 1582.

[5] *Murūj*, sec. 1598. In *Tanbīh*, pp. 293–94, Mas'ūdī reports that 'Uthmān lost the Prophet's ring, which earlier Caliphs had worn. The implications of this loss are obvious.

[6] *Murūj*, sec. 1597.

[7] *Murūj*, sec. 1605.

example, 'Amr ibn al-'Āṣ, who, in Mas'ūdī's account, is seen as an unprincipled hypocrite caring only to advance his own fortunes.[1] Another is al-Mughīra ibn Shu'ba who fails to win 'Alī over to his cunning schemes and leaves him for Mu'āwiya.[2] Al-Zubayr and Ṭalḥa are hypocrites and liars, bitter opponents of 'Uthmān while he lived and champions of his cause after his death.[3] The rebellion of these latter, joined by 'Ā'isha, is a sordid episode, pitting against 'Alī's men opponents who were too proud to give up the struggle even as they acknowledged that they were in the wrong.[4] 'Alī on the other hand is the head of a party which includes most of the Prophet's Companions both among the Muhājirūn as well as the Anṣār.[5] At every turn, 'Alī upholds the divine law while his opponents, cynical and greedy for power, scheme to deprive him of his legitimate authority. In every confrontation, 'Alī is never the one to strike the first blow, but strives to avoid the shedding of blood.[6]

In the momentous conflict with Mu'āwiya, Mas'ūdī regards 'Alī as blameless. His failure, it is often suggested, is due not to any defect in his character but rather to the disobedience of some of his followers. When his army at Ṣiffīn urges him to accept arbitration in accordance with the dictates of the Koran, and his own arguments to the contrary fall on deaf ears, he tells his followers, "Yesterday I gave orders; today I receive them. You have chosen to disobey".[7] Unable to command obedience, 'Alī cannot wage war effectively against his enemies. In Mas'ūdī's account, 'Alī foretells his future and the future of the Islamic community, but even this power of prophecy cannot sway the wayward and stubborn among his followers.[8]

Mu'āwiya and his party are treated very harshly by Mas'ūdī. When arbitration is discussed in 'Alī's camp, 'Alī, speaking of Mu'āwiya, 'Amr ibn al-'Āṣ and their party, tells his followers, "These

1 *Murūj*, sec. 1624.

2 *Murūj*, sec. 1625.

3 *Murūj*, secs. 1626, 1628.

4 *Murūj*, sec. 1634.

5 See, e.g., the extraordinary description of 'Alī and his followers marching before the Battle of the Camel in *Murūj*, sec. 1631.

6 *Murūj*, secs. 1632, 1719.

7 *Murūj*, sec. 1695. See also *Murūj*, sec. 1715.

8 E.g., *Murūj*, secs. 1684, 1721, 1742.

are men neither of religion nor of the Koran. I know them better than you. I lived with them and knew them as children and as men. They were the worst of children and the worst of men".[1] The real villain for Mas'ūdī is 'Amr ibn al-'Āṣ who is pictured as a cynical man leading a sordid and irreligious life. Other leaders of the Umayyad party are also described as criminals fleeing from justice or greedy and unprincipled adventurers. Some follow Mu'āwiya merely because they gave their word to do so although, like Ṭalḥa and al-Zubayr in the earlier war, they know that they are in the wrong and 'Alī's cause is just.[2]

Mas'ūdī then recounts 'Alī's war against the Khawārij where, again, 'Alī's orders are not obeyed, for he had urged his followers to pursue Mu'āwiya rather than be distracted by the Khawārij. Mu'āwiya meanwhile poisons al-Ashtar, 'Alī's trusted lieutenant, and kills his governor of Egypt in a foul manner.[3] The conspiracy to murder 'Alī is related in detail as are his last days and his death. The section on his Caliphate is then ended with a chapter devoted to his sayings and his virtues.

It is evident from this examination of Mas'ūdī's account of the first four Islamic Caliphates that the figure of 'Alī occupies a predominant position. Being so patently superior to all his contemporaries, he is nevertheless rejected and opposed by men of base motives and a community which in large part is too stupid to distinguish right from wrong. Indeed, Mas'ūdī's attitude to the masses of the community at large is frequently one of contempt. Thus the Syrian multitudes who followed Mu'āwiya are caricatured as simple-minded and totally ignorant of the issues and personalities of the conflict.[4] In a passage which quotes a speech by 'Alī, Mas'ūdī writes of the masses:

> It is a trait of the multitude (*'āmma*) to bring to power those who are unworthy of it, to exalt men other than the best and to ascribe wisdom to the ignorant. The multitude follow whoever leads without distinction of virtue or vice and without knowing right from wrong... If you observe the multitude when they congregate, you will always see them gathered around a man leading a bear

[1] *Murūj*, sec. 1695.

[2] *Murūj*, sec. 1683.

[3] *Murūj*, sec. 1726.

[4] *Murūj*, sec. 1838.

> about or another who beats on a drum to make a monkey dance, or anxious for pleasure and frivolity or attending to a charlatan holy man... The Prophet spent twenty-two years calling men to God. Revelation descended upon him and he dictated it to his followers, who wrote it, took it down and gathered it word by word. God only knows where Mu'āwiya was all this while. Then, a few months before the death of the Prophet, Mu'āwiya acted as his scribe. So the multitude acclaimed him and exalted his standing by making him a recorder of revelation and glorified him with that title which they ascribed to him while denying it to others and omitting to mention their names.[1]

'Alī's failure, then, was the result of circumstances over which he had no control. The disobedience of his own followers, the guile of his opponents and the fatuity of men frustrated his attempt to reassert legitimate rule in Islam. The question of his own sinlessness, a cardinal tenet of Shī'ite doctrine, is not resolved in a positive or explicit manner by Mas'ūdī. But since no blame is attached to any of 'Alī's words or deeds and no hint of censure is ever intimated, 'Alī's sinlessness is distincly suggested. This, coupled with the Prophet's explicit designation of him as his successor, lends further weight to the strong Shī'ite views expressed previously by Mas'ūdī in his account of the creation in chapter 3 above.

'Alī's wisdom and virtue are further emphasized in the chapter devoted to his sayings with which the account of his Caliphate is concluded.[2] 'Alī expounds an ascetic view of the world, frequently to be met with among the sages and philosophers of antiquity:

> Among God's creatures are some who live as though they see the people of Paradise eternally blessed in Paradise and the people of Hell tormented in the fire. They shroud their inner self and preserve their secrets. Their souls are abstemious and their needs are meager.[3]

The world is a fickle place and the duty of the true believer is to be patient and to prepare himself for the afterlife. Mas'ūdī describes

[1] *Murūj*, secs. 1847–49. One may note that the term *al-'āmma* in Shī'ite usage meant the Sunnīs.

[2] *Murūj*, secs. 1744–57.

[3] *Murūj*, sec. 1746.

'Alī as second only to the Prophet in wisdom and virtue and refers his reader to other works in which 'Alī is more fully extolled.[1]

To conclude this section, it will be instructive to compare briefly Mas'ūdī's treatment of the era of the first four Caliphs with that of certain other Muslim historians. Our task is made easier since the genesis and character of early Muslim historiography on the 'Alī-Mu'āwiya conflict is the subject of a recent study which seeks to examine and identify the various strands of partisanship among historians.[2] It was also found that a comparison with Ya'qūbī and Dīnawarī in particular yielded fruitful results in the attempt to determine Mas'ūdī's own place and views within that historiographical tradition.

Dīnawarī's treatment of the first four Caliphs is rich in detail and possesses much literary merit.[3] Considerable sympathy is accorded to Abū Bakr and 'Umar and the conquests are treated at great length, especially in the Mesopotamian and Persian regions. 'Uthmān however, is given less than two pages and is neither praised nor condemned.[4] His murder is mentioned but without any elaboration. The Caliphate of 'Alī, on the other hand, occupies some eighty pages, and copious information is provided on his reign and the civil war.[5] The historian's sympathy for 'Alī is apparent but it cannot be considered an essentially Shī'ite account. 'Alī, for example, is made to justify his succession to the Caliphate in Sunnite terms, that is, according to the rules established by orthodox theory.[6] No mention is made of any explicit delegation of authority from the Prophet (*naṣṣ*), a point upon which Shī'ite authors have stood firm. On the question of 'Alī's sinlessness, Dīnawarī also seems to digress from strictly Shī'ite dogma, since 'Alī is made to commit sins.[7] While Mu'āwiya is clearly

[1] *Murūj*, secs. 1755–56.

[2] Erling Ladewig Petersen, *'Alī and Mu'āwiya in Early Arabic Tradition* (Copenhagen: Scandinavian University Books, 1964), (hereafter referred to as *'Alī*).

[3] For a full treatment of Dīnawarī's account of the 'Alī-Mu'āwiya conflict, see Petersen, *'Alī*, pp. 159–68.

[4] Dīnawarī, *Akhbār*, pp. 147–49.

[5] *Ibid.*, pp. 149–230.

[6] Petersen, *'Alī*, p. 164.

[7] The *'iṣma* of 'Alī is not treated by Petersen, although it represents an important test of a historian's Shī'ite views. Dīnawarī makes 'Alī commit the crime of burning the house of Jarīr ibn 'Abdallāh al-Bajalī (Dīnawarī, *Akhbār*, pp.

in the wrong in opposing 'Alī, one does not detect in Dīnawarī the same degree of hostility to his every word and deed as may be found in Mas'ūdī. One may, therefore, accept the verdict of a recent scholar on Dīnawarī as a historian of the 'Alī-Mu'āwiya conflict that "On the whole . . . Dīnawarī attempts to combine the moderate Shī'ism's veneration for 'Alī with soundly orthodox views".[1]

Ya'qūbī's Alid sympathies are far more pronounced than Dīnawarī's. Abū Bakr and 'Umar are treated with sympathy although the former is said to have regretted his treatment of Fāṭima, daughter of the Prophet.[2] Unlike Dīnawarī, however, 'Uthmān is harshly dealt with. Stories about his corrupt governors are related at length.[3] 'Uthmān is described as a spend-thrift who regards the public treasury as his own.[4] 'Alī, on the other hand, is treated with even greater sympathy than in Dīnawarī. Mu'āwiya's actions and motives are condemned. Nevertheless, Ya'qūbī too cannot be described as an advocate of a strictly Shī'ite standpoint, and his Abbasid sympathies have been noted in a recent study.[5] In addition, he records that 'Alī prescribed "strange" (*'ajība*) legal punishments.[6] And while the Ghadīr Khumm episode is mentioned,[7] 'Alī's succession to the Caliphate is not justified by an explicit delegation of authority from the Prophet.

Upon examining the evidence, it becomes clear that Mas'ūdī differed from these two pro-Alid historians in several essential respects. The messianic aura which surrounds 'Alī in Mas'ūdī; the explicit delegation from the Prophet; the strong suggestion of 'Alī's sinlessness; the attribution of 'Alī's failure to the utter baseness of his enemies and the almost universal stupidity of the community — all this suggests that Mas'ūdī was trying to present a Shī'ite view of the early history

171–72). Dīnawarī also reports al-Ḥasan's criticism of his father (*Akhbār*, pp. 154–55) as well as the refusal of a Persian princess to marry al-Ḥasan (*Akhbār*, pp. 163–64).

1 Petersen, *'Alī*, p. 168.

2 Ya'qūbī, *Historiae*, 2: 142.

3 *Ibid.*, 2: 190.

4 *Ibid.*, 2: 195, 201–2.

5 Petersen, *'Alī*, pp. 172–73.

6 Ya'qūbī, *Historiae*, 2: 251. This has a direct bearing on the question of 'Alī's sinlessness.

7 *Ibid.*, 2: 125.

of Islam. Unlike Ya'qūbī, Dīnawarī and Ṭabarī, who have been described as the proponents of a compromise between orthodoxy and moderate Shī'ism, Mas'ūdī, it appears, was reviving and continuing an earlier and more thoroughly Shī'ite historical viewpoint.[1]

The Umayyads

The remainder of this chapter will be taken up with an examination of Mas'ūdī's views on the Umayyad and Abbasid dynasties and his attitudes towards two major theological movements of his day, Mu'tazilism and Shī'ism. In the course of this analysis, an attempt will be made to describe Mas'ūdī's views on Islamic history as a whole, its past glory and present decline, and the reasons offered for his interpretation.

It will be noted, to begin with, that Mas'ūdī's treatment of Islamic Arab history, especially from the Umayyad period onward, is more orderly in presentation than the pre-Islamic section. The reigns of the Caliphs are treated in order and approximately the same kind of basic information is furnished for each Caliph: his full name, his ancestry, his age at the time of his accession, his age at death, the length of his reign, his chief aides and counsellors and so forth. The chronology is therefore maintained by considering the Caliphates as self-contained historical units. In essence, each Caliphate is made up of stories and anecdotes about the chief characters. These serve to construct a subtle psychological portrait of each character and provide important clues to Mas'ūdī's verdicts on any given reign, since outright condemnation is rare. In appearance, therefore, Mas'ūdī remains faithful to his self-imposed task of "relating of men only the reports that do them most credit".[2] In reality, however, the stories recorded are often strong indictments of a particular ruler's character or deeds.[3] This is especially in evidence in Mas'ūdī's treatment of the Umayyads.

1 Petersen, *'Alī*, p. 173, argues that Dīnawarī, Ya'qūbī and Ṭabarī were all attempting to achieve a compromise between differing opinions, suppressing the more extreme Shī'ite views of the civil war. The earlier Shī'ite historiography is described in Petersen, *'Alī*, pp. 100–108, *passim*.

2 *Murūj*, sec. 3609. This was a common literary etiquette of the period. See Ṣūlī, *Awrāq*, p. 210.

3 Mas'ūdī thus informs his reader that he must "deduce from what we have recorded our intent, which we omitted to record." (*Murūj*, sec. 1877).

To begin with, only one Umayyad ruler, 'Umar ibn 'Abd al-'Azīz, is dignified with the title of Caliph. All the other reigns of the dynasty are referred to as "the kingdom" (*mulk*) or simply "the days" (*ayyām*). This represents a rejection of their claims to legitimacy.[1] In Mas'ūdī's view, they had usurped the legal authority, maintaining their sway by terror, by the discipline of their followers and through the stupidity of the masses.[2] Most of the Umayyads are described as despicable. 'Abd al-Malik is blood-thirsty and miserly. Sulaymān is a glutton and a lover of pleasure. Hishām is crude and vicious. Walīd II is an unbeliever.[3] But perhaps the most revealing reason offered for the eventual collapse of the Umayyad dynasty is the injustice of the rulers.[4] Mas'ūdī reports the following verdict, pronounced by remnants of the Umayyad family themselves:

> We were diverted by pleasures from devoting ourselves to what needed our attention. So we were unjust to our subjects and they despaired of our justice and wished to be rid of us. Taxpayers, overburdened with taxation, abandoned us. Our domains fell into decay, our treasuries were empty. We trusted our ministers but they preferred their own interests to ours and conducted the affairs of state independently of us and without our knowledge. We were late in paying our soldiers so they overthrew their allegiance. When our enemies called them, they made common cause with them and warred against us. We sought out our enemies but could not apprehend them because our followers were few. The fact that the news was hidden from us was one of the most important reasons for the overthrow of our kingdom.[5]

1 Ya'qūbī likewise refers to the reigns of the Umayyads as 'days' and uses the verb 'to reign' (*malaka*) in regard to their rule. (See, e.g., *Historiae*, 2: 256 and *passim*.) For further reference see Goldziher, *Muhammedanische Studien*, 2: 31 ff. (*Muslim Studies*, ed. Stern, trans. Barber and Stern, 2: 40 ff.).

2 The stupidity of the Syrians is emphasized in *Murūj*, secs. 1786, 1839–40. The discipline and obedience of Mu'āwiya's followers when he proposes his son Yazīd as his successor are described in *Murūj*, sec. 1827 ff. See also *Murūj*, sec. 1851 ff. for Mu'āwiya's ability to command or placate men.

3 E.g., *Murūj*, secs. 1973, 2154 ff., 2219 ff., 2245, for Mas'ūdī's verdicts on these four Umayyads respectively. Yazīd I is said to have been so unjust that "Pharoah was more just than he" (*Murūj*, sec. 1922).

4 The words *ẓulm* and *jūr*, both of which mean 'injustice,' are used frequently in conjunction with Umayyad reigns (e.g., *Murūj*, secs. 1922, 2114, 2198, 2237).

5 *Murūj*, sec. 2266.

This passage, when carefully analyzed, reveals many of the important lessons to be learned from political history as explained by Mas'ūdī and set forth in chapters 3 and 4 of the present study. The injustice of the Umayyads is emphasized more than any other defect which characterized their reign. This injustice consisted, in the beginning, in usurping a power which they knew did not rightfully belong to them.[1] It was also manifested in their harsh dealings with their subjects,[2] their arbitrary judgements and actions and their excessive personal vices. Added to this is the neglect of the affairs of state which, according to Mas'ūdī, often accompanies injustice and leads to the social and economic ruin of a country. The fabric of the empire was torn, in the end, by a recrudescence of the Nizārī-Yamanī rivalry which hastened the coming of the Abbasids.[3] These interpretations offered by Mas'ūdī for the eventual collapse of Umayyad rule echo his views, treated in earlier chapters, on the causes of the decline of states.

The above, however, does not do complete justice to Mas'ūdī's treatment of the Umayyads. 'Umar ibn 'Abd al-'Azīz is described, significantly enough, as a "just" Caliph.[4] His piety led him to stop the cursing of 'Alī and to revere his descendants.[5] His governors followed his pious and ascetic example. Aside from 'Umar, one detects in Mas'ūdī a grudging admiration for the political sagacity of Mu'āwiya, 'Abd al-Malik and Hishām.[6] This is especially true of Mu'āwiya. Lengthy anecdotes are related concerning his foresight, forbearance, self-control and caution. His ability to win his opponents over by carefully calculated acts of clemency is stressed frequently.[7] These qualities were lacking in most of his successors.

Nevertheless, Mas'ūdī's verdict on the Umayyads is a harsh one.

1 See, e.g., the report of 'Amr ibn al-'Āṣ reminiscing with Mu'āwiya about the Battle of Ṣiffīn in *Murūj*, sec. 1808. In *Tanbīh*, p. 309, Marwān is said to be "the first who seized the Caliphate with the sword."

2 Mas'ūdī devotes an entire chapter to the blood-thirsty governor of Iraq, al-Ḥajjāj ibn Yūsuf al-Thaqafī (*Murūj*, secs. 2052–2112).

3 On this rivalry, see *Murūj*, secs. 2267-72.

4 *Murūj*, secs. 2194–95, 2198.

5 *Murūj*, secs. 2171, 2174.

6 *Murūj*, sec. 2234.

7 E.g., *Murūj*, secs. 1836–38, 1860–61, *passim*.

The foundation of their rule was itself an act of injustice and they maintained this rule by terror. The people of Syria, who constituted the base of their power, are ridiculed by Mas'ūdī as stupid and irrational in their loyalty. The Alids cast their shadows over the history of the Umayyads, rising occasionally in futile but legitimate rebellion and providing all the while stark contrast between the degenerate and worldly Umayyads on the one hand and the legitimate heirs of authority on the other.[1] We shall deal at greater length with the Alid Imāms below.

The Abbasids

Mas'ūdī's treatment of the Abbasids is more complex than his treatment of the Umayyads. To understand Mas'ūdī's views on the claims of the Abbasids to assume the leadership of the Muslim community, one must examine his views on the Rāwandiyya, the politico-religious party of the Abbasids, and compare these views with those of historians sympathetic to the Abbasids like Dīnawarī and Ya'qūbī.[2]

According to Dīnawarī, the beginning of the Abbasid movement can be traced to the Imām Muḥammad ibn 'Alī ibn 'Abdallāh ibn al-'Abbās in 101 A.H. The meeting of the Imām with a few followers is described as a fulfillment of ancient prophecies. The Imām tells his followers that at the end of every century in a nation's history, God interferes to restore right and expose evil.[3] Thereafter, as the movement spreads, the Imām is said to have foretold the future at every juncture, as does his son, the Imām Ibrāhīm.[4] In Dīnawarī, then, the succession of the Abbasids is not tainted with any doctrinal doubts on the part of the historians, despite his obvious sympathy for the Alids.

[1] For stories of Alid Imāms and their martyrdom, see *Murūj*, secs. 1927, 1991, *passim*.

[2] On the Rāwandiyya see, e.g., Nawbakhtī, *Firaq*, pp. 42 ff. For strongly pro-Abbasid accounts of the Abbasid movement, see the extract from a chronicle by an anonymous eleventh-century author entitled *Nubdha min Kitāb al-Tārīkh*, ed. in facsimile by P. Griaznevich (Moscow: U.S.S.R. Academy of Sciences, 1960) and the history of an anonymous, ninth-century author entitled *Akhbār al-dawla al-'Abbāsiyya*, ed. by 'Abd al-'Azīz al-Dūrī (Beirut: Dār al-Ṭalī'a, 1971).

[3] Dīnawarī, *Akhbār*, pp. 334 ff.

[4] Dīnawarī, *Akhbār*, pp. 336, 340, 343.

The same may also be asserted of Ya'qūbī, whose Alid sympathies are, if anything, even more clearly pronounced than Dīnawarī's. The letter of 'Abdallāh ibn al-'Abbās to Yazīd ibn Mu'āwiya is an interesting example of Ya'qūbī's handling of Abbasid and Alid claims. Ibn al-'Abbās declares that both his family as well as that of his cousins (the Alids) have a better title to the Caliphate than the Umayyads.[1] In addition, Ya'qūbī recounts in detail the transmission of the *waṣiyya* from the Alids to the Abbasids, from Abū Hāshim, 'Abdallāh ibn Muḥammad ibn al-Ḥanafiyya to Muḥammad ibn 'Alī ibn 'Abdallāh ibn al-'Abbās.[2] Ya'qūbī's Alid sympathies did not prevent him from accepting the legitimacy of Abbasid claims.

Mas'ūdī is far less sympathetic to Abbasid claims. 'Abdallāh ibn al-'Abbās, the most important ancestral figure in the Abbasid movement,[3] is represented in Mas'ūdī as a staunch Alid who never advances his own family's claims to legitimate succession. When Mu'āwiya asks him to describe the most eminent of the Prophet's Companions, he waxes so eloquent in praise of 'Alī that Mu'āwiya tells him, "You have praised your cousin excessively. What have you to say about your father?" He praises his father but in terms much less exalted than those used for 'Alī.[4]

When Mas'ūdī comes to review the doctrinal aspects of Rāwandiyya, the only book which he mentions by name as an exposé of that doctrine is a book by Jāḥiẓ entitled *Kitāb Imāmat Wuld al-'Abbās*. According to Mas'ūdī, however, that book was written in jest since Jāḥiẓ, we are told, wrote other treatises defending the party of 'Uthmān and the party of Mu'āwiya.[5] In addition, Mas'ūdī views the Rāwandiyya as the successors of the Kaysāniyya,[6] a movement which Mas'ūdī treats with considerable hostility. The most important leader and advocate of the Kaysāniyya, al-Mukhtār ibn Abī 'Ubayd al-Thaqafī, is described as a hypocrite and opportunist.[7] Nor does

1 Ya'qūbī, *Historiae*, 2: 294–96.

2 *Ibid.*, 2: 356–58.

3 On 'Abdallāh ibn al-'Abbās, see Laura Veccia Vaglieri, "'Abd Allāh b. al-'Abbās," in *Encyclopaedia*, ed. Gibb et al., 1: 40–41.

4 *Murūj*, secs. 1879–80; see also *Murūj*, secs. 1766–67.

5 *Murūj*, sec. 2280. In a similar vein, Mas'ūdī ridicules the attempt of the Caliph al-Amīn to declare his son the expected Imām (*Murūj*, sec. 2645).

6 *Murūj*, sec. 2283.

7 *Murūj*, sec. 1935.

Abū Muslim, the military leader of the Abbasid movement, fare much better at Mas'ūdī's hands than al-Mukhtār. His mysterious career and eventual downfall are treated in detail but without any sympathy. Furthermore, unlike Ya'qūbī, for example, who records the transmission of the *waṣiyya* from Abū Hāshim the Alid to Muḥammad ibn 'Alī the Abbasid as a historical fact,[1] Mas'ūdī in the *Murūj* merely reproduced this as a doctrinal claim of the Rāwandiyya.[2]

The reservations which Mas'ūdī expresses concerning the legitimacy of Abbasid succession do not, however, prevent him from describing their rule as a *khilāfa*, in contrast to the Umayyad usurpation. His attitude to the various Caliphs seems to be determined largely by their treatment of the Alids, whose careers and rebellions continue to be recorded with care by Mas'ūdī. As a whole, the character of the Caliphs is still depicted mainly through anecdotes, although stories of purely literary interest occupy an increasingly sizeable portion of the whole.[3] This is especially true of the later Abbasid period, when the Caliphs lose much of their power and prestige and literary anecdotes and digressions seem more worthy of recording than the activities of the Caliph.

To facilitate our task of assessing Mas'ūdī's views on the Caliphs, it would be appropriate to describe briefly his reasons for praising or censuring the various Caliphs. The reign of the Caliph al-Manṣūr provides an interesting insight into Mas'ūdī's ethical judgements. Al-Manṣūr, like certain Umayyad Caliphs, is able to command the loyalty of his followers who obey him even when he fights the Alids. The remark of one of his courtiers that the greatest proof of his loyalty was that he obeyed his orders to kill the descendants of the Prophet recalls to mind a similar remark made by a tribal leader

[1] See above, p. 132, n. 2.

[2] *Murūj*, sec. 2283. But cf. *Tanbīh*, p. 338.

[3] There is a graceful discussion of Mas'ūdī's literary excellence in treating the Abbasids in Ernest Renan, "Les Prairies d'Or de Maçoudi," in *Oeuvres Complètes de Ernest Renan*, ed. by H. Psichari (Paris: Éditions Calmann-Lévy, 1947), 2: 502–19. Renan's essay first appeared in 1873 and deals primarily with volume 7 of *Les Prairies d'Or*, ed. by C. Barbier de Meynard et Pavet de Courteille (Paris: Société Asiatique, 1861–77). See also Grunebaum, *Medieval Islam*, pp. 284–85.

to Mu'āwiya during the Battle of Ṣiffīn.[1] When al-Manṣūr delivers his speech following the revolt of al-Nafs al-Zakiyya, he details the failings of the Alids in terms which are clearly at variance with Mas'ūdī's own account.[2] Examples are also given of al-Manṣūr's duplicity and blood-thirstiness. However, al-Manṣūr is also described as a just and shrewd ruler who knew the affairs of his kingdom in intimate detail.[3]

Many of the same reasons, whether for praise or for censure, occur in Mas'ūdī's treatment of other Abbasid Caliphs. Hārūn al-Rashīd's reign is described in glowing terms but we find that the real rulers of the kingdom were the Barmakids, whom Mas'ūdī praised lavishly and who were Alid sympathizers.[4] With their downfall, however, the affairs of the kingdom were badly managed and the Caliph was exposed as an inferior ruler and administrator.[5] The wisdom of al-Ma'mūn is compared to that of Anūshirwān.[6] As he explains to a Ṣūfī, he holds his power only as long as the community think him best fit to rule or until a superior claimant is found.[7] It is significant, therefore, that he intended to make the Imām 'Alī ibn Mūsā al-Riḍā his successor, an episode which Mas'ūdī records in detail.[8] Only the envy of the Abbasid family and later, of course, the Imām's death, forestalled his designs.

Al-Mu'taṣim and al-Mutawakkil are praised for their justice which brought material prosperity in its wake.[9] Al-Muntaṣir, despite his complicity in the plot to murder his father, is praised lavishly, in contrast, for example, to the hostile treatment he received from Ya'qūbī.[10] The reason for Mas'ūdī's praise seems, again, to be the

1 Cf. the remark made to al-Manṣūr in *Murūj*, sec. 2409 to the words addressed to Mu'āwiya in *Murūj*, sec. 2119. See *Murūj*, sec. 1851, for the ability of Mu'āwiya to transcend family loyalty.

2 *Murūj*, sec. 2413 ff.

3 E.g., *Murūj*, secs. 2385, 2431.

4 *Murūj*, secs. 2559–2618.

5 *Tanbīh*, p. 346.

6 *Murūj*, sec. 2701.

7 *Murūj*, sec. 2727.

8 *Murūj*, secs. 2745-47.

9 On al-Mu'taṣim, see *Murūj*, sec. 2805; on al-Mutawakkil, see *Murūj*, secs. 2873 ff., 2960 ff.

10 *Murūj*, sec. 2992. Cf. Ya'qūbī, *Historiae*, 2: 602–3.

Caliph's generous treatment of the Alids. The Turkish commander Bughā who was instrumental in destroying the power of the Caliphate receives, nevertheless, a favorable verdict from Mas'ūdī because Bughā was sympathetic to the Alids.[1]

As Mas'ūdī brings his history closer to his own day, the disintegration of the Caliphate becomes more evident. Both al-Muhtadī, for example, with his strict piety and his other-worldliness, and al-Mu'tamid, with his negligence and love of pleasure, are equally unfit and incapable of resuscitating the power of the Caliphate.[2] The same factors which precipitated the decline of Umayyad rule are at work in the Abbasid Caliphate. All these are succinctly summarized in Mas'ūdī's description of the reign of al-Muqtadir:

> His reign witnessed certain events unprecedented in the history of Islam. For example, he succeeded to the Caliphate at an age at which no other Muslim ruler had succeeded, since he came to the Caliphate at the age of thirteen ... He reigned for twenty-five years less fifteen days, longer than any other Caliph or ruler before him. He appointed twelve wazīrs, of whom some were appointed twice or three times. Such a number of wazīrs was unknown before his reign. Then there was the dominance of women over the kingdom and administration so that a slave girl of his mother's... used to preside over assemblies of *maẓālim*... attended by the wazīr, the secretary, the judges and the scholars. In 317 the pilgrimage was cancelled ... although no pilgrimage had ever been cancelled since the beginning of Islam.[3]

The characters of later Caliphs like al-Muttaqī, al-Mustakfī and al-Muṭī' are unworthy of description for Mas'ūdī, since they are little better than puppets and their country has fallen into ruin.[4]

From this outline of Mas'ūdī's treatment of the Abbasid Caliphs, certain conclusions may be drawn which seem to coincide with his views (described in earlier chapters) relative to the governance and decline of states. In the first place, Mas'ūdī reserves his esteem for

[1] *Murūj*, secs. 3054–55.

[2] On al-Muhtadī, see *Murūj*, secs. 3111, 3130, and *Tanbīh*, pp. 366–67; on al-Mu'tamid, see *Tanbīh*, p. 367.

[3] *Tanbīh*, p. 378.

[4] *Tanbīh*, p. 400.

Caliphs whose conduct was characterized by justice and intimate knowledge of affairs, which led to peace and prosperity of the realm. But Mas'ūdī's own Alid leanings seem to dispose him favorably towards Caliphs who were sympathetic to the Alids, even when these Caliphs are not otherwise distinguished for their justice and political sagacity. On the other hand, the decline of the Caliphate stems from the neglect of government and the consequent rise of powerful contenders and rebels. This leads to a state of affairs which Mas'ūdī often likens to the era of Mulūk al-Ṭawā'if, when the Persian empire was dismembered and local potentates paid only nominal loyalty to their sovereign.[1] In addition, racial and sectarian divisions among the population of the empire hastened the collapse of Caliphal power.

Throughout that period, Alid revolts break out, headed by men whom Mas'ūdī frequently describes as "rising in rebellion to re-establish the truth".[2] Again and again, these rebels are let down by their followers and killed by the Abbasids. As Mas'ūdī chronicled the arbitrary choice of Caliphs by army commanders, the internal power struggles and palace intrigues, so he regarded these Alids as the only men who could have rallied the people to a cause so patently right and just. The fact that men did not rally to the Alids stemmed from their inability, described above, to distinguish between right and wrong, or to decide upon the best and most worthy candidate for political power.

Mu'tazilism and Shī'ism

It was stated at the beginning of this chapter that the student of Mas'ūdī can, through close examination of his views on Islamic history in particular, shed light not only on his political sympathies but also on his theological views. Some of these have already been described above, for instance, his strong Shī'ite inclinations as expressed in his treatment of Umayyad and Abbasid history. This problem must now be explored further and linked with another, equally important problem: his attitude towards the Mu'tazilite movement. This must be done, not only because Mas'ūdī himself seems deeply

[1] *Tanbīh*, p. 400. See also *Murūj*, secs. 335 and 504.

[2] For Alid rebellions see, e.g., *Murūj*, secs. 2401 ff., 2741 ff., 3574 ff.

interested in Mu'tazilism, but also because he was particularly interested in the relationship between Shī'ism and Mu'tazilism, a relationship which was the subject of one of his books, the *K. al-Ibāna 'an Uṣūl al-Diyāna.*[1] The analysis of this problem forms a fitting conclusion to our study, since it will help to clarify the theological basis of Mas'ūdī's thought.

Various aspects of Mas'ūdī's Shī'ite convictions have been described thus far in this study. The story of the creation in chapter 3 and the treatment of 'Alī and of the Umayyad and Abbasid empires in the present chapter reveal a strong theological commitment to Shī'ite doctrine. Mas'ūdī, like Ya'qūbī, devotes a section to each Imām of the Twelver Shī'ites in the various reigns. Many of these Imāms possess hidden powers. Many are able to foretell the future, or to frighten their enemies or to ward off even the lions sent to devour them.[2] It is also noticeable that most of them die by poison,[3] perhaps in order to emphasize the stealth and corruption of their enemies (who were afraid to do them physical violence).[4] Other Alid leaders who rise in revolt are treated favorably by Mas'ūdī, but the Twelve Imāms remain the main upholders of Alid legitimacy.[5] Extremist Shī'ite sects (*ghulāt*) are vigorously attacked and Mas'ūdī detects in some of them Indian, dualist or Magian influences and ideas.[6]

[1] *Murūj*, sec. 2256.

[2] E.g., *Murūj*, secs. 1927, 2220, 2504–05.

[3] E.g., *Tanbīh*, p. 301; *Murūj*, secs. 2532, 2747, 3080.

[4] E.g., *Murūj*, secs. 1927, 3080.

[5] This is clearly the implication of *Murūj*, secs. 2259-61.

[6] We must at this point deal with the contention of Miquel, *La Géographie humaine*, pp. 205–8, that Mas'ūdī may well have been an Ismā'īlī emissary (*dā'ī*). He advances five main arguments, none of which seems convincing:

A. Mas'ūdī travelled in Zanzibar and 'Umān, both places having large Ismā'īlī communities. He also travelled to Baṣra where he may have contacted Ikhwān al-Ṣafā'. However, it is doubtful that the itinerary of the body can ever provide a useful clue to the itinerary of the mind.

B. Mas'ūdī knew the Qarmatians at first-hand. There is little in this argument since Mas'ūdī knew the beliefs of many other religious sects at first-hand.

C. Mas'ūdī pleaded for *ra'y*, *qiyās* and *ijtihād*. But these cannot be considered the sole property of Ismā'īlī thought.

D. His liberty of spirit may contradict Ismā'īlī rigidity and he even attacks the *ghulāt* (a reference to *Murūj*, secs. 1135–37). But this could be 'dissimulation' (*taqiyya*) on his part, since he qualifies his condemnations with sympathy in other

Mas'ūdī's interest in the problems of Islamic theology is not very pronounced in the *Murūj* or the *Tanbīh*. The reason for attempting to describe or elicit certain of his theological views is that he seems to have dealt at length with theology in some of his lost books.[1] But our analysis must perforce remain tentative unless or until one or more of these books is brought to light.[2] We shall proceed, therefore, by analyzing the scattered remarks made in his two surviving works, in the belief that a pattern of thought eventually will emerge.

Of the theological schools of his day, there can be little doubt that Mas'ūdī occupied himself primarily with the Mu'tazila. This is evident, on the simplest level, in his recording of the deaths of prominent Mu'tazilites and also in his detailed outline of the Mu'tazilite creed.[3] His intimate knowledge of Mu'tazilite theology is suggested by numerous allusions to his other works in which their beliefs are said to have been set forth in detail.[4] As to his attitude to some of

passages. This is a doubtful argument since he shows equal sympathy, or at least objectivity, towards many other religious movements.

E. Mas'ūdī states that his book is a "book of historical report, not of research and critical enquiry." Therefore, this means that his other books were books of critical enquiry and polemics. This may be so but there is no evidence that these polemics were Ismā'īlī.

The basic weakness of Miquel's arguments is that he relies on circumstantial evidence rather than on careful examination of Mas'ūdī's texts. But only this examination can give the student of his thought a clue to Mas'ūdī's own theological inclinations. For a brief and recent critique of Miquel's contention, see Charles Pellat, "Mas'ūdī et l'Imamisme," in *Le Shī'isme Imāmite*, ed. by Robert Brunschvig and Toufic Fahd (Paris: Presses Universitaires de France, 1970), p. 70.

1 The *K. al-Ibāna*, (*Murūj*, sec. 2256), is one example of his interest in theology. Another is the *K. al-Maqālāt fī Uṣūl al-Diyānāt* which treats of the views of the Kaysāniyya (*Murūj*, sec. 1945); the Khawārij (*Murūj*, sec. 2078), the Mu'tazila (*Murūj*, sec. 2256), the Khurramiyya (*Murūj*, sec. 2399) and many other theological schools and sects. For a description of the approximate content of his lost writings, see Appendix B of the present study.

2 We find the method used by Charles Pellat in his "Mas'ūdī et l'Imamisme," in *Le Shī'isme Imāmite*, pp. 69–90, to be somewhat unusual. Pellat attempts to determine Mas'ūdī's Shī'ite leanings largely by analyzing a work (*K. Ithbāt al-Waṣiyya*) whose attribution to Mas'ūdī remains doubtful. We believe that there can be no substitute for a thorough scrutiny of the *Murūj* and the *Tanbīh*, unless or until a definitive work of Mas'ūdī's which bears on this question is unearthed.

3 For the notices on the deaths of Mu'tazilites, see, e.g., *Murūj*, secs. 2420, 2898, 2916–18. For Mas'ūdī's description of Mu'tazilite dogma, see *Murūj*, secs. 2254-57.

4 See n. 1, above.

their basic tenets, Mas'ūdī seems to have disapproved of the public discussion of abstruse theological questions. Of the inquisition (*miḥna*) at the time of al-Wāthiq, he writes, "He [i.e., the Caliph] occupied himself with scrutinizing the religion of the people. He thus confused their hearts and drew their curses upon himself."[1] Such an attitude is understandable when one bears in mind Mas'ūdī's deep-seated suspicion of the common man and his low estimate of the intelligence of the masses. But this does not prevent Mas'ūdī from praising al-Wāthiq for his love of reason and his aversion to "imitation".[2] In fact, Mas'ūdī's attitude to the Mu'tazila is not at all as clear, cut as some modern scholars suggest.[3] He seems, on the one hand, to espouse the Mu'tazilite doctrine of *al-wa'd wa al-wa'īd,* the divine and irrevocable promise of bliss and threat of damnation. In describing the sins of the Umayyad Caliph Yazīd ibn Mu'āwiya, he writes:

> Of Yazīd and others, strange tales are told of many shameful deeds like the drinking of wine, the murder of the Prophet's grandson, the cursing of the *waṣiyy* [i.e., 'Alī], the destruction and burning of the Ka'ba, the shedding of blood, infamy and depravity, and other deeds for which revelation has prescribed the threat of being without the hope of Divine mercy (*qad warada fīhi al-wa'īd bi al-ya's min ghufrānihi*), just as revelation has prescribed this threat against anyone who denies God's unity and rejects His Prophet.[4]

In addition, Mas'ūdī goes out of his way to explain that the Umayyad al-Yazīd ibn Walīd, surnamed 'the deficient' (*al-Nāqiṣ*), was a follower of the Mu'tazila and was not deficient in body or mind but earned his nickname because he decreased the pay of his troops.[5] Yazīd ibn Walīd is treated with rare consideration by Mas'ūdī.

Mas'ūdī also shows favor to many prominent Mu'tazilites. Typical of this are 'Amr ibn 'Ubayd and Aḥmad ibn Abī Du'ād. The former is eulogized for his piety and asceticism; the latter is described

1 *Tanbīh,* p. 361. See also *Tanbīh,* pp. 190–91.

2 *Murūj,* sec. 2857.

3 E.g., by S. Maqbul Ahmad as in p. 115, n. 2, above.

4 *Murūj,* sec. 1931. His espousal of *al-wa'd wa al-wa'īd* may well have stemmed from his belief in the principle of justice, as set forth in chap. 3 above.

5 *Murūj,* sec. 2254.

as generous and charitable.[1] Mu'tazilites with Alid sympathies are particularly favored by Mas'ūdī,[2] while Alid Imāms like Muḥammad al-Jawād are said to have believed in *al-wa'd wa al-wa'īd.*[3] In sum, therefore, Mas'ūdī was attracted to the Mu'tazila in so far as they upheld the importance of critical inquiry (*naẓar*) as opposed to imitation and stressed the unity and irrevocable decree of God. We cannot be more specific than this since Mas'ūdī does not express himself explicitly on many other tenets of the Mu'tazila school.[4]

Mas'ūdī differs from the Mu'tazila, first and foremost, in regards to the problem of the *imāma*, which remained throughout the centuries one of the main bones of contention between the Shī'ites and the Mu'tazila.[5] This difference is illustrated by Mas'ūdī in the form of two debates between the Shī'ite Hishām ibn al- Ḥakam and the Mu'tazilites 'Amr ibn 'Ubayd and Abū al-Hudhayl al-'Allāf.[6] We know from a Mu'tazilite source in the ninth century that the polemics of these central figures in their respective movements were of considerable importance in defining the relationship between the two movements.[7] The debate between Hishām and Abū al-Hudhayl concerned the problem of movement (*ḥaraka*) and the question of divine attributes (*ṣifāt*). The debate between Hishām and 'Amr centered on the *imāma*. In the first, Abū al-Hudhayl was shown

[1] *Murūj*, secs. 2420, 2898.

[2] E.g., al-Iskāfī in *Murūj*, sec. 2282 and Muḥammad ibn Hārūn al-Warrāq in *Murūj*, sec. 2920. On these two Mu'tazilites, see especially Johann Fück, "Some Hitherto Unpublished Texts on the Mu'tazilite Movement from Ibn al-Nadīm's *K. al-Fihrist*," in *Professor Muhammad Shafi' Presentation Volume*, ed. S. M. Abdullah (Lahore: on behalf of the Majlis-e-Armughān-e-'ilmī, 1955), pp. 66–67, 71.

[3] *Murūj*, sec. 2890.

[4] Two additional but tentative suggestions may be made at this point. The story (related in *Murūj*, sec. 3132 ff.) of how an old man worsts the Mu'tazilite Qāḍī ibn Abī Du'ād in a debate about the creation of the Koran, may well reflect Mas'ūdī's anti-Mu'tazilite views in this matter. On the other hand, the phrase of Mas'ūdī in *Murūj*, sec. 1432 referring to God ("the minds of men are incapable of confining Him within attributes") may reflect Mu'tazilite influence. But without further elaboration from Mas'ūdī, one cannot pronounce with certainty on these two questions.

[5] Wilferd Madelung, "Imāmism and Mu'tazilite Theology," in *Le Shī'isme Imāmite*, p. 13.

[6] These debates are recounted in *Murūj*, secs. 2917–19.

[7] See, e.g., al-Khayyāṭ, *Intiṣār*, index, s.v. Hishām ibn al-Ḥakam; Abū al-Hudhayl. On Hishām, see Wilferd Madelung, "Hishām b. al-Ḥakam," in *Encyclopaedia*, ed. Gibb et al., 3: 496–98.

the falsity and contradiction of his views while in the second Hishām was able to demonstrate to 'Amr the logical necessity of the *imāma.* These debates are significant, not so much for their content as for what they reveal of Mas'ūdī's sympathies in the polemics of Shī'ism and Mu'tazilism. The second debate is particularly important since it demolishes what was, for the Shī'a, the chief obstacle in the way of a rapprochement with their opponents. It is interesting to add that, as far as the first debate is concerned, non-Shī'ite sources claim that Hishām was worsted by Abū al-Hudhayl.[1] By means of these debates, Mas'ūdī strove to vindicate Shī'ite beliefs against the attacks of the Mu'tazila.

That Mas'ūdī was influenced by certain Mu'tazilite beliefs there can be little reason to doubt.[2] But he also approached that movement with a considerable degree of independence. We now possess a study of the relationship between Shī'ism and Mu'tazilism which sheds light on Mas'ūdī's own position in this regard.[3] That study demonstrates that certain Shī'ite intellectual circles in Iraq in the tenth century approached the Mu'tazilite movement with an independence of spirit that seems to characterize Mas'ūdī's own viewpoint. The main representatives of this current in Shī'ite thought were the Banū Nawbakht, who accepted certain tenets of the Mu'tazila school while rejecting others. This is how their relationship with the Mu'tazila is defined:

> With their wide learning and interests in philosophy and the doctrines of various religions they approached the Mu'tazilite schools of their time with considerable independence. In their doctrine of the imāmate they remained, of course, essentially opposed to Mu'tazilism although they denied, perhaps under Mu'tazilite influence, the possibility of miracles of the imāms while at the same time endeavouring to prove rationally their

1 Baghdādī, *Farq*, p. 48; al-Khayyāṭ, *Intiṣār*, p. 103; Ibn al-Murtaḍā, *Ṭabaqāt*, p. 44.

2 In addition to the influences cited above, it appears that his arguments for the temporality (*ḥudūth*) of the world in *Murūj*, secs. 1431–32 are ultimately derived from Mu'tazilite sources. On the origin and development of arguments for the temporality of the world, see Majid Fakhry, "The Classical Islamic Arguments for the Existence of God," *Muslim World* 47 (1957): 133–45.

3 Wilferd Madelung, "Imāmism and Mu'tazilite Theology," in *Le Shī'isme Imāmite*, pp. 13–30.

sinlessness, infallibility and perfect knowledge of all arts and all languages.[1]

Mas'ūdī's views do not tally in every respect with those of the Banū Nawbakht.[2] But the same independence of spirit seems to animate both these Shī'ite intellectuals as well as Mas'ūdī. From our own study of Mas'ūdī's thought in this as well as previous chapters, it would appear likely that his theological views had much in common with his Shī'ite contemporaries, the Banū Nawbakht. Such a conclusion fits the fragmentary passages of theological speculation assembled above.

1 *Ibid.*, p. 16.

2 Mas'ūdī knew the work of al-Ḥasan ibn Mūsā al-Nawbakhtī, citing him in one instance as a Shī'ite theologian who attacked Jāḥiẓ for his anti-Alid works (*Murūj*, sec. 2282), and criticizing him in another for insufficient information on India (*Murūj*, sec. 159). In one other passage in the *Tanbīh* (p. 396) it is asserted that Mas'ūdī knew Nawbakhtī personally.

CONCLUSION

This study has attempted to sketch a portrait of Mas'ūdī as a historical thinker rather than to assess him as a historical source. The two aspects of his work are no doubt closely related. Some early critics, like Ibn Khaldūn, praised him for his insights but criticized him as a source. Ibn Khaldūn's praise has been largely ignored, whereas his criticisms have been remembered and repeated by countless readers. A reappraisal of Mas'ūdī, such as this study has attempted to provide, may well begin with Ibn Khaldūn's remarks of praise:

> Let us now adduce a valuable point with which to round out this chapter. History consists of the recording of the *particular* events of an era or a generation. As for the *general* conditions of far-away places, generations and eras, these constitute a *basis* for the historian upon which most of his objectives are built and according to which his reports are classified. Men once devoted themselves to this genre of writing as did Mas'ūdī in his *Kitāb Murūj al-Dhahab*, in which he explained the conditions of nations and far-away places, both east and west, down to his own days in the fourth decade of the fourth century, A.H. He mentioned their creeds and customs and described countries, mountains, seas, kingdoms and states and distinguished Arabic from non-Arabic nations. He thus became an *imām* for historians who refer to him and a *basis* upon whom they depend to verify many of their reports [Italics my own]. [1]

In this extract, Ibn Khaldūn, despite frequent criticisms elsewhere, pays homage in careful language to a man whom he calls the *imām* of historians and he does so by indicating precisely that attention to "principles" which distinguishes the historian from the

[1] Ibn Khaldūn, *Muqaddima*, p. 52.

mere chronicler of the particular event. Mas'ūdī's reflections on the meaning and purpose of his discipline was ultimately what impressed Ibn Khaldūn and what has constituted the main theme of this study.

Mas'ūdī was not a philosopher of history — at least not the Mas'ūdī of the *Murūj* and the *Tanbīh*. He was, nonetheless, the earliest Muslim historian to reflect on history and to apply certain principles of scientific method and philosophical reasoning to history, within what one might term an encyclopaedic frame of reference. His main concern was obviously to define for his community the historical image he thought best represented its heritage. A religious community like Islam, when seeking to understand and elaborate its relationship to the world, must inevitably draw upon its historical roots. The need to define this image became particularly acute when the Abbasid Empire began to assimilate the heritage of both the Hellenistic West and the Persian-Indian East. This was largely the result of the triumph of Pan Islamism over Arab oligarchy. The product, a universal culture expressing itself in Arabic, sought to define its inner core as well as its constituent elements, the infra-structure of religion and the super-structure of diverse cultures. The scholars who attempted to formulate such definitions were the Muslim "scholastics", who faced the challenge of interpreting the world in Islamic terms. A new school of historians, culminating in Ibn Khaldūn, restated almost the whole of previous cultural history in their effort to meet the challenge. Where Ibn Khaldūn detected laws, earlier historians had detected patterns and deduced insights. Ibn Khaldūn's philosophy of history was ultimately derived from their thoughts and reflections.

What were these thoughts and reflections in Mas'ūdī's case? To begin with, he recognized the limitations of his predecessors and did his best to correct them in his own writings. In other words, he believed that intellectual progress was limitless and that the Muslim historian could not be satisfied with mere imitation but was always called upon to innovate. In order to do so, he must use the specialized skills of colleagues, the tools of research in other disciplines, particularly science and philosophy, and the conclusions arrived at must reflect the spirit of "research and reasoning" that must guide him. Having done so, the historian will detect a pattern emerging from the rise and fall of kingdoms and nations. The Divine principle of justice, which has its counterpart in the proper ordering of society, is disturbed especially when men, for pursuit of private gain, follow leaders or doctrines in blind imitation and in disregard of independent reasoning. In addition, Mas'ūdī believed that Islam was the embodiment of all that was best in pre-Islamic culture. Therefore he felt no compunction about appropriating the views of the "ancients" and casting them as part of the foundation upon which to create his image of the Muslim past.

But Mas'ūdī was also a sectarian Muslim, a Twelver Shī'ite who held to the often unpopular tenets of a sect frequently accused of "excesses" and worse. This commitment to Shī'ism undoubtedly influenced his judgement of certain figures in Islamic history. In common with other Abbasid historians, the Umayyad dynasty was described as, at best, an unworthy interregnum between the "Rightly-Guided" Caliphs and the Abbasids. Indeed the whole of Umayyad history needs to be rescued from the jaws of Abbasid historiography. But this was a task that Mas'ūdī did not want to do and did not even feel needed to be done.With the advent of the Abbasids the legitimacy of the House of 'Alī became a different problem. Mas'ūdī now had to tread softly because the Abbasids possessed a counter-legitimacy of their own and argued for it, at least at first, in almost the same messianic terms as the Alids. Nevertheless, his verdict on the Abbasids while not as harsh as his earlier verdict on the Umayyads, was equally coloured with sectarianism. He passed over in silence the atrocities of Caliphs and other public men because of their favoritism to the Alids, while he condemned the actions of others, perhaps more worthy of praise, largely because of their lack of sympathy for the Alid cause. His value as a source on Arabic-Islamic history lies not so much in his judgements of reigns but rather in the anecdotes and other bits of information included, which are often gleaned from the recollections of literary colleagues and are found nowhere else in Arabic historiography.

But to do him justice, a phrase he would have fancied, it must be added that his sectarianism was not of the narrow, imitative or "juristic" kind. He believed in a world order where the elevation of a certain family to the status of recipients of divine inspiration, the Alid imāms, was a necessary, indeed rational component. That God was not simply the Creator-Judge but also a constant Guide was, to Mas'ūdī, almost self-evident. Islam consummated Divine revelation in a prophetic sense but introduced Divine guidance in a messianic sense. Humanity, always in need of direction and order: political, economic and religious, could not be trusted to change its nature even after the advent of the "Seal of the Prophets." Even the Sunnites came to believe that a reviver of religion arrives every hundred years to interpret the faith anew. As a rationally-held belief, this sectarianism did not, for Mas'ūdī, interfere in his retelling of world history. On the contrary, it helped him to clarify it. The absence of a just ruler, for example, almost always signalled the onset of social chaos and political disorder.

For the rest, that is, his occasional inaccuracies and his reports of fables, a few words of explanation are in order. The reader must decide for himself whether these failings seriously impugn his value both as a source and as a thinker. Most of the fables he lists are set down in one section: *Murūj*, secs. 1419-25. There is no explicit or categorical approval of any of them, even if we set aside for the moment his view that history should also entertain. The supernatural or unique was an accepted part in much of medieval Muslim, or for that matter Christian speculation. The Muslim scholar of Mas'ūdī's bent of mind believed that he possessed, in the Koran, an evident miracle of God. If He could create miracles, He could with even less pomp create marvels of nature or human artifact. This did not of course excuse the historian from the task of defining "custom" and "nature" in order to distinguish them from the "breaking of custom" and the the supernatural; hence the repeated emphasis on experience and rational inquiry, reinforced by extensive travels. No breaking of custom as such was impossible to God. Nevertheless, nature did obey laws of its own, as set for it by God. A divine, ultimately inexplicable order was set above a natural order. Shī'ism for Mas'ūdī was a constant reminder in the natural order of the existence of the divine. In medieval Islam,this particular attitude of mind was not uncommon and Muslim historical thinking is a rich field for the student of the historical relationship between these two over-used but indispensable terms, Reason and Revelation.

As for Mas'ūdī's inaccuracies, his own *apologia* provides perhaps the most appropriate conclusion (*Murūj*, secs. 4-5):

> We apologize for any shortcomings, if any there are, and disclaim responsibility for any oversight that may occur, since our journeys

and desert treks have caused in us a tumult of ideas and emotions. At times by sea, at others by land, we came to know the marvels of nations by witnessing them and the characteristics of regions by personal experience. We thus crossed the regions of the Sind, the Zanj, the Ṣanf, China and Zābij and we plunged into East and West. At times we were in furthest Khurāsān, at others in central Armenia, Adharbayjān, al-Rān and Baylaqān . . . where we met various kings with varying customs, policies and lands and came to know every single aspect of their governance. But the heritage of the sciences has been eroded, their light has been dimmed. The ignorant are many, the learned are few.

APPENDIX A

Fragments of a Biography

The full name of our author as he cites it is Abū al-Ḥasan ʿAlī ibn al-Ḥusayn ibn ʿAlī ibn ʿAbdallāh al-Masʿūdī (*Murūj*, sec. 522). His family is said by many sources to have traced its ancestry to the famous Companion of the Prophet, ʿAbdallāh ibn Masʿūd. It is noteworthy that he traces the ancestry of ʿAbdallāh ibn Masʿūd back to Muḍar ibn Nizār (*Tanbīh*, p. 294). According to Ibn Ḥazm (*Jamhara*, p. 197), Masʿūdī's descent from the Prophet's Companion is as follows: ʿAlī ibn al-Ḥusayn ibn ʿAlī ibn ʿAbdallāh ibn Zayd ibn ʿUtba ibn ʿAbdallāh ibn ʿAbd al-Raḥmān ibn ʿAbdallāh ibn Masʿūd. There is no reason to doubt this pedigree.

Masʿūdī was born in Baghdād (*Murūj*, sec. 987; *Tanbīh*, pp. 19, 42), but of a Kūfan family, according to Ibn Ḥazm (*Jamhara*, p. 411). He seems to have received an excellent education. Among those from whom he received instruction or heard reports were:

1. Abū Jaʿfar Muḥammad ibn Jarīr al-Ṭabarī (d. 310/923). *Tanbīh*, p. 267. Historian and Traditionist.

2. Abū Bakr Muḥammad ibn Yaḥyā al-Ṣūlī (d. 335/946). *Murūj*, sec. 3364. Historian and literary critic.

3. Abū Bakr Muḥammad ibn Khalaf Wakīʿ al-Ḍabbī (d. 306/918). *Tanbīh*, p. 293. See Sezgin, *Geschichte*, 1: 376. Historian, grammarian and poet.

4. Abū al-Ḥasan Aḥmad ibn Saʿīd al-Dimashqī al-Umawī (d. 306/918). *Tanbīh*, p. 300. See Yāqūt, *Muʿjam*, 3: 46–49. Man of letters and friend of ʿAbdallāh ibn al-Muʿtazz.

5. Abū Khalīfa al-Faḍl ibn al-Ḥubāb al-Jumaḥī (d. 305/917). *Murūj*, sec. 2242. See Yāqūt, *Muʿjam*, 16: 204–14. Poet, jurist and historian.

6. Abū Bakr Muḥammad ibn al-Ḥasan ibn Durayd (d. 321/934). *Murūj*, sec. 764. See Brockelmann, *Geschichte*, 1: 111; Brockelmann, *Supplement*, 1: 172; Sezgin, *Geschichte*, 1: 217; Yāqūt, *Mu'jam*, 18: 127–43. Grammarian and poet.

7. Abū Bakr al-Qāsim ibn Muḥammad ibn Bashshār al-Anbārī al-Naḥwī (d. 304/916). *Murūj*, sec. 3382. See Yāqūt, *Mu'jam*, 16:316–19. Traditionist and man of letters.

8. Abū 'Abdallāh Ibrāhīm ibn Muḥammad ibn 'Arafa Nifṭawayhi (d. 323/935). *Murūj*, sec. 3391. See Yāqūt, *Mu'jam*, 1:254–72. Grammarian.

9. Abū Isḥāq Ibrāhīm ibn Jābir (or Sarī) al-Zajjāj al-Naḥwī (d. 311/923). *Murūj*, sec. 3324. See Brockelmann, *Geschichte*, 1: 110. Philologist and student of al-Mubarrad.

10. Abū al-'Abbās Aḥmad ibn 'Ubaydallāh ibn 'Ammār (d. 314/926). *Murūj*, sec. 1951. See Yāqūt, *Mu'jam*, 3: 232–42. Traditionist and historian.

11. Muḥammad ibn Sulaymān ibn Dāwūd al-Minqarī. *Murūj*, secs. 2085, 2088–90, 2092. See Rosenthal, *Muslim Historiography*, p. 509, n. 5. Historian. His date of death could not be ascertained.

12. Abū Muslim Ibrāhīm ibn 'Abdallāh ibn Muslim al-Kashshī (d. 292/904). *Tanbīh*, p. 254. See al-Dhahabī, *Mushtabih*, p. 553. Traditionist.

13. Sinān ibn Thābit ibn Qurra (d. 331/943). *Tanbīh*, p. 73. See Brockelmann, *Geschichte*, 1: 218; Brockelmann, *Supplement*, 1: 386. Philosopher and scientist.

To this list of historians, traditionists, grammarians and scholars, one may add another list of scholars with whom Mas'ūdī was personally acquainted:

1. Abū 'Alī Muḥammad ibn 'Abd al-Wahhāb al-Jubbā'ī (d. 303/915). *Tanbīh*, p. 396. See Sezgin, *Geschichte*, 1: 621–22. Mu'tazilite theologian.

2. Abū al-Qāsim 'Alī ibn Aḥmad al-Balkhī (d. 319/931). *Tanbīh*, p. 396. See Sezgin, *Geschichte*, 1: 622–23. Mu'tazilite theologian.

3. Al-Ḥasan ibn Mūsā al-Nawbakhtī (d. circa 310/922). *Tanbīh*, p. 396. See Sezgin, *Geschichte*, 1: 539–40. Shī'ite theologian.

4. Abū al-Ḥasan ʿAlī ibn Ismāʿīl al-Ashʿarī (d. 324/935). *Tanbīh*, p. 396. See Sezgin, *Geschichte*, 1: 602–04. Heresiographer and theologian.

5. Abū al-ʿAbbās ʿAbdallāh ibn Muḥammad al-Nāshi' (d. 293/905 or 906). *Tanbīh*, p. 396. See Ibn Khallikān, *Wafayāt*, 2: 277–79. Muʿtazilite theologian, poet and grammarian. On al-Nāshi', see Josef Van Ess, *Frühe Muʿtazilitischen Häresiographie* (Beirut/Wiesbaden: Fritz Steiner Verlag, 1971), pp. 1-17.

His contact with these scholars, among whom were some of the most illustrious of his generation, was continuous and lively. Thus it is related that he debated with Abū Bakr Muḥammad ibn Zakariyyā al-Rāzī (d. 320/923) on the temporality (*ḥudūth*) of the world (Ibn Abī Uṣaybiʿa, *ʿUyūn*, 1: 321). His frequent debates with non-Muslim scholars are cited in chapter 1. Taking into consideration the date of death of some of his authorities, it is possible to conjecture that Masʿūdī was born about the year 280/893.

Regarding Masʿūdī's travels, little can be added to the exhaustive treatment of this question by a recent scholar (see S. Maqbul Ahmad, "Travels of Abū al-Ḥasan ʿAlī ibn al-Ḥusayn al-Masʿūdī," *Islamic Culture* 28 [1945]: 509–21). His travels seem to have begun in the year 303 and to have ended in 336. During this period, he travelled over much of the eastern Islamic world but seems not to have visited Spain and North Africa. It also appears that he did not visit Iraq after 315 and that he spent the last thirty years of his life in Egypt and Syria. Seeing that he began the first edition of the *Murūj* in 332 in Egypt after having already finished several works on theology, law and history, it seems probable that his writing activity began after the year 315 (see Appendix B, no. 10).

On his life and works, the Arabic sources offer comparatively little information which, moreover, is often contradictory. We have arranged the most important of these sources in chronological order below:

1. Ibn al-Nadīm (d. after 377/987).

Ibn al-Nadīm describes Masʿūdī as a man from al-Maghrib, records only five of his works, and misquotes or wrongly attributes all these titles, as cited by Masʿūdī himself (see *Fihrist*, p. 154).

2. Aḥmad ibn 'Alī al-Najāshī (d. 450/1058).

This Shī'ite biographer lists fourteen titles, seven of which are accurately cited, i.e., as cited by Mas'ūdī, but records that he died in 333 (*Rijāl*, p. 192). Al-Najāshī further cites Mas'ūdī in an *isnād* (*ibid.*, p. 260). The information here is more accurate than in Ibn al-Nadīm.

3. Yāqūt (d. 626/1228).

Yāqūt corrects the biographical information of Ibn al-Nadīm by quoting Mas'ūdī's own words concerning his place of birth. He lists eleven titles of his works, nine of which are accurate, but records nothing concerning his life or date of death (see *Mu'jam*, 13: 90–94).

4. Al-Dhahabī (d. 749/1348).

Records his death as occurring in Jumādā II, 345. (See *'Ibar*, 2: 269; *Duwal*, 1: 167).

5. Ibn Shākir al-Kutubī (d. 764/1363).

Lists eleven titles, nine of which are cited accurately, but records his date of death as 326 (see *Fawāt*, 2: 94–95).

6. Tāj al-Dīn al-Subkī (d. 772/1370).

Lists seven titles, of which five are accurately cited. Identifies Mas'ūdī as a Baghdadi who resided for a long time in Egypt. Al-Subkī names two of his teachers, mentions that he was reportedly a Mu'tazilite and records a story about his transmission of a *fatwā* from the famous Shāfi'ite jurist Abū al-'Abbās ibn Surayj (d. 306/918) (see *Ṭabaqāt*, 2: 307).

7. Ibn Ḥajar al-'Asqalānī (d. 853/1449).

Ibn Ḥajar records that in his day Mas'ūdī's works, with the exception of the *Murūj*, were rarely to be found. He records his date of death as 346. He also identifies him as a Shī'ite and cites his preference for 'Alī as evidence (see *Lisān*, 4: 224–25).

8. Ibn al-Taghrībirdī (d. 875/1470).

Records his death as occurring in Jumādā II, 345, on the authority of the historian al-Musabbiḥī (see *Nujūm*, 3: 315–16).

9. Ḥajjī Khalīfa (d. 1069/1657).

Uses the *Murūj* to cite correctly sixteen titles of Mas'ūdī's works (see *Kashf*, 1: 185–86, 271, 434, 494; 2: 82, 439; 3: 18–19, 137, 325, 339, 593; 5: 137, 166, 500; 6:50), adds two titles which are dubious (see *ibid.*, 4: 187; 5: 509–10), and four which are ascribed simply to "al-Mas'ūdī" (*ibid.*, 2: 239, 645; 4: 108, 368). He records his death as occurring in 346.

10. Ibn al-'Imād (d. 1090/1679).

Records his death as occurring in Jumādā II, 345, and distinguishes him from a Shāfi'ite jurist also called al-Mas'ūdī (see *Shadharāt*, 2: 371).

The dearth of information on Mas'ūdī's life and works in these sources is surprising. One reason that may be suggested here is that his prolonged absence from his native land made him a relatively unknown figure to Iraqi biographers who would presumably have been those most interested in his life. His translator, Barbier de Meynard, asserts that numerous frauds were ascribed to Mas'ūdī by Arab copyists (see his comments in *Journal Asiatique*, 9th ser., 8 [1896]: 154) and this too must be attributed to the fact that he was a shadowy figure to the scholars of his native land. It is noteworthy that the Egyptian biographers in general provide more accurate information on him than other biographers. Relying largely on Egyptian sources, we may safely assume that he died in Jumādā II, 345/September 956.

APPENDIX B

Reconstruction of Lost Works

This Appendix seeks to describe the contents of Mas'ūdī's lost works and to specify, where possible, the relationship, both thematic and chronological, among his various works. It is not an exhaustive list of references to all citations of Mas'ūdī's works by other writers, but is based on Mas'ūdī's own citations of his works. The description of the contents of his lost works shows the breadth of his interests and learning, while the proper determination of the relationship of his works to each other has an important bearing on Mas'ūdī's achievements and methods of research.

It has thus far been generally assumed that the *Murūj* and the *Tanbīh* are "epitomes" or "extracts" or a "précis" of his other works (see, e.g., Gibb, *Arabic Literature*, p. 82; Miquel, *La Géographie humaine*, pp. 204, 210; Nicholson, *Literary History*, p. 353). Such a view is based upon Mas'ūdī's statements in the *Murūj* and the *Tanbīh* in which he seems to imply that these two works were abridgements or summaries of his other works, now lost (*Murūj*, sec. 2; *Tanbīh*, pp. 5–6). Being no longer in possession of his lost works, one cannot, of course preclude the possibility that the *Murūj* and the *Tanbīh* were epitomes of earlier and more extensive works. This, however, was not what Mas'ūdī himself intended them to be, since he considered both the *Murūj* and the *Tanbīh* to be independent works offering the fruits of novel thought and research (see, e.g., *Murūj*, secs. 880, 2150, 3014, 3534; *Tanbīh*, pp. 45, 97). One may test the accuracy of this assertion by briefly comparing the contents of the *Murūj* and the *Tanbīh*. The reader of these works will find that entire topics or periods treated in one work are either treated briefly or not at all in the other. Thus, the creation and the history of the prophets down to Muḥammad are told at length in the *Murūj* but there is no mention of them in the *Tanbīh.* On the other hand, the principles of astronomy, for example, are explained in great detail in the *Tanbīh* but receive summary attention in the *Murūj*. Perhaps the most convenient place to compare the two books is in the information that each book provides on the reigns of the Caliphs, both Umayyad and Abbasid. Some duplication here is of course inevitable but the *Tanbīh*, which deals far less extensively with each reign, consistently describes the physical characteristics of each caliph together with the inscription on his seal, whereas the *Murūj* contains little or no information of this nature. With regard at least to the *Murūj* and the *Tanbīh*, it would be inaccurate to consider the latter a précis of the former. Rather, the *Tanbīh* appears as complementary to the earlier and more comprehensive work.

The total number of his works mentioned by Mas'ūdī, excluding the *Murūj* and the *Tanbīh*, is thirty four. Of these, twenty three were written Before the *Murūj* (*BM*), five were probably written After the *Murūj* but Before the *Tanbīh* (*AM*, *BT*), and six were written possibly After the *Murūj* but Before the *Tanbīh* (*BT*, *AM*?). We shall proceed by describing the contents of each work and by indicating where it stands chronologically by use of the abbreviations explained above.

1. *K. Akhbār al-Zamān wa man Abādahu al-Ḥidthān min al-Umam al-Māḍiya wa al-Ajyāl al-Khāliya wa al-Mamālik al-Dāthira* [The Book of the History of the Ages and of the Ravages which Time has Wrought upon Past Nations, Ancient Generations and Desolate Kingdoms] *BM*. This is probably Mas'ūdī's largest work and the first in the historical series as given at the beginning of the *Tanbīh.* No evidence has yet been unearthed that any portion of it has survived. The purported edition of this book by 'Abdallāh al-Ṣāwī entitled *K. Akhbār al-Zamān* (Cairo: Maṭba'at al-Ḥanafī, 1938) cannot be identified with Mas'ūdī's work. It was shown to be a popular book of marvels in the translation of this work by Carra de Vaux under the title *L'Abrégé des merveilles* (Paris: Librairie Klincksieck, 1898); cf. *idem*, "Note sur un ouvrage attribué à Maçoudi," *Journal Asiatique*, 9th ser., 7 (1896): 133–44. There is an important discussion of this problem of attribution in Dunlop, *Arab Civilization*, pp. 110 ff.

The very frequent references to this book in the *Murūj* and *Tanbīh* suggest that it had basically the same plan as these two works, i.e., that it began with the creation and included much information on pre-Islamic nations, foreign lands, the various sciences and, finally, the Islamic period. The subject matter, however, was treated at far greater length. It was in fact divided into thirty chapters (*fann*; *Murūj*, secs. 299, 304). The first included a discussion of black tribes, their habitat, customs and history (*Murūj*, sec. 880); the second dealt with, among other things, the various theories about the origin of seas and rivers (*Murūj*, secs. 299, 304, 776). Chapter 14 included an account of Magian theories on how Adam avoided transgression in marrying his progeny to each other (*Murūj*, sec. 50), and chapter 30 was devoted to the Abbasid dynasty and the Alid rebellions (*Murūj*, sec. 2741). It was thus a book devoted to history (*āthār*; *Murūj*, sec. 1877). It is probable that the Islamic section was annalistic in form (*Murūj*, secs. 1498, 3240).

2. *Al-Kitāb al-Awsaṭ* [The Intermediate Book] *BM*. This was written after the *Akhbār*, the second in the historical series. The work, again, seems to have provided more ample information on subjects treated in the *Murūj* and the *Tanbīh* and to have had the same plan. It included information on ancient nations and kingdoms (e. g., *Murūj*, secs. 355, 441, 521, 529), was probably annalistic in the Islamic section (*Murūj*, sec. 1498), discussed the opinions of various sects (*Murūj*, secs. 212, 2076), had ample biographical information and necrologies (*Murūj*, secs. 15, 3353), provided detailed information on the Islamic conquests (*Murūj*, sec. 1668), and dealt at length with the various sciences (*Murūj*, sec. 1369).

The *Akhbār al-Zamān* and the *Awsaṭ* were both composed prior to the *Murūj*. Therefore, the *terminus ad quem* of the early editions of these two lost works is 332. But several references to events occurring after 332 which the author says are to be found in these two works suggest continuous additions right up to 345 (*Tanbīh*, p. 400). It must therefore be presumed that Mas‘ūdī made continuous and simultaneous additions to his historical works.

3. *K. Murūj al-Dhahab wa Ma‘ādin al-Jawhar* [The Book of the the Meadows of Gold and Mines of Gems]. The *Murūj* was written in 332 (*Tanbīh*, pp. 97, 155–56) and constantly revised between 332

and 336 (e.g., in *Murūj*, sec. 3458, he records the current date as 333). In 345, he substantially revised and added to the 332–336 edition (*Tanbih*, pp. 97, 155-56, 175–76), although by this time the 332–336 edition was already in wide circulation (*Tanbīh*, p. 97). All the extant MSS of the *Murūj* are of the 332–336 edition. The 345 edition was many times larger (*aḍʿāf*) than the earlier editions but seems to have preserved the same plan (*Tanbīh*, pp. 110–11). At least one reference in the *Tanbīh* made to this last edition concerning an event cannot be found in the extant edition (*Tanbīh*, p. 105). The last edition was divided into 365 sections (*ajzā'*), each of which Masʿūdī considered to be self-contained. This division cannot be determined in the extant edition.

4. *K. Funūn al-Maʿārif wa mā jarā fī al-Duhūr al-Sawālif* [The Book of the Types of Sciences and the Events of Past Ages] *AM*, *BT*. This is probably the fourth in the historical series. It appears to have filled in the gaps largely in the field of Greek and Byzantine history and culture (*Tanbīh*, pp. 121, 144, 151, 153, 158, 160, 174, 182), but it also provides more ample accounts of North African history and of the Prophet's ambassadors to kings and potentates (*Tanbīh*, p. 261).

5. *K. Dhakhā'ir al-ʿUlūm wa mā kāna fī Sālif al-Duhūr* [The Book of the Treasures of the Sciences and the Events of Past Ages] *AM*, *BT*. This is the fifth in the historical series. It seems to have been basically a larger version of the *Tanbīh* (pp. 400–401). It provides more detailed information on Byzantium, its religion, buildings, churches, reigns of kings and wars with Persia and Islam (*Tanbīh*, p. 176). It also has more information on *Mulūk al-Ṭawā'if* (*Tanbīh*, p. 97).

6. *K. al-Istidhkār limā jarā fī Sālif al-aʿṣār* [The Book of the Remembrance of the Events of Past Ages] *AM*, *BT*. This is the sixth in the historical series. This work seems to have been larger than numbers 4 and 5 above, judging chiefly by the more frequent references to it. It dealt at length with pre-Islamic as well as Islamic history, and seems to have provided especially ample information on Iraq and Byzantium (*Tanbīh*, pp. 53–54, 102, 137, 144, 176). The Islamic section took in such topics as the Prophet's expeditions (*Tanbīh*, pp. 271, 279), the decline of the caliphate (*Tanbīh*, p. 401) and the problems of dating

(*Tanbīh*, pp. 213, 329). The *Tanbīh* was in fact based on this work and we may well assume that they both had the same plan (*Tanbīh*, p. 84).

7. *K. al-Tanbīh wa al-Ishrāf* [The Book of Notification and Review]. The work passed through two editions, the first and shorter in 344, and the final one, which we possess, in 345 (*Tanbīh*, p. 401). This is Mas'ūdī's last work and the seventh and final in his historical series.

8. *K. al-Maqālāt fī Uṣūl al-Diyānāt* [The Book of the Opinions Concerning the Principles of Religions] *BM*. This is a book devoted to sects and their opinions, both Islamic and non-Islamic. Among the Islamic sects discussed are the various branches of the Shī'a, the Khawārij, and the Mu'tazila (*Murūj*, secs. 1945, 1994, 2078, 2225, 2256, 2291, 2399, 2420, 2741, 2800). Among the non-Islamic sects, Mas'ūdī discusses the views of the Maronites, Sabians, Dualists and Khurramiyya (*Tanbīh*, pp. 154, 161–62; *Murūj*, sec. 2399). Certain specific legal and theological questions are also dealt with, such as the conflict regarding the faith of 'Abd al-Muṭṭalib, the views of men regarding jinn and demons, the conflict over the arbitration at Ṣiffīn, and the conduct of the faithful with the pagans (*Murūj*, secs. 783, 1138, 1205, 1715). It appears that this book was polemical in tone and did not confine itself to the mere narration of opinions. The many references to it suggest its importance.

9. *K. al-Qaḍāyā wa al-Tajārib* [The Book of Problems and Experiences] *BM*. This work appears to have been one of his most interesting, since it dealt with all that Mas'ūdī had encountered and experienced on his journeys (*Murūj*, sec. 815) concerning the workings of nature and its marvels. It dealt apparently with such geographical, chemical and physical phenomena as the climatic effect of every region on its inhabitants, its flora and fauna (*Murūj*, sec. 369), the effect of certain types of water on animal life (*Murūj*, sec. 705), the chemical qualities of certain minerals (*Murūj*, sec. 2247), the genetics of animals and plants (*Murūj*, sec. 817) and the peculiar qualities of certain animals (*Murūj*, sec. 846). Of all his works, this seems to have provided the most valuable information on his scientific method and views.

10. *K. Sirr al-Ḥayāt* [The Book of the Secret of Life] *BM*. Written after 313 but before 332, since he refers to a debate held in Takrīt

with a Christian in 313 and recorded in this work (cf. the faulty reading of this passage in Miquel, *La Géographie humaine*, p. 209 and n. 4). This book seems to have been largely devoted to the various views on the soul, its fourfold division (*Murūj*, secs. 533, 1248), its transmigration (*Murūj*, secs. 1195, 2800) and its longings and desires (*Murūj*, sec. 988). It also took in the views of Christians on the Trinity, of the Shī'a on the *ghayba* of the last Imām, and debates he held with the Khurramiyya on the occult (*Tanbīh*, p. 155; *Murūj*, sec. 3156; *Tanbīh*, p. 353). It seems to have been polemical as well as expository in tone.

11. *Risālat al-Bayān fī Asmā' al-A'imma al-Qaṭ'iyya min al-Shī'a* [The Essay Concerning the Elucidation of the Names of the Imāms among the Qaṭ'iyya Sect of the Shī'a] *BM*. This work was devoted to the lives of the Twelve Imāms of the Twelver Shī'a sect. It included information on their descent, the names of their mothers, the manner of their death, their ages at death, how long each lived with his father and grandfather, and the site of their tombs. The opinions of the Shī'a regarding all these matters was also recorded (*Murūj*, secs. 2532, 2798; *Tanbīh*, p. 297).

12. *K. al-Zulaf* [The Book of Stages] *BM*. This book deals primarily, but not exclusively, with the soul and may belong to the same period as *K. Sirr al-Ḥayāt* (no. 10 above). It discusses the fourfold division of the soul (*Murūj*, sec. 533); the four humors of the body and how they as well as the animal and plant life are affected by the sun and moon (*Murūj*, secs. 1325, 1335); the reasons why men of ancient nations lived longer and had larger bodies; and why certain animals and minerals cannot exist in certain countries (*Murūj*, sec. 928). It also dealt with the qualities essential to kingship and the various opinions expressed on this matter by Persian and Greek sages (*Murūj*, sec. 630). Its tone appears expository rather than polemical.

13. *K. al-Mabādi' wa al-Tarākīb* [The Book of Principles and Compositions] *BM*. There is only one reference to this work and we can pass no meaningful judgement on its contents except that it included a discussion of the effects of the sun and moon on earth and specially on the four humors of the body (*Murūj*, sec. 1325). It may have dealt with cosmology.

14. *K. al-Intiṣār* [The Book of Triumph] *BM*. This appears to have been a polemical work devoted entirely to a refutation of Khārijite doctrine. Mas'ūdī informs us that he dealt, among other topics, with the arbitration at Ṣiffīn (*Murūj*, sec. 2190).

15. *K. Naẓm al-Jawāhir fī Tadbīr al-Mamālik wa al-'Asākir* [The Book of the Necklace of Gems Regarding the Administration of Kingdoms and Armies] *BT*, *AM*?. The only reference to the contents of this work is very vague. It seems to have included information similar to the one found in the *Tanbīh* (pp. 400–401).

16. *K. Ṭibb al-Nufūs* [The Book of the Medication of Souls] *BM*. This work dealt with such topics as the effect of laughter and amusements on the soul, and also with the reasons for the soul's longing for its homeland (*Murūj*, secs. 988, 1247).

17. *K. Naẓm al-Adilla fī Uṣūl al-Milla* [The Book of the Necklace of Proofs Regarding the Principles of the Islamic Religion] *BM*. This work, along with others, probably preceded the historical series described above. Mas'ūdī provides a detailed description of its contents which indicates that it dealt largely with Islamic jurisprudence (*fiqh*). It encompassed discussion of such topics as the principles of analogy (*qiyās*) and independent legal judgement (*ijtihād*), the manner of consensus (*ijmā'*) and a review of traditions from the Prophet dealing with legal questions. The book appears to have been polemical in part since Mas'ūdī indicates that he recorded debates with opponents on these matters and that he was able to win their partial agreement to his views (*Tanbīh*, pp. 4–5; *Murūj*, sec. 5).

18. *K. al-Ṣafwa fī al-Imāma* [The Book of Quintessence Concerning the Imāma] *BM*. This work appears to have dealt primarily with the most important theological questions relating to the *imāma*. It dealt with the diverse views of the sects relative to this question, from the esoteric *ghulāt* of the Shī'a (*Murūj*, sec. 6) to more legal problems like temporary marriage (*mut'a*) and its historical precedents (*Murūj*, sec. 1952). It also dealt with the problem of the faith of the Prophet's ancestors, in particular 'Abd al-Muṭṭalib, where Mas'ūdī records that opinions on his faith diverged among sects like the Imāmiyya, Mu'tazila, Khawārij and Murji'a (*Murūj*, sec. 1138). As a corollary, the book also dealt with the faith of 'Alī ibn Abī Ṭālib,

whether he was an unbeliever before he embraced Islam and whether or not he was sinless (*Murūj*, sec. 1463). The book appears to espouse an Imāmī viewpoint but to have been unpolemical in tone.

19. *K. al-Istibṣār fī al-Imāma* [The Book of Discernment Regarding the Imāma] *BM*. It appears to have dealt with almost the same topics as no. 18 above (*Murūj*, secs. 1138, 1463, 1952), but to have been more polemical in tone, since it includes a refutation of the Khārijite position as expressed during the Arbitration controversy (*Murūj*, sec. 2190). It also dealt with the views and arguments of many sects concerning the *imāma* and whether its legality is based on explicit delegation from the Prophet (*naṣṣ*) or on election (*ikhtiyār*) (*Murūj*, sec. 6).

20. *K. al-Da'āwī al-Shanī'a* [The Book of Abominable Views] *BM*. Judging by the title and the sole reference to this work, it appears to have been a polemical tract which attacked, *inter alia*, the views of pre-Islamic Arabs and other nations on the transmigration of souls (*Murūj*, sec. 1195).

21. *K. Ḥadā'iq al-Adhhān fī Akhbār Ahl* (or *Āl*) *Bayt al-Nabī wa Tafarruqihim fī al-Buldān* [The Book of the Gardens of Intellects Concerning the History of the Prophet's Family and Their Dispersal in Various Countries] *BM*. This book appears to have detailed the history, not only of the Twelve Imāms, but also of the rebellions of various Alid pretenders and their deaths all over the Muslim world. In fact, it appears to belong to the literature of 'virtues' (*manāqib*), with the Prophet's family as the object of praise and veneration (*Murūj*, secs. 1013, 1943, 2506, 2742, 3023).

22. *K. al-Wājib fī al-Furūḍ al-Lawāzim* [The Book of What is Necessary in Obligatory Duties] *BM*. This, again, seems to be a legal work which discusses such topics as temporary marriage, for which copious precedents and traditions are cited, and the wiping of sandals (*al-masḥ 'alā al-khuffayn*), both topics being points of dispute between Sunnite and Shī'ite jurists (*Murūj*, sec. 1952).

23. *K. Waṣl al-Majālis bi Jawāmi' al-Akhbār wa Mukhallaṭ* (or *Mukhtaliṭ*) *al-Athār* [The Book of the Collection of Assemblies Relating to General History and Miscellaneous Traditions] *BT*, *AM*. Mas'ūdī refers to this book in the *Murūj* as one which he intended to compose immediatly after the *Murūj*. He deliberately intended it to

have no precise plan but rather to include diverse pieces of historical information (*Murūj*, secs. 3014, 3428, 3608). The sole reference to its contents in the *Tanbīh* suggests that it was a work of history which included information on the rulers of Andalus, their wars with their neighbors and Andalusian history from the conquest down to Mas'ūdī's own times (*Tanbīh*, p. 333).

24. *K. Maqātil Fursān al-'Ajam* [The Book of the Deaths of non-Arab Knights] *BT*, *AM*?. This is a work of polemics written to counter the work of Abū 'Ubayda Ma'mar ibn al-Muthannā on the deaths of Arab knights. The sole reference to its contents mentions the death of a Persian knight and refers to the deaths of other knights, treated at length (*Tanbīh*, p. 102).

25. *K. Taqallub al-Duwal wa Taghayyur al-Ārā' wa al-Milal* [The Book of the Vicissitudes of Dynasties and the Changes of Opinions and Religions] *BT*, *AM*?. We cannot pronounce with certainty on the character and contents of this work. The sole reference to its contents states that it included information on the wars between the Aghlabids and Fatimids in North Africa and the rebellion of Abū Yazīd al-Zanātī (*Tanbīh*, p. 334). It must therefore have been partly historical in nature.

26. *K. al-Masā'il wa al-'Ilal fī al-Madhāhib wa al-Milal*]The Book of Questions and Proofs in Doctrines and Religions] *BT*, *BM*?. This work seems to have dealt polemically with certain topics in law and theology, both Muslim and non-Muslim. It included an account of Mas'ūdī's debates with a Christian in Takrīt on the Trinity (*Tanbīh*, p. 155), but also detailed the diverse views of jurists regarding the principles of religion (*uṣūl al-dīn*), analogy, opinion (*ra'y*) and so forth (*Tanbīh*, pp. 4–5, 155).

27. *K. Khazā'in al-Dīn wa Sirr al-'Ālamīn* [The Book of the Treasures of Religion and of the Secret of the Worlds] *BT*, *AM*?. A work which seems to be similar in content to *K. al-Maqālāt* (*Tanbīh*, pp. 161–62; see no. 8 above) and to be essentially a work devoted to the theological views of various sects. Of special interest is his lengthy reference to a discussion of Qarmatian doctrines (*Tanbīh*, p. 395) and to an explication of the differences between Manichaeanism, Zoroastrianism and Mazdakism (*Tanbīh*, p. 101).

28. *K. Naẓm al-aʿlām fī Uṣūl al-Aḥkām* [The Book of the Necklace of Information Regarding the Principles of Legal Judgements] *BT*, *AM*?. A work on jurisprudence which outlined diverse views of jurists on legal questions (*Tanbīh*, pp. 4–5).

29. *K. al-Ibāna ʿan Uṣūl al-Diyāna* [The Book of the Explication of the Principles of Religion] *BM*. A work of polemics which dealt in part with the differences between Imāmism and Muʿtazilism (*Murūj*, sec. 2256), but also sought to counter the arguments and opinions of such sects and religions as Mazdakism, Manichaeanism, Dayṣāniyya and Khurramiyya (*Murūj*, sec. 212; *Tanbīh*, p. 354).

30. *K. al-Nuhā wa al-Kamāl* [The Book of Wisdom and Perfection] *BM*. It dealt in part with the effect of laughter and amusements on the soul and the four humors (*Murūj*, sec. 1247).

31. *K. al-Ruʾūs al-Sabʿiyya* [The Book of Septenary Principles] *BM*. The title as it appears is probably incomplete, since the text of Masʿūdī supplies variant additions to it. Nonetheless, it appears to be a work of philosophy, political philosophy and science, dealing with oddities in nature and the influence of heavenly bodies (*Murūj*, secs. 1222–23), the reasons for longevity among ancient nations and for the absence of certain animals from Andalus. It contains as well a discussion of the minerals and plants therein (*Murūj*, sec. 928), the secrets of tracking (*qiyāfa*) (*Murūj*, sec. 1232) and philosophic questions, e.g., the soul, substance (*hayūlā*) and the four elements (*isṭaqissāt*) (*Murūj*, sec. 1336).

32. *K. al-Istirjāʿ fī al-Kalām* [The Book of the Resumption on Theology] *BM*. It appears to have dealt, in part, with refuting Zoroastrian and Manichaean arguments on the dualism of light and darkness (*Murūj*, sec. 1223).

33. *K. Maẓāhir al-Akhbār wa Ṭarāʾif al-Āthār fī Akhbār Āl al-Nabī* [The Book of the Radiant History and Singular Traditions regarding the History of the Family of the Prophet] *BM*. This work appears to be similar in design to *K. Ḥadāʾiq al-Adhhān* (see no. 21 above). It detailed the virtues of ʿAlī, his life and his speeches (*Murūj*, sec. 1755), but also included information on the Alids (*Murūj*, sec. 3032) and even on some of their most prominent supporters, e.g., ʿAmmār ibn Yāsir (*Murūj*, sec. 1677).

34. *Al-Akhbār al-Mas'ūdiyyāt* [The Mas'ūdian History] *BT*, *BM*?. This appears to be a work of history. Its title is puzzling and may or may not have been a continuation of a family history (see Carra de Vaux, *Le Livre de l'Avertissement*, p. 343, n. 1; Dunlop, *Arab Civilization*, p. 101). It included, in any case, historical information on the rulers of Andalus (*Tanbīh*, p. 333) and also on pre-Islamic Arab history (*Tanbīh*, p. 259).

35. *K. al-Zāhī* [The Radiant Book] *BM*. We cannot pronounce with certainty on the contents of this work. The sole reference to its contents is to the question of the faith of 'Alī ibn Abī Ṭālib and whether he was sinless or an unbeliever before his conversion. Diverse views are recorded (*Murūj*, sec. 1463).

36. *K. Rāḥat al-Arwāḥ* [The Book of the Repose of Souls] *BM*. This was a work of history which dealt with, according to Mas'ūdī, the history of the kings of nations and their deaths, which were not mentioned in his *Akhbār al-Zamān*. Among the kings treated is Nebuchadnezzar (*Murūj*, sec. 819).

This survey of Mas'ūdī's works does not take into account the five other titles mentioned by Ibn al-Nadīm, Yāqūt and in Brockelmann, *Geschichte*. These five are cited in Miquel, *La Géographie humaine*, p. 202, n. 3-a, and are described below.

1. *K. al-Tārīkh fī Akhbār al-Umam min al-'Arab wa al-'Ajam* [The Book of the History of Nations, Arabs and non-Arabs]. Ibn al-Nadīm, *Fihrist*, p. 154. Judging by Ibn al-Nadīm's faulty information on Mas'ūdī's life and works, this reference may well be to the *Akhbār al-Zamān*.

2. *K. Akhbār al-Khawārij* [The Book of the History of the Khawārij]. Yāqūt, *Mu'jam*, 13:94. This is almost certainly to be identified with *K. al-Intiṣār* (see no. 14 above).

3. *K. Rasā'il* [A Book of Epistles]. Ibn al-Nadīm, *Fihrist*, p. 154. This is cited by Ibn al-Nadīm. The attribution to Mas'ūdī appears doubtful.

4. *K. fī Ithbāt al-Waṣiyya li 'Alī ibn Abī Ṭālib* [The Book of the Establishment of the Regency of 'Alī ibn Abī Ṭālib]. Brockelmann, *Geschichte*, 1: 152; Sezgin, *Geschichte*, 1: 336. The attribution of this

work to Mas'ūdī appears doubtful as C. Pellat himself, who uses this work as his main argument for establishing Mas'ūdī's Shī'ite viewpoint, recognizes in his "Mas'ūdī et l'Imamisme," in *Le Shī'isme Imāmite*, pp. 69–90. Examination of the contents of this work shows wide variations in details of events described in the *Murūj* and the *Tanbīh* as well as a distinct difference in style.

5. *Fī Aḥwāl al-Imāma* [Of the Modes of the Imāma]. Brockelmann, *Geschichte*, 1: 152. The attribution, here again, seems doubtful. To this list, one may add:

6. *K. al-Masālik wa al-Mamālik* [The Book of Routes and Kingdoms]. Ibn Abī Uṣaybi'a, *'Uyūn*, 1: 56, 82. The two references are to reports which cannot be found in Mas'ūdī's extant works and may either be part of a work of Mas'ūdī that Mas'ūdī himself does not cite or of another work cited erroneously by Ibn Abī Uṣaybi'a.

From this survey of Mas'ūdī's works, it appears that the bulk of his polemical and nonhistorical works was written before the historical. More particularly, internal evidence suggests (see, e.g., no. 10 above and *Murūj*, secs. 5–6; *Tanbīh*, pp. 2–7) that the nonhistorical works belong to the period 313–32. This survey also confirms our opinion that his various works were constantly added to and revised and that some works were written to fill in the lacunae of others in a constantly expanding scholarly activity.

INDEX

Aaron, 120. *See also* Hārūn

Abbasid Caliphate/dynasty/empire/era, XIII, 144; Mas'ūdī's authorities in the period of, 10; belles lettres under, 15; compared to the Umayyads, 17; Mas'ūdī's views on, 128; disintegration of, 135; in Mas'ūdī's books, 155

Abbasids, 130, 145; Mas'ūdī's treatment of, 131-36

Abbott, Nabia, 7*n*, 8*n*, 24*n*, 25*n*, 56*n*, 57*n*, 58*n*

'Abd al-Jabbār ibn Aḥmad (al-Qāḍī), XIX, 48*n*, 54*n*

'Abdallāh ibn al-'Abbās, 56, 132

'Abdallāh ibn Mas'ūd, 148

'Abd al-'Azīz ibn Marwān, 100

'Abd al-Malik (ibn Marwān), 30, 129

'Abd al-Muṭṭalib, 8*n*, 61, 157, 159

Abhandlungen zur arabischen Philologie (Goldziher), 15*n*, 16*n*, 17*n*, 18*n*

Abraham, 89*n*; knowledge of God, 8*n*, 68*n*; Mas'ūdī's views of religion of, 69*n*; in Ṭabarī's *Annales*, 83*n*

L'Abrégé des merveilles (de Vaux), 43*n*, 154

al-'Absī, Khālid ibn Sinān, 119, 119*n*

Abū al-'Atāhiya, 20, 21

Abū Bakr (Caliph), 62*n*, 120; Mas'ūdī's description of reign of, 121; Dīnawarī's attitude to, 126; Ya'qūbī's treatment of, 127

Abū al-Hudhayl al-'Allāf, 48*n*; debate between Hishām ibn al-Ḥakam and, 140-41

Abū Hāshim 'Abdallāh ibn Muḥammad ibn al-Ḥanafiyya, 132, 133

Abū Muslim (al-Khurāsānī), 133

Abū Sufyān, 122

Abū Tammām: Ṣūlī's assessment of, as poet, 20; Mas'ūdī's assessment of, as poet, 21

Abū 'Ubayda Ma'mar ibn al-Muthannā, 12, 161

Abū Yazīd al-Zanātī, 161

'Ād, 46

al-'ādāt wa al-tajārib, 38

adab, 102, 113; characteristics, 6, 22, 23; and historical writing, 14 ff., 23, 26, 33

Adab al-Kuttāb (Ṣūlī), XXV

Adam, 69*n*, 84, 103, 155; in Mas'ūdī's account of the creation of the world, 56, 58, 59; in his account of the prophets, 60, 63; ancestor of the Persians, 85

Adharbayjān, 147

Africa, 98, 99, 100

Agathodemon, 65

Aghlabids, 161

aḥkām, 75, 76*n*

Aḥmad b. aṭ-Ṭayyib as-Sarakhsī (F. Rosenthal), 40*n*

Ahmad, S. Maqbul, 30*n*, 36*n*, 40*n*, 69*n*, 103*n*, 115*n*, 139*n*, 150

'Ā'isha, 123

akhbār al-āḥād, 41, 42

Akhbār (Dīnawarī), 8*n*, 62*n*, 69*n*, 92*n*, 126*n*, 127*n*, 131*n*. *See also Kitāb al-Akhbār al-Ṭiwāl*